VICTOR DAVIS HANSON

An Autumn of War

Victor Davis Hanson was educated at the University of California, Santa Cruz, and the American School of Classical Studies at Athens, and received his Ph.D. in Classics from Stanford University. He farmed full-time for five years before returning to academia in 1984 to initiate a Classics program at California State University, Fresno. Currently, he is Professor of Classics there and Coordinator of the Classical Studies Program.

Hanson has written articles, editorials, and reviews for the *New York Times, Wall Street Journal, Daily Telegraph, International Herald Tribune, American Heritage, City Journal, American Spectator, National Review, Policy Review, The Wilson Quarterly, The Weekly Standard,* and *Washington Times,* and has been interviewed on numerous occasions on National Public Radio and the BBC, and appeared with David Gergen on *The NewsHour with Jim Lehrer.* He writes a biweekly column about contemporary culture and military history for *National Review Online.*

He is also the author of some eighty scholarly articles, book reviews, and newspaper editorials on Greek, agrarian, and military history, and contemporary culture. He has written or edited eleven books, including *The Western Way of War, The Soul of Battle,* and *Carnage and Culture.*

He lives and works with his wife and three children on their forty-acre tree and vine farm near Selma, California, where he was born in 1953.

Also by VICTOR DAVIS HANSON

Warfare and Agriculture in Classical Greece

The Western Way of War: Infantry Battle in Classical Greece

Hoplites: The Ancient Greek Battle Experience (editor)

The Other Greeks: The Agrarian Roots of Western Civilization

Fields without Dreams: Defending the Agrarian Idea

*Who Killed Homer? The Demise of Classical Education
and the Recovery of Greek Wisdom* (with John Heath)

The Wars of the Ancient Greeks

*The Soul of Battle: From Ancient Times to the Present Day,
How Three Great Liberators Vanquished Tyranny*

The Land Was Everything: Letters from an American Farmer

Bonfire of the Humanities (with John Heath and Bruce Thornton)

Carnage and Culture: Landmark Battles in the Rise of Western Power

An Autumn of War

An
Autumn
of
War

*What America Learned
from September 11 and the War
on Terrorism*

VICTOR DAVIS HANSON

Anchor Books

A DIVISION OF RANDOM HOUSE, INC.

NEW YORK

FIRST ANCHOR BOOKS EDITION, AUGUST 2002

Copyright © 2002 by Victor Davis Hanson

The essays in this work were originally published in:
City Journal, The Claremont Review of Books, the *Daily Telegraph,*
Military History Quarterly, National Review magazine,
National Review Online, and the *Wall Street Journal.*

Library of Congress Cataloging-in-Publication Data
Hanson, Victor Davis.
An autumn of war : what America learned from September 11 and
the war on terrorism / Victor Davis Hanson.— 1st Anchor Books ed.
p. cm.
ISBN 978-1-40003-113-9
1. September 11 Terrorist Attacks, 2001.   2. War on Terrorism, 2001–
3. United States—Foreign relations—1989–   4. World politics—1995–2005.
5. United States—Foreign relations—Middle East.   6. Middle East—
Foreign relations—United States.   I. Title.
HV6432 .H377 2002
973.931—dc21   2002023156

Author photograph © Susan McClearan
Book design by Fritz Metsch

www.anchorbooks.com

Printed in the United States of America
10   9   8   7   6

For Cara

Contents

Chronology of Events

September

9/11 Suicide bombing of the World Trade Center and Pentagon; some 3,000 killed

9/12 President Bush promises a "monumental struggle of good and evil"

9/18 Anthrax letters postmarked and sent to major media

9/19 Military issues orders for military deployment in Afghanistan

9/20 President Bush addresses a joint session of Congress; announces war on terror

9/21 Ex-Soviet generals predict that America cannot win in Afghanistan

9/24 President Bush moves to freeze terrorists' asssets

9/28 Jesse Jackson changes plans and will not go to Afghanistan to mediate crisis

October

10/1–7 Alice Walker, Susan Sontag, and others voice criticism of American retaliation

10/6 Bush announces "time is running" out on Taliban to give up bin Laden

10/7 American aircraft begin bombing Taliban and al-Qaeda strongholds

10/9 Senator Daschle's office receives anonymous anthrax letter

10/13 Al-Qaeda official promises more terrorist attacks on American skyscrapers

10/16 Secretary of State Powell offers to work with "moderate Taliban"

10/21 Taliban captures and executes opposition leader Abdul Haq

10/31 R. W. Apple in the *New York Times* compares Afghanistan to a
Vietnam quagmire

November

11/1 Taliban spokesman warns that every Afghani has a rifle and will
fight to the death

11/5 U.S. diplomat in Pakistan relates that Taliban feel they "have the
means to win"

11/9 Sudden abandonment of Mazar-i-Sharif

11/11 Fall of western city of Herat

11/12 Three U.S. servicemen killed in accidental bombing at Kandahar

11/16 Mullah Omar rejects peace offers and vows to fight to death

11/17 Muslim holy month of Ramadan begins; bombing continues;
fall of Kabul

11/23 Taliban give up Kunduz

11/25 Kunduz inmate uprising and killing of CIA agent; Marines land
in Kandahar

11/27 American al-Qaeda member John Walker Lindh captured in
Kunduz

December

12/1 Mullah Omar vows to fight for Kandahar until "Judgment Day"

12/2 Ten Israeli teens blown up in Jerusalem by suicide bombers;
twenty-five during the week

12/5 Mullah Omar offers $50,000 for each dead Western journalist

12/7 Fall of Kandahar; Mullah Omar and bin Laden in hiding

12/13 Tape released of bin Laden lauding the terrorists' attacks on 9/11

12/18 Organized resistance at Tora Bora caves ends; Americans begin
search and destroy

12/19 Last fires at the wreckage of the World Trade Center are extin-
guished

12/22 Hamad Karzai forms new government of reconciliation in
Afghanistan

Introduction:
Why September 11 Won't Go Away

THE UNITED STATES was attacked at a time of peace on September 11, 2001. Islamic fundamentalists—sponsored by the al-Qaeda organization, with the implicit support of the Taliban regime in Afghanistan, to the applause of thousands in the Middle East, and with the silence of millions more—destroyed the towers of the World Trade Center in New York City, severely damaged the Pentagon in Washington, crashed four jumbo jetliners in suicidal fury, and murdered nearly three thousand unsuspecting Americans. We shall never know the full extent of the initial planned attack, but it might have been far worse. Brave passengers on a Washington-bound jet seem to have overpowered the hijackers before they could destroy either the Capitol building or the White House. And the immediate arrest of hundreds of terrorist suspects in the days after September 11 probably prevented other subsequent operations.

On the afternoon of the attack, I began to compose several essays for a variety of newspapers and magazines—and thereafter wrote each day until the cessation of general hostilities in Afghanistan, the formation of a new government in Afghanistan, and the final extinction of the smoldering fires at Ground Zero in New York in late December. By that time the Taliban regime was thoroughly destroyed, the al-Qaeda terrorists had been either killed, captured, or scattered, and the United States was pondering its next season of war in its global counterattack against terrorism.

At the very outset, I was convinced that September 11 was a landmark event in American history, if not the most calamitous day in our nation's 225 years. Not only did it represent the most grievous single-day foreign attack on the shores of the United States, but the bombings marked a far more climactic and devastating strike than all the prior precursors to American wars—greater in severity than Lexington and Concord, Fort Sumter, Havana Harbor, the sinking of the *Lusitania*, Pearl Harbor, and the Tonkin Gulf. The dead were for the most part civilians—slaughtered completely unaware at work or in transit. Their murderers were almost immediately canonized by many in the Middle East, and the architect of such evil was within hours greeted as a hero on the streets of the Islamic world. Four general consequences from the events of September 11 characterize these essays and provide themes for the book at large.

September 11 was not merely an act of terrorism per se—isolated and disgruntled individuals of a small clique mad at the state of their world, and so taking out their frustrations against innocents in the United States. Rather, if al-Qaeda did not exist, it would have to have been invented to assuage the psychological wounds of hundreds of millions of Muslims who are without much consensual government, freedom, and material security. Bin Laden is the ultimate representation of Islam's failure to come to grips with the dizzying and sometimes terrifying pace of globalization and the spread of popular Western culture. In that context September 11 must be seen as the opportunistic response of fundamentalists to funnel collective frustration against the United States, which for most of the world represents the epitome of Westernism and modernism all in one.

The terrorists acted against America because of who we are, *not* what we did—despite various claims that our troops in Saudia Arabia were modern "Crusaders" and rumors that Jewish-American women were walking in Muslim countries in suggestive attire. Rampant capitalism, radical equality between the sexes, secular rationalism, and unbridled freedom are not merely antithetical to Islam but appeal to the senses, appetites, and aspirations of millions of Muslims far more effectively than Islamic traditionalism can repress them. It is difficult to suggest that the words of the Koran alone can withstand the hideous and foul West when thousands of Muslims voluntarily eat at Western fast-food franchises in Cairo, the *Star Wars* saga is popular in Amman, and millions want to be in lecture halls in Europe and America. The frustrated terrorists themselves were not poor and ignorant, but rather, upscale and educated. Their fury toward the West was incited, not tempered by, their own affinity for and familiarity with us.

Our response to September 11 also revealed another fault line in American thinking: the great divide between a tragic appreciation of the universe and a confidence that all humanity's problems of the age are solvable through the proper therapeutic and enlightened response. The former view reminds us that as mere humans we cannot rid the universe of all its pathologies in a mere lifetime, and that sometimes we may resemble devils when we try to be omnipotent avenging angels; the latter offers us the god Reason as a worldly religion that can eradicate everything from disease and illiteracy to car exhaust, handguns, cigarettes, and unkind words. As a student of classical literature, I was deeply influenced by the epics of Homer, the plays of Sophocles, Thucydides' history, and the dialogues of Plato, which all seem to offer time-honored alternatives to modern behaviorism, Freudianism, Marxism, and social construction. In the Hellenic view, the *wrong* questions to ask in this present conflict are "Why is there war?" "Why do they hate us?" or "What did we do to them?"

The Greeks would instead answer that war is terrible but innate to civilization—and not always unjust or amoral if it is waged for good causes to destroy evil and save the innocent. By the same token, we must return to the idea that terrorists and their sponsoring states are not simply economically driven to conflict, rationally seeking redress from real exploitation, poverty, or inequality. Rather, bellicose theocratic and autocratic nations can be like people—immature, rash, and mercurial—and so rush to battle out of classical motives like Thucydidean fear, envy, and self-interest that in turn are fueled by a desire for power, fame, and respect. Although war is often fought rationally, the causes for its outbreak are seldom rational.

The glum ancients would expect, rather than be shocked by, September 11, realizing that human nature is unchanging and thus predictable through the ages—its essence being raw, savage, and self-serving just beneath the veneer of civilization. In the arena of conflicting and sometimes malevolent powers, national weakness invites attack more often than thanks and appreciation of past self-restraint. Even our magnanimity in sending food to the Taliban was as frequently interpreted as irresolution as it was seen as charity. And military restraint in not responding to prior bombings can be dismissed as timidity rather than praised as sobriety.

Similarly, we need to be reminded of the tragic limitations of the human condition—and how rare Western culture is in its efforts to ameliorate the savagery innate to all peoples at all times. Kabul was not Paris or San Francisco when we arrived, and it will not be so when we leave. We wish peace and some sort of human order in Afghanistan, but we accept that without a Madison or Lincoln or the Federalist Papers there may well be unclean water, harsh police, and only one radio station for some time to come. Our mission in this war is not to right wrongs that cannot be righted given the limits of our wisdom and power, but rather to leave millions in Afghanistan and elsewhere better off than when we arrived, offering hope to other states that their towers will not be toppled and their citizens vaporized should a fanatical enclave decide to target their culture.

Acceptance of this dark vision of human nature need not be pessimistic if one understands that a transcendent morality—the desire to protect the unsuspecting, aid the attacked, and leave behind for others more than one has received—is the foundation for such an unsparing worldview. Thus we accept the tragedy of the human condition in order to ensure that we do *not* allow evil people to act out what they desire and sometimes are surely capable of accomplishing.

Such a realistic acceptance of war seemed to me far more humane (not to mention safe) than believing that we can reinvent the nature of man each generation through state planning, psychoanalysis, counseling, or any of the other social and behavioral sciences that seek to alter—often through coercion—the very way we humans think and act on some universal scale. Mr. bin Laden killed thousands of Americans because he was depraved and thought it more likely that he could gain fame and power than court death and destruction. We were Britain to his Hitler, a power not in any way culpable for past transgressions, but an obstacle nonetheless by virtue of our democracy and liberality to his mad dreams of grandeur. He envisioned a medieval Caliphate under his sway. And he was convinced by the past restraint of the United States that the world's sole superpower either could not or would not retaliate against him, despite his long history of murdering.

I also tried to make sense of our own subsequent response to September 11 from an equally different view of class and status. I am a classicist, but also a farmer, who was born, lives, and works on a family farm in California's Central Valley. From that agrarian vantage point, itself handed down from some five previous generations who lived on our small 120 acres, I have had doubts about what passes for intellectual life in America today—particularly as manifested in the contemporary university. Physical work, close acquaintance with the poor, and affinity with the innate dangers that confront millions of Americans are all a complete mystery to many of the most vocal critics of America in this current conflict; those who do not disk the south forty, hammer nails, or pump out cesspools, it seemed to me, had a greater propensity (not to mention more time) to ponder the legal ramifications of trying John Walker Lindh—and were more likely to see him as a confused idealist from Marin County than an abject traitor.

So I felt much of what the university had to say about September 11 would reflect its general isolation from the material conditions facing most Americans—and I was not disappointed. Almost all the working-class people I know—farmers, mechanics, union electricians, and students at California State University, Fresno—were solidly behind the United States' response. In contrast, nearly all of the opposition to our conduct in this war was expressed by professors and those in law, the media, government, and entertainment, who as a general rule lead lives rather different from those of most Americans.

Many critics, of course, were well-meaning pacifists and principled opponents of the use of force in response to violence. I am not interested so much in refuting such positions as in explaining how frequently they seem to be held by the most comfortable and secure members of American society—whether in the corporation, law firm, or university. Those who were tenured, highly paid, or leisured, both Republican and Democrat, I think have forgotten how hard it is to survive and raise a family—how often daily life is muscular and dangerous, and how frequently evil people can and must be stopped only through physical strength from hurting those who are helpless. Rarely do our professional classes meet or live by those who have few lifelines and therefore understand this brutality and the slim margin of error that sometimes separates survival from catastrophe. Many enlightened and well-educated Americans—often among the most influential of our society—simply cannot believe that awful men abound in the world who cannot be cajoled, bought off, counseled, reasoned with, or reported to the authorities, but rather must be hit and knocked hard to cease their evildoing if the blameless and vulnerable are to survive.

Yet the vast majority of Americans accept this pragmatic creed—90 percent of them supported bombing the Taliban and al-Qaeda according to many polls taken throughout the autumn of 2001. Too many of our more educated and upscale did not. They felt that we should have done very little militarily, but quite a lot in consultation with the United Nations, our allies, and moderate states to convince al-Qaeda to stop. Class as an indicator of America's differing political responses to September 11 was rarely remarked upon by social critics. So this war has reminded citizens that a great many progressives are more likely to be privileged than sweaty, eager to craft bromides from the suburb rather than the farm or coal mine, and quite ready to embrace abstract cure-alls as penance for the vast distance they have put between themselves and their objects of empathy. Domestically, such hypocrisy and naïveté are problematic, but in a war with deadly adversaries like al-Qaeda and their supporters, utopianism is near suicidal.

These essays reflect a deep belief that September 11 has reminded us how Western civilization and its more radical manifestation of liberty and capitalism in the United States are very different from other cultures past and present. Multiculturalism taught us that all peoples are more or less equal, one society not qualitatively better or worse than any other. Cultural relativism added that it is wrong to judge a people on its habits and practices—there being no real objective standard of good or evil behavior, since both concepts are not absolute, but simple "constructions" or "fictions" of the day, created by those in power to maintain their control and privilege.

Or so we were told in our schools, books, and universities. September 11 suggested otherwise. There is not—and never has been—a single true democracy in the Islamic world other than a sometimes constitutional, secular, and Westernized Turkey. There may be four or five words for various types of female veils in the languages of the Middle East— *burqa, chador, niqab, hyab,* and others—but no indigenous vocabulary for constitutional and consensual government. That fact alone makes a real difference in the lives of a billion people. Freedom to worship, the rule of law, the right to inquire apart from religion and government, the existence of a voting middle class, the opportunity to own property and pursue profit—all these are mostly Western ideas and, to the degree they are followed anywhere, permit a people prosperity and happiness. If such values are thwarted by either religion, tribalism, statism, or sheer anarchy, far too frequently and unnecessarily men and women get sick, kill each other, die early, and live in squalor.

Consequently, many of the following chapters deny that the misery of the Middle East is simply a result of colonialism, racism, or Ameri-

can hegemony—much less attributable to the bogeyman Israel—
rather than the predictable result of widespread failure to adopt free
institutions, democracy, open markets, and civilian audit. In that
sense, *realpolitik* alone will not see America through the war against
the terrorists. Instead, in the tumult to follow September 11, overwhelming military force must be coupled with humane considerations and straight talk. All people born onto this planet seek freedom
and security, and since the Western paradigm alone provides man a
chance to realize these innate aspirations, it is the duty of Americans
to be neither cynical nor insensitive in their approach to the Islamic
world, but rather in confidence and without apology to support popular governments and democratic revolutionaries wherever possible.
The more the present repressive regimes now hate America, the more
their freed peoples will later admire us. Now is the time for promoting
consensual government in the Middle East and cessation of our support for autocrats; later we can worry about the arrogance or naïveté
of embracing Western nation-building.

Finally, the three-millennia story of Western civilization on the
battlefield has proved to be one of abject terror for its enemies. Europe
and its cultural offspring have across time and space fashioned a
deadly form of warfare that transfers ideas of freedom, rationalism,
consensual government, and egalitarianism to lethally trained civic
militaries—highly disciplined, well led, technologically advanced, and
superbly armed. Much of what I wrote in the military context was
intended to remind Americans that they had little to fear from the Taliban and the terrorists. If we stayed true to our ideals of freedom and
democracy, and were not afraid to incur sacrifice in lives and capital
in the use of our forces, then history teaches us that the ultimate victory was never in doubt. Americans, I have learned, are completely
unaware of the vast extent of their nation's military power.

The essays appear in the rough order that they were composed
between September 11 and December 22, 2001. The only occasional
changes I made in the original texts from what appeared in print were
corrections of occasional typographical and grammatical errors, and
the elimination of some redundancies that became clear only when
the essays were assembled together. In a few cases an essay has retained
my original title, rather than that which appeared in print and was
supplied by an editor. Readers should note that the records of the

number of fatalities from September 11 were reassessed almost daily during the final four months of the year, ranging from an original guess of some 10,000-plus dead, to losses of between 7,000 and 4,000 before careful analysis revealed a figure of some 3,000 killed in the air, at the Pentagon, and in New York.

I also left things as I wrote them in hopes that these essays, as a contemporary record of ongoing events, will show some prescience in light of what actually transpired—and, more important, will encourage Americans not to listen to the future gloomy prognoses of so many of their most esteemed experts and pundits on both the left and the right. It is hard now to remember that a great many prominent thinkers believed that we either would not or could not respond to our attackers, and that if we did, we would probably be unsuccessful and so only create more problems than we solved. Some conservatives at times were convinced that we were failing to wage real war, even as their liberal counterparts were appalled that we were bombing as much as we did. September 2001 was an especially chaotic time, when panic and sophistry ruled the airwaves and papers.

The great majority of these articles first appeared in *National Review Online*. I would like to thank the editors there as well as *National Review* magazine, the *Wall Street Journal*, the *Daily Telegraph*, *City Journal*, *Military History Quarterly*, and *The Claremont Review of Books* for permission to reprint the other essays. My thanks also go to Cara Hanson, Bruce Thornton, Kathryn López, Myron Magnet, Edward Craig, Kristi Hill, Sabina Robinson, and my editor at Anchor, Andrew Miller, for help in editing and assembling a number of the essays.

I.

September

(The destruction of the World Trade Center; the attack on the Pentagon; the explosion of four jet airliners; President Bush's promises of a worldwide war on terror; dispatch of American carriers to the Indian Ocean; initial criticism of proposed American response both at home and abroad)

DURING THE THREE-WEEK lull between September 11 and our military response in early October, it was not clear when and if America would strike back. Despite our president's immediate and firm assurance that we would battle terrorists across the globe for years to come, critics both here and abroad immediately questioned the morality of our tactics in bombing the terrorist enclaves in Afghanistan and the military feasibility of finding the al-Qaeda camps—and then destroying them without either killing scores of innocent civilians or causing such disruption as to precipitate wide-scale starvation and disease.

In addition, we did not know exactly the number of our own dead, as casualties on September 11 were at first feared to be in the tens of thousands, before generally being reduced to a round figure of between seven thousand and three thousand killed—a total by January 2002 that would be generally recognized as around three thousand fatalities. Both friends in Europe and neutrals and enemies in the Middle East demanded "proof" that bin Laden had, in fact, masterminded the attacks. Yet throughout these dark days, the Taliban and al-Qaeda alike promised annihilation for any Americans foolish enough to enter Afghanistan and raised the specter of further terrorist attacks here and abroad against the United States.

In the numbing aftermath of September 11, Americans were presented with a daily variety of myths—military, cultural, and political—designed to temper our military response. I was chiefly worried that we were awash in a sea of false knowledge concerning everything from the military history of Afghanistan, the lessons of Vietnam, misinformation about the Northern Alliance, half-truths about the effectiveness of our air forces, the purportedly hopeless struggle against a "new" form of terror, the reasons for al-Qaeda's assault, and the nature of American foreign policy in the Middle East.

September was perhaps the most hectic and depressing month in our nation's history. In the following nine essays, composed in those times of chaos and uncertainty, I employed occasional parody, posed counterfactual scenarios, and drew on classical history—as well as the careers of General Sherman and Winston Churchill, the 2,500-year Western military tradition, the heroism of the New York policemen and firefighters, and our struggle against the Japanese during World War II—all to argue that we had no choice but to counterattack long and hard in Afghanistan.

I.

What Are We Made Of?

THE GUTS TO RESIST EVIL

THE UNITED STATES finally entered World War I due to the nation's lingering outrage over a few hundred floating bodies of Americans from the sunken ocean liner *Lusitania,* which was torpedoed as a part of Germany's unrestricted submarine warfare. Over two decades later, on December 7, 1941, we declared war against the Japanese Empire after twenty-four hundred American sailors were surprised and killed on a Sunday morning at Pearl Harbor. In the aftermath of each attack, the United States did not seek the sanction of world opinion, nor did it worry about the feelings of either its allies or newfound enemies. Instead America unleashed the dogs of war, precipitously so against countries that had promised and delivered our people death.

In the days after Pearl Harbor a dazed American public saw newsreels of victorious Japanese, shouting "Banzai!" with arms outstretched on conquered American outposts, the precursors of suicidal kamikaze pilots who would soon promise the annihilation of our fleet and sailors. What terrible foes, we thought, to hate us so—so adroit at surprising us, so deadly at killing despite our defenses. Yet, the generation of our fathers was not impressed by either images or rhetoric. In response, a rather innocent and unprepared nation in less than sixty months left both Germany and Japan in smoldering ruins. Both fascism and Japanese militarism were incinerated and have not plagued the world for over a half-century.

Today, September 11, the United States was similarly attacked, in acts every bit as cowardly and without warning. The only difference between Pearl Harbor and the firing on the Pentagon and destruction of the towers of the World Trade Center is one of magnitude. Ours now is the far greater loss. No enemy in our past, neither Nazi Germany nor imperial Japan, has killed so many American civilians and brought such deadly carnage to our shores as these suicidal hijackers who crashed the very citadels of American cultural, economic, and military power in our nation's two greatest cities. While preliminary reports of casualties are still unclear, our enemies may have killed more Americans—nearly all of them civilian men, women, children, and the aged—than died at Shiloh or Pearl Harbor. And unless sizable numbers of the targeted fifty thousand escaped, our casualties could in theory approach the aggregate numbers of Vietnam war dead. It may well be that more Americans died today than fell at Gettysburg or Antietam, or in fact on any single day in American history. Surely, by any fair measure of history, we should now be at war.

But are we and shall we be? This generation of Americans is at a crossroads in our nation's history. We must decide whether we shall continue to be the adolescent nation that fretted the last six months over the risqué details of Congressman Condit's private life while our enemies were plotting death on the scale of a Guadalcanal or Tet under our very noses. Or are we still the children of our fathers, who accepted the old, sad truth that "the essence of war is violence, and moderation in war is imbecility."

The voices of our therapeutic culture will caution otherwise. Indeed, they already have. We all know the old litany of inaction and self-loathing. Such seething hatreds are inevitable, we are told, given our world swagger, and are the bothersome wages of global activism. Should not we look inward, others will remind us, to examine why so many despise us so much?—as if people who practice neither democracy nor religious tolerance nor equality are our moral superiors. And are not these isolated terrorists emissaries of a new war for which we are so ill-equipped and do not understand?—as if we, the greatest military power in the history of civilization, do not fathom the unchanging and eternal nature of blood and iron. Is not our support for Israel the source of our calamity?—as if we should abandon the only democratic island in a sea of fanaticism and autocracy.

As in the case of the Marine barracks in Lebanon, the Lockerbie airliner downing, the cowardly murder of our servicemen in Saudi Arabia, the ruination of the embassies in Africa, the suicidal ramming of the USS *Cole*, and the earlier near carnage of the World Trade Center, we know well the vocabulary of prevarication practiced by our political and media pundits. We shall "track down and punish" the terrorists; we must "bring to justice the perpetrators," who can "run but not hide"; we will "act swiftly and deliberately"—but, of course, at all times "soberly and judiciously." And so on. Out will follow the old nostrums: Europe must be consulted, moderate Arab states entreated, and the United Nations petitioned. Few will confess that we are in our own outright bloody war against tyranny, intolerance, and theocracy, an age-old fight against medieval foes who despise modernism, liberalism, and freedom, and all the hope that they bring to the human condition.

But Americans now must ignore the old lie, because at last they also know the new truth: despite the braggadocio of the past years, we have in fact done very little—and so invited war onto our shores. Worse still, we have disguised that little in the rhetoric of the criminal justice system, as if these enemy warriors are local misguided felons to be handed over to our courts. Or our diplomatic experts would quietly return us to a comfortable stasis by the usual whispers about the consequences of "polarizing" the Arab world or "radicalizing" moderate societies—folk perhaps such as the Palestinians who were celebrating today in their streets on news that thousands of bodies lay strewn in ours. Far worse even still, after the launching of a few impotent cruise missiles, we can go on cloaking that nothing in the immoral vocabulary that we are either too civilized to punish evil, or perhaps too comfortable, or too sophisticated to kill killers. And so Americans die, they are forgotten, and we do nothing—hoping that our enemies will at least do their cowardly work on our distant ships or barracks rather than at our doorsteps.

Yes, we are at a great juncture in American history. We can go to battle, as we once did in the past—hard, long, without guilt, apology, or respite until our enemies are no more. It was our ancestors who passed on to us that credo and with it all that we hold dear, and so just as they once did, we too must confront and annihilate these killers and the governments that have protected and encouraged them. Only that way can we honor and avenge our dead and keep faith that they have not died in vain. Only with evil confronted and crushed can we ensure that our children might still someday live, as we once did, in peace and in safety.

Written on September 11 and published in National Review, *week of October 1.*

2.

Western Nations Are Slow to Anger,
but Lethal in Their Fury

WE IN THE United States have suffered a great loss. But the incineration of innocent civilians in our cities was not due to our intrinsic weaknesses but rather, like the Greeks in the weeks before Thermopylae, attributable to our naïveté and unpreparedness.

Yet Osama bin Laden has made a fatal miscalculation. Like everybody who scoffs at the perceived laxity of Western democracies, these murderers have woken an enormous power from its slumber, and retribution will shortly be both decisive and terrible. The bloody wages of this ignorance of the power of a free people aroused are age-old and unmistakable—Xerxes's sixty thousand washed ashore at Salamis, eighty thousand of the sultan's best floating in the waters off Lepanto, one hundred thousand lost in the streets of Tokyo.

Western nations at war, from the Greeks to the present, are not weak but enormously lethal—far out of proportion to their relatively small population and territory. This power is not an accident of geography, much less attributable to natural resources or genes, but rather found in its very ideas and values. The foundations of Western culture—freedom, civic militarism, capitalism, individualism, constitutional government, and secular rationalism—when applied to the battlefield have always resulted in carnage for their adversaries.

Such ideals were apparent almost immediately this time around—with the decision of doomed airline passengers to storm their hijackers; with Congress freely voting vast sums of capital for military operations; with individual rescue workers, aided by sophisticated and huge machines, on their own initiative devising ad hoc methods of saving victims and restoring calm to a devastated city.

Neither the genius of Hannibal nor the diseases of Africa nor the fanaticism of the Mahdists have stopped Western armies. Occasional lapses such as last week's have prompted not capitulation, but responses far more deadly than their enemies' temporary victories.

In our peace and affluence, and in awe at the suicidal fanaticism of our enemies, we Americans of this complacent age have forgotten these iron laws of the Western way of war—Alexander the Great destroying an empire of seventy million with an army of forty thousand, Cortés wrecking an imperial people of two million in less than two years, or a small band of British redcoats ending the power of Cetshwayo and his Zulus for good in less than a year. The arsenal at tiny sixteenth-century Venice—based on principles of market capitalism and republican audit—launched far better and more numerous galleys than those of the entire Ottoman navy. At Midway, American code breakers—the products of free universities, nursed on egalitarianism and able to investigate without political and religious censure—helped to win the battle before it had even begun.

In the months to come, American ground and air forces, with better weapons, better supplies, better discipline and more imaginative commanders—audited constantly by an elected Congress and president, criticized by a free press—will shatter the very foundations of Islamic fundamentalism. Indeed, the check on the great power of Western armies through the ages has rarely been enemy spears or bullets, but the very voices of internal dissent—Bernardino de Sahagún aghast at his people's cruelty in Mexico, a Bishop Colenso remonstrating against the British government about the destruction of Zululand or an American co-ed marching to end the war in Vietnam.

The Taliban and other hosts of murderers at bases in Pakistan, Iraq, and Syria may find reprieve from Western clergy and academics, but they shall not from the American military. America is not only the inheritor of the European military tradition, but in many ways also its most powerful incarnation. Our multiracial and radically egalitarian society has taken the concepts of freedom and market capitalism to their theoretical limits. While our critics often ridicule the crassness of our culture and the collective amnesia of our masses, they often underestimate the lethal power that accrues from such an energetic and restless citizenry, where past background means little in comparison with present ambition, drive, and ingenuity.

Our creed is not class, breeding, or propriety, but rather machines, brutal competition, and unchecked audacity. These are intimidating assets when we turn, as we shall shortly, from the arts of production to those of destruction. The world, much less the blinkered fundamentalists, has not seen a United States unleashed for a long time and so has forgotten all this. Americans are kind, and they are a generous people. But when wronged, held in contempt, and attacked in peace, they define victory as the absolute annihilation of their adversaries.

So we are a schizophrenic people of sorts, a nation of amateurs that can almost magically transform itself into a culture of professional killers. In 1860, Grant was a clerk and Sherman a failed banker and then teamster; in 1865, they were cruel masters in the art of unmitigated carnage, their huge armies the most deadly of the age.

My father was a peaceful farm boy in 1941. Within a mere twenty-four months, he had been turned into a brutal agent of the apocalypse as he and other tyros in thousands of monstrous new B-29s rained death upon the cities of Japan—without guilt or apology, proud that their napalm was ridding the world of Japanese militarism. When we, as confident students of the 1970s, remonstrated against him for his past vengeance, he scoffed at our naïveté: "I'd be proud and ready to do it again." And so he would, and so we may now as well.

Written on September 12 and published in the Daily Telegraph
on September 21.

3.

Cornered

THE TALIBAN IS NEITHER NEW NOR SCARY

WITHIN THE LAST several hours the Taliban in Afghanistan have been variously reported as in hiding, preparing their forces for a border war, denying bin Laden was in their custody, offering to let a "neutral" Islamic "court" adjudicate his future, calling for a jihad against the United States, and threatening Muslim neighbors who ally themselves with the United States. It would be a grave mistake to listen seriously to any of this prattle, worse still to think their apparently contradictory and inexplicable behavior represents real power or danger.

In fact, their passive-aggressive bluster is typical of the usual last howls of all cornered thugs and dictators. Goebbels continued to broadcast doom to the Allies hours before he blew his brains out. As American armies raced through the carcass of Germany, Admiral Dönitz in the last minutes of Nazism still issued threats and demands to the Allies concerning the conditions of German capitulation. Japanese fanatics under General Anami promised to overthrow the brokered surrender and lead Japan to eternal victory amid the ashes of Hiroshima—shortly before committing suicide as the American fleet made ready to sail into Tokyo Bay.

In the past, we scoffed at all these desperate attempts of murderous and illegitimate governments to salvage their eroding power. So too we must with the Taliban, who possess neither the skill nor terror of those whom we obliterated in World War II. The only difference is that they have panicked even before we have fired a shot.

The empty rhetoric of the Taliban offers even greater lessons still. In the months to come we must not delude ourselves that the "new" enemy of Islamic fundamentalism has suddenly arisen to change entirely the rules of war. Their terrorism, fanaticism, and even suicide bombers are not novel. They find parallels throughout history from the conquest of Mexico to the siege of Cyprus in 1571 to the kamikaze attacks on the American fleet off Okinawa.

Instead, we must remember in this present crisis that military precedent and behavior, based as they are on the unchanging nature of man, always endure. In this case they teach us that all illegitimate and murderous regimes, when they are at last stripped of their terror and the illusion of power, threaten even as they broker to save their own skins. The Taliban will do the same until the last bullet finally puts an end to their evil. As Afghanistan's neighbors—untrustworthy states like Iran and Pakistan, who until days ago harbored terrorists but now are themselves in deadly fear of U.S. bombs—seal their borders, the threats of the cornered Taliban will become even more surreal as they are empty. This is a good sign that they recognize, as we do, that their end is near.

We are witnessing a great change in the balance of power in the world. Formidable states like India and Russia, both secular democracies with historical ties to Europe, will gravitate to us even as the Arab world—with ruined economies and without a single elected government—finds itself weakening by the day. The United States has awoken from its moral slumber and found itself not feeble, but fearsome beyond its wildest imagination. We have suffered a grave defeat—more dead than at Pearl Harbor—not because we were intrinsically weak, but rather because we, like the Greeks on the eve of Thermopylae, were naive and unprepared. The Taliban sound ferocious, but that is because the most dangerous place in the world in the next few weeks will be Kabul, not Manhattan.

Written on September 15 and published in National Review Online
on September 19.

4.

Great Leaders Are Forged in War

"GREAT BATTLES," Winston Churchill remarked, "change the entire course of events, create new standards of values, new moods, in armies and in nations." And so too has our first defeat of this new conflict. We have suffered a calamitous tragedy on September 11—more than the dead of Shiloh—only to have awakened to the world turned upside down. Old orthodoxies are obsolete; what is to follow is still unsure and untried. In the battles to come we will not have the luxury of the moral smugness of our past, and so no need for the tired voices of conciliation and impotence. The terrible cloud over Manhattan has ended the era of hesitancy—of kind, predictable, and cautious men whose sobriety proved to be their weakness, their reluctance to act now revealed as the recklessness of inaction.

President Bush appears a different sort. He was said to be inarticulate and incapable of leadership. Neither is true. He radiates instead seriousness, even anger. His sternness is so far without arrogance. The president's mettle shows signs that it may prevail in the setbacks to come, when the universities and media revile him, or even endure our successes when the diplomats and experts warn him to prevaricate and cease. What are we, then, to look for in our president and his subordinates in the months to come?

First an unquestioned faith in victory, without which no great captain can marshal his troops. Pericles rebuked his demoralized and plague-ridden Athenians when Spartans were in sight of his walls and reminded them that they, not their enemies, were to be feared. Churchill predicted the destruction of Germany even as bombs fell on London. Such confidence in total victory must be near religious in a leader, requiring the acceptance of nearly anything when calculating "the terrible arithmetic" of battle. Bush in his avowals about the fate of his presidency seems already to grasp that singular leadership requires a sense of personal fatalism, that all of one's past ambitions and aspirations hinge solely now on the triumph of the moment.

Leadership in democracy also demands transcendence—the constant reminder to a free and affluent citizenry that their killing and dying is nevertheless for a purpose beyond mere victory. At Salamis the Athenians chanted "free your native soil" as they speared drowning Persians. In the months to come we must be retold that we war to remember the dead, to save the innocent, and to end the violence. Democracies are derided as decadent and soft. They are neither when aroused, but it requires vision to convince a complacent citizen that moderation in war is imbecility, that tragically real humanity is to put to rest those who would slay the helpless.

For our generals to achieve successful battle command there must not be merely confidence, but at times understated arrogance as well. Caesar, Wellington, Nelson, and Grant were not much concerned with what the enemy might do—are our European allies on board? might our response prompt greater conflagration in the Muslim world? can we conquer this new face of terror?—but focused instead on what they knew they would and could do to the enemy. When told that the Athenians opposed his great trek to free the Spartan helots, the philosopher-general Epaminondas scoffed to his Theban soldiers to dismiss such empty threats. Instead, he wagered that it was more likely that they might well take a detour into Athens, dismantle her majestic temples, and reerect them atop the Theban acropolis.

Great leaders are at times not only unpredictable, but often a little frightening. Reagan at times surely was, but so too on brief occasions were Truman and Kennedy. Bush has shown such flashes of anger, and on occasion real emotion, whose unpredictability has already registered among the Taliban. Still, we have been lectured by moderate Arab regimes on what we cannot do, even to the extent that the naming of our campaign "Infinite Justice" is inappropriate. We are waiting for leaders who will advise them sternly that nomenclature is the least of their worries, when three thousand of our kin are killed in the streets by men from their shores. Periodic scariness is not a vice in military leadership.

Leaders in a democracy must mingle with the rest of us, just as our president walked amid the rubble and hugged our brave rescue workers. But unlike President Clinton, who discussed the nature of his underwear and donned shades to play the saxophone, great leaders are not entirely one with the people they lead. Pericles, Wellington, Don Juan at Lepanto, Montgomery, and Patton were all beloved by their rank and file, but such affinity grew out of knowledge that these more articulate and polished men sought to elevate their soldiers rather than to descend below them.

Every great army has a soul; it is nourished on military competence, of course, along with success, but without an identity and élan it eventually starves. In that regard, commanders must possess real personality, if not eccentricity, both natural and induced. Wellington's nose, Churchill's jowls, Roosevelt's cigarette, Montgomery's beret, and Patton's pistols are essential in a leader, whose speech and very manner instantly identify him as exceptional.

So history's battlefield stalwarts are rarely consensus builders. While not insubordinate, they are often at odds with their overseers who strive to monitor and rein in their zeal. Bush must recognize and accept this as a law of war. In the coming crucible, the nation's real benefactors may prove the most odious to organization and bureaucracy. Sherman was advised by both his superiors that it was not wise to go into Georgia, and then made his case and marched. He proved to be no Halleck. When Alexander the Great was advised by Parmenio that he should not dare fight against the odds at Gaugamela, Alexander retorted, "I would not either if I were Parmenio."

We have enough handlers and experts to curb our leaders' exuberance, but in our present age far too little audacity. We need generals who this time may well resign if told not to go to Baghdad. They may well misspeak in public. Pericles and Patton were all at last relieved of command; Sherman and Grant came close; Bradley and Hodges, never. History, not the popularity of contemporaries, ultimately decides who were the real peacemakers.

All past criteria of merit also fade when the shooting starts. George McClellan was a dapper executive salaried at $10,000 a year before 1861, only to give way to the slovenly ex-grocer Grant and the unstable Sherman—men whose temperament and comportment made them unfit for high service in times of peace. We do not require merely A-students with impressive recommendations, but perhaps more often scrappers who have been overlooked amid the order and routine of the past—the more eager and desperate, the better—who know opportunity and fate are not ordained but fleeting and of the moment.

Scipio Africanus was an untried and ignored youth when Hannibal entered Italy; he crushed him at Zama a few years later. An uncouth, cigar-chomping Curtis LeMay frightened us in peace; we may not have won without him in war. Nathan Bedford Forrest was an atrocious man of the antebellum South; his genius unleashed in war nearly saved his cause.

Are there still such leaders among us, in this, the age of our greatest affluence and cynicism? Perhaps. Some, like the once discounted mayor of New York, have already come to the fore; other, more anonymous people at the Department of Defense have shown admirable resolve. Our president with flashing eyes, it turns out, may as well.

Written on September 17, published in the Wall Street Journal
on September 24.

5.

War Myths

WHAT NOT TO BELIEVE

1. We have incurred legitimate hatred from the radical Islamic states.

NOTHING COULD BE further from truth. The Taliban, the mullahs in Iran, and other assorted fundamentalists despise the United States for its culture and envy it for its power. The wealth, technology, and freedom of America's global culture—from bare navels to the Internet—have challenged fundamentalists, who are wedded to a medieval world of perpetual stasis. That terrorists use frequent-flier miles and cell phones to kill us only sharpens that paradox, and accentuates their dual sentiments of envy and inadequacy. For the record, in the last ten years, the United States freed the Arab and Islamic state of Kuwait, opposed Saddam Hussein and his murder of Islamic Kurds and Shiites, prevented Muslim Afghanistan from becoming a Soviet satrapy, and saved the Muslims of Bosnia and Kosovo from extinction—as European and "moderate" Arab states watched the carnage of their neighbors and kin. The majority of the terrorists that surround bin Laden are from the upper and middle classes of Arab society, are highly educated, and are driven to murder by hatred and envy, not hunger or exploitation. They are a world apart from the starving in South America and Africa, who do not crash airliners into office towers. These terrorists hate us for who we are, not what we have done.

2. The Arab and Muslim worlds are formidable.

IN FACT, DESPITE being over a billion strong, they are not monolithic and are at their weakest since the fifteenth or sixteenth century.

Like the Ottomans of the past, who made poor copies of Venetian cannon, so too the fundamentalists are parasitic upon Western culture, their societies unable to mass-produce, or even create, a single one of the weapons they employ. The economies of the larger Muslim world—from Indonesia and Iran to Lebanon and Palestine—are in shambles, ruined by either autocracy or theocracy. Moreover, new coalitions are emerging that will only further isolate Muslim states, in which even mainstream clerics and intellectuals have not successfully reconciled the unfettered dynamism of global capitalism and technology with the doctrines of the Koran. In response, the United States will gradually gravitate toward tough nuclear powers like Russia and India, whose secular democracies have long-standing affinities with the West—and deep enmity toward Islamic fundamentalism.

3. The moderate Arab countries are our friends.

WE ALSO NEED to revisit the myth of the "moderate" Arab countries. Most are moderate in only a relative sense, the way an opportunist like Franco was a moderate fascist in comparison to Hitler, or a wily Tito a moderate Communist as opposed to Stalin. We must accept the bitter truth that states like Palestine, Egypt, Syria, and others—despite American deference and occasional aid—are not our friends, much less our allies. Their citizens do not vote freely; their media is controlled and censored; women are not fully liberated, if at all; and they are growing less, not more, tolerant of religious and cultural diversity. While the United States should not gratuitously incite societies like Jordan (a supporter of Iraq in the Gulf War), Egypt, or Saudi Arabia, we must reexamine our relationships with them—from military assistance to foreign aid to travel and immigration. We should pay close attention to what the upscale parents of the terrorists now profess to European journalists: They may well be representative of Arab "moderates" in Egypt and Lebanon, and yet, with perfect consistency, either deny their progeny's involvement, spin myths about CIA conspiracies, or suggest that the attacks were warranted.

4. Fundamentalist terrorism cannot be eliminated.

THIS FEAR TOO is erroneous. Terrorist organizations like bin Laden's, Hezbollah, and Islamic Jihad are not as formidable as either

German Nazism or Japanese militarism, both of which were exterminated within five years of America going to war and have not plagued the planet since. The Waffen SS, the Gestapo, the kamikazes, and the Japanese army at Bataan were all more horrific than the Taliban. Terrorism is a tumor with tentacles, but these can be excised by frequent and continued air strikes, coupled with sudden ground incursions and ongoing counterinsurgency. The hosts can be given a series of ongoing ultimatums: to surrender suspects, demolish camps, and cease monetary support or face the month-by-month, systematic destruction of their military assets, banks, and communications. Add in financial, economic, and cultural ostracism, and terrorism can and will be crushed—if the United States is willing to give treasure and lives for the greater good and for our children's future.

5. The crisis is an international problem.

IN THEORY, OF course it is, and we should welcome assistance from our traditional allies and enlist indigenous resistance groups in Iraq and Afghanistan. But the United States must be prepared to act alone, especially as casualties mount and terrorist reprisals increase. Nor should we welcome alliances with past terrorist culprits that will haunt us later and erode the moral high ground.

The United Nations is not only as impotent as the old League of Nations, but lacks the former's idealism and has become ever more morally bankrupt. Once the fighting starts, despite initial pledges of support, the Europeans will probably extend words of encouragement but lend no real material or military assistance of any value. We cannot expect the French to remember Normandy Beach or the Germans the Berlin airlift—at least to the extent of incurring real sacrifice in lives and social unrest. Indeed, most Europeans have mostly forgotten American intervention on their doorstep to stop the recent holocaust in the Balkans. We should neither lament nor be angered by their hypocrisy, but rather expect it, and realize what a different country America is and always has been compared to its European allies. We must be ready to be lectured by the Swedes, who passed on World War II; ignored by the Swiss, who profited from it; and hectored by the French, who nearly lost it. America needs and welcomes friends, but the absence of such should not deter our response to avenge our own dead and protect our innocent.

6. War has never solved anything.

QUITE THE CONTRARY. The three greatest scourges of the twentieth century—Nazism, Japanese militarism, and Soviet Communism—were defeated through war or continued military resistance. More were killed by Hitler, Stalin, and Mao outside of combat than died in World Wars I and II. War, as Sherman said, is all hell, but as Heraclitus admitted, it is also "the father of us all." Wickedness— whether chattel slavery, the gas chambers, or concentration camps— has rarely passed quietly into the night on its own. The present evil isn't going to either.

Written on September 18 and published in National Review Online
on September 20.

6.

Pseudo-Military History

THE BOMBINGS OF the last two weeks have raised a number of analogies with wars of the past—nearly all of them false and, in fact, dangerous.

Afghanistan

WE ARE HECTORED ad nauseam about the horror of a dreaded landlocked and rugged Afghanistan, the quagmire that has swallowed Alexander the Great, the 19th-century British colonialists, and Soviet Communists alike. Yet Alexander, in fact, did overrun Afghanistan— and with fewer than thirty thousand troops, despite factional rivalry within his army and his self-destructive murders of his own top lieu- tenants. Britain withdrew because of errors of arrogance, logistics, and tactical incompetence; the Soviets, largely on account of the billions in aid and weapons sent to their enemies from the United States, and their own foolhardy and evil attempt to wipe out Islam. The Russian army in the last decade of Communism was not the force that stopped Hitler in the far more difficult street-fighting at Stalingrad.

Also unlike the prior invaders, Americans are prepared to strike with no illusions about the ease of their task and with no wish for conquest, lucre, or obeisance. We are not arrogant or naive, as past armies were, and we have no interest in occupying the country or in turning the people from medieval Islam to the benefits of popular American culture. Our mission is simply to destroy the Taliban; the tragic chaos that follows will be no worse than what exists now. The destruction of the Taliban can be accomplished through concerted air attacks against their conventional military installations and terrorist camps as counterinsurgency teams and commandos target their leadership, and as mobile ground forces, perhaps with indigenous forces, advance on the major cities.

Vietnam

THE CHIMERAS OF Vietnam are often raised. Few conflicts are more misunderstood. Then we were fighting a distant war against foes supplied on their borders by our two chief nuclear rivals, China and the Soviets. Our target list against the North was small and it often shrank. We defined victory as creating a democratic, enlightened culture where none had existed before. The draft ensured that our elite youth in universities would take to the streets. Even with all that, our military forces fought superbly. At the so-called bloodbath at Hue, the U.S. Marines lost 147, killed over 5,000 of the enemy, and freed the city in the worst street-fighting since the Korean War. The siege of Khe Sahn was an enemy failure and resulted in 50 communist dead for each American lost. In the horrific Tet offensive, a surprised American military inflicted 40,000 fatalities upon the attackers while losing fewer than 2,000.

Vietnam itself was a defeat, but this was largely due to politics. Yet the political landscape of contemporary America is hardly comparable. Our home soil has now been attacked; we have lost more civilians than we did soldiers at Pearl Harbor. Nor is the country likely to see an American war as the nexus of racial, sexual, and cultural unrest. Instead, most Americans are slowly accepting the grim reality that our enemies, far from apologizing for the slaughter, wish to kill even thousands more of us at work, in our streets, and in our beds.

Israel

OTHER CHORUSES HAVE chanted, "Israel could not wipe out terrorism, so how could we?" Again, the analogy is false—and should be apparent immediately in the grim reality of the post–September 11 world: It is safer to fly on El Al than on United, and the towers of Tel Aviv are apparently more secure than those in lower Manhattan. Israel's collective losses from the much-feared Palestinian uprising are far less than those inflicted against the terrorists. Indeed, Middle Eastern fundamentalists have now killed more Americans than terrorists have killed Israelis in the last three decades, and perhaps since the inception of the Jewish state. But far more important, in the past a tiny Israel has been isolated—with no financial, cultural, or economic assistance in its struggle from Europe or others in the eastern Mediterranean, states that at least could have ostracized terrorist hosts and supporters. In contrast, we have the power to shut down—or, better yet, physically destroy—banks, communications, and corporations that facilitate, encourage, or tolerate the terrorism of our enemies.

Unending War

A DECADE OF war is often promised. But rarely in history do we see such lengthy fighting. The European civil conflicts of the Seven (1756–1763), Thirty (1618–1648), or Hundred Years' Wars (1337–1453) were marked by cyclical rather than continual battles; even the nightmares of the Civil War, and the two world wars of the past century, lasted less than five years. The tragic fact is that since classical times, war in Western society is truly destructive when it pits Western power against Western power. Caesar and Pompey and their followers killed more Romans than did Hannibal; more Greeks were killed in single intramural battles in the Peloponnesian War than in all the fighting against Persians at Marathon, Thermopylae, Salamis, and Plataea combined. Alexander lost fewer than one thousand soldiers in three pitched battles against the Persians while destroying an empire of seventy million. His greatest worry was not Afghani tribesmen or Bactrian cavalry but tough Greek mercenaries.

Zealots

THE MUCH FEARED Cetshwayo and his dreaded Zulu militarist state of some two hundred thousand were annihilated in less than a year at a cost of fewer than two thousand British dead. The Mahdists, ensconced at Khartoum and swollen with British blood, promised a jihad to end all jihads; instead they were annihilated by Kitchener. Hernán Cortés, despite seeing the beating hearts of his men ripped out at Tenochtitlán, wrecked an enraged empire of millions with fewer than twenty-five hundred Castilians. We should not always be proud of these bloody accomplishments, but in military terms they remind us that, for good or evil, the chief fear of a Western army is one like itself. Yet, that horrific scenario seems unlikely in the present conflict. Real powers that have elements of Westernized discipline, advanced weapons, logistics, and training—Russia, India, and China—are more likely to aid or remain neutral than to oppose us. If anything, the United States may find itself closer to such strong states as it distances itself from weak and " moderate" Arab regimes.

Microbes, Nerve Gas, and Atoms

WE ARE TOLD that we must worry constantly about biological or nuclear weapons. Such caution is prudent and will remain wise advice for the next decade. Microbes and atoms are formidable threats, which, unlike conventional arms, leave lethal, material aftershocks that ripple outward from their points of explosion. Yet Americans must pause to digest fully the magnitude of their own catastrophe of September 11—more than three thousand dead in our cities, far more than what terrorists' nerve gas killed in Japan, and more than the toll of Saddam's reported use of biological agents before and after the Gulf War. Physicists could do us a great favor by calculating the magnitude of the explosions on September 11. The combined destructive power of thousands of tons of metal and fuel in the airplanes striking the towers of the World Trade Center at high speed surely was equivalent to two or three kilotons of TNT—in other words, comparable to the ruin left by a small, primitive nuclear device of the type perhaps now in terrorists' hands. We should be vigilant—and angry—but realize that we have endured a horrible attack and yet are still more powerful, not enfeebled, for our ordeal. Indeed, knowing that our enemies have access to biological weapons and perhaps nuclear bombs, and even wish to kill our children, should make our resolve stronger, not weaker.

What Is Ahead?

AN *ANNUS TERRIBILIS* is upon us—the most unpredictable year since 1941, ushering in a frightening contest that we did not seek, but now must enter and win. Yet the study of military history should offer us more reassurance than dejection. This is the first occasion since World War II on which we can and should use the entire arsenal of our defense. The strategies of halting before Baghdad and lecturing Saddam Hussein have been shown bankrupt; cruise missiles shall bring us no comfort, much less deterrence. The world has been turned upside down; with that upheaval, the voices of proportionality, accommodation, and consultation are discredited and now relegated to increasingly rare appearances on late-night television. Good and kind men like Sandy Berger, William Cohen, Warren Christopher, and Colin Powell have been shown not prudent, as they promised, but in fact reckless through their past inaction.

The terrorists, in their eagerness for blood, have blundered terribly, both in their barbarity and in their timing. It is hard to arouse Americans, especially in the last two decades of their greatest wealth, leisure, and license. Yet they have accomplished a radical reversal in temperament and ideology in mere days by killing innocents and striking both at the heart of American power and prestige and at the very heartstrings of innate American kindness. There is a new administration different in character from the past that in turn now governs a changed citizenry. The next bloody months will not be the easy police actions of Grenada and Panama. Perhaps they will require more sacrifice than the fighting in the Balkans and the Gulf War, whose combined American dead was comparable to a bloody week on our freeways. But our war to come will not be Vietnam either. And this time, if we choose to, we shall prevail. The terrorists and their sympathetic hosts have no idea what they have unleashed.

Written on September 19 and published in National Review Online
on September 20.

7.

General Sherman, the Western Way of War, and September 11

FEW FIGURES IN American history have been more misunderstood—or hated—than General William Tecumseh Sherman. Between November 1864 and April 1865 he led an enormous Union army into the heart of the Confederacy, leaving a swath of destruction through the center of Georgia and the Carolinas that led to the collapse of the South, the end of the Civil War—and his own lasting infamy.

The tally of his material damage in Georgia alone, however, needs no exaggeration. In terms of the costs of destruction, the roughly one month of marching from Atlanta to Savannah was staggering. As one Union soldier put it, "The destruction could hardly have been worse if Atlanta had been a volcano in eruption and the molten lava had flowed in a stream sixty miles wide and five times as long." Although only 12 percent of the Georgia countryside had been canvassed by Union columns, Sherman claimed his troops had inflicted $100 million of damage—$20 million of which, he said, "has inured to our advantage." In the march's aftermath the price of Georgia farmland crashed, losing up to 70 percent of its value.

The assessed valuation of slaves who would be eventually liberated in Georgia alone was close to $275 million—a figure that Sherman largely was responsible for. "This may seem a hard species of warfare," Sherman wrote when he finished, "but it brings the sad realities of war home to those who have been directly or indirectly instrumental in involving us in its attendant calamities." In this view, an elite Southern gentry had started the conflict, and Sherman was ending it.

In our present crisis the general would suggest to us that a great many in Afghanistan must be taught both the wages of their support for the Taliban, and where the logic of cheering the news of three thousand incinerated Americans ultimately leads—and all that can be done without killing them, but by demonstrating how even tacit support for promulgators of war has real material costs in the here and now. As Sherman gazed out at his men who marched into the streets of Savannah, he observed, "They regard us just as the Romans did the Goths and the parallel is not unjust."

Vandals they were, for one calculation put Sherman's work at 100,000 hogs stolen, 20,000 cattle driven off, 15,000 horses confiscated, and 500,000 bushels of corn and 100,000 bushels of sweet potatoes consumed—all food destined for Confederate armies in the field. The army itself arrived in Savannah with 200 more wagons than when it started and thousands more in livestock. In actual mileage, given the terrain and variety of routes, some of his men had marched between 350 and 550 miles, averaging between 12 and 15 miles a day—a phenomenal rate given the fact that the army was actively destroying infrastructure as it moved through enemy territory.

Besides the booty in Atlanta, the matériel Sherman's men confiscated in Savannah alone was considerable. Sherman had bragged to Lincoln that he had found 25,000 bales of cotton and 150 heavy guns. In fact, there was probably an additional 10,000 to 20,000 bales that were either randomly destroyed or turned up later. The government later sold Sherman's cotton for $30 million, ensuring after the plundering of the Georgia countryside that the entire march had essentially been self-supporting and cost the federal government nothing. The Confederates, in addition, left behind in Savannah nearly 200 railcars, thirteen locomotives, nearly 30,000 artillery rounds, and more than 50,000 rifle cartridges. But the most amazing aspect of Sherman's march was the paucity of deaths on either side.

His army suffered about 100 dead, a little over 700 wounded or missing, and another 1,300 captured—in other words, an army of more than 60,000 men lost only about 60 men a day from its fighting strength for over a month as it went through the heart of the Confederacy. In contrast, six months earlier at Cold Harbor, Grant had lost more than three times that total number of casualties in less than twenty-four hours.

Most of Sherman's casualties were those caught out of formation and laden with plunder, who were either summarily executed or taken

to horrific prisoner-of-war camps in rural Georgia or forcibly con-
scripted into the Confederate army. Few were killed in fights with
enemy soldiers. Sherman reported that his army had fired 1,245,000
cartridges—or about only twenty rounds per man during the entire
march. Each soldier on average shot his rifle less than once a day—
mostly on chickens and livestock—and arrived at Savannah with 90
percent of his allotted cartridges unfired. In Sherman's new kind of
war, an army was to be in better shape after its campaign than before.

If Sherman's capture of Atlanta had guaranteed Lincoln his elec-
tion in November, then the subsequent March to the Sea in the last
months of Lincoln's life ensured the newly reelected president soaring
popularity and the assurance of the people's lasting faith in his policy
of absolute victory. There would be no more whispers of negotiated
settlements, no further talk with the rebels about anything other
than unconditional surrender. All of Sherman's earlier expectations in
the late summer of 1864 had come to full fruition by winter on the
Atlantic coast: his lieutenant Thomas had essentially destroyed Hood's
army in Tennessee, Grant was holding Lee firm in Virginia, and the
Southern populace was aghast but also terrified over the ruin that
their comrades had experienced in Georgia.

Worse still for the Confederacy, after Georgia Sherman made
ready to march systematically northward through the Carolinas to
meet Grant, to destroy the remaining Confederate armies, to occupy
more capitals at Columbia, Raleigh—and perhaps Richmond itself—
and to punish severely the people of South Carolina, who had inaugu-
rated the war. As Sherman put it years later, the march through
Georgia was all along the beginning, not the end.

I only regarded the march from Atlanta to Savannah as a "shift
of base," as the transfer of a strong army, which had no opponent, and had finished its then work, from the interior to a
point on the sea-coast, from which it could achieve other
important results. I considered this march as a means to an
end, and not as an essential act of war. Still, then, as now the
march to the sea was generally regarded as something extraor-
dinary, something anomalous, something out of the usual
order of events; whereas, in fact, I simply moved from Atlanta
to Savannah, as one step in the direction of Richmond, a move-

ment that had to be met and defeated, or the war was necessarily at an end. Were I to express my measure of the relative importance of the march to the sea, and that from Savannah northward, I would place the former at one, and the latter at ten, or the maximum.

Just as revolutionary as Sherman's unconventional attack on the Confederacy was the nature of his army and his use of psychological warfare. The South bragged that it was an agrarian nation of spirited landowners. But in truth only a few Southerners owned the vast majority of the most fertile land in the Confederacy; most free whites were without viable farms and could not compete against the enormous slave-run estates. Far more agrarian were the yeomen of Sherman's army—the bulk of it from just a few western states. Over half the army was from Ohio, Illinois, and Indiana alone; in fact, only 33 of Sherman's 218 regiments were from the East—less than 15 percent of the aggregate strength of his Army of the West. It turned out that the real farmer-soldiers in the war down South were not local, but from the northern Midwest—and Sherman's officers made it clear to the rank and file that they were a different sort of folk on a moral mission of retribution.

If the results of Sherman's march are clear in economic and strategic terms in collapsing the South, what was the moral defense of such a brutal invasion? Sherman had many, but mostly he argued for the necessity of his invasion on three grounds—moral, practical, and sociological. The South was a slave society and had started the war; his army was a force of liberation and was ending it. He made this clear in both a number of letters to Southern generals and in essays of explication to Northern journalists and politicians. Whatever Sherman's occasional insensitivity to blacks, there was no doubt this army freed more slaves than any Union force. This fact was not lost on Sherman, who reminded his abolitionist critics that midwesterners, who had initially been reluctant to go to war, were freeing far more blacks than New Englanders, who had been calling for a crusade against the South for years.

Sherman's army of burners was seen by Union and Confederate soldiers alike as an ideological force, and the zeal to ruin a slave society spread from its top down. Accordingly, in our present war, if we are to wreck the infrastructure of the Taliban and its terrorist allies, and to instruct the Afghani people of the folly of even tacitly supporting such murderous leadership, then we must make it clear that we wish to overthrow fascists, allow freedom again for women, stop terrorist murder, and have no wish to kill civilians who do not actively oppose us.

Second, in a practical sense Sherman's march was bringing the Civil War to a close, while the mass slaughter in northern Virginia between Grant and Lee gave no signs of letup throughout 1864 and early 1865. Moreover, Grant embraced a brutal simplicity in destroying Confederate armies, one that did not involve the myriad problems of expanding the war beyond the battlefield, and thus he left no assurance that in a decade or two the population of the South, its infrastructure intact, its people still proud, might not once more field armies to champion states' rights. Yet in Sherman's view the way to ensure the absence of subsequent terrorism was to make "war so terrible" that the South would never consider raising arms again.

In general, he was proved correct. After Sherman's march through Georgia and the Carolinas, every child of the South would come to know that the will of the Confederate people, not merely its army, had been crushed. The hatred of Sherman, the destroyer of the plantations, not of Grant, the devourer of Confederate manhood, is proof enough of that. In short, the South despised Sherman, not because he had defeated them, but because he had humiliated them in the process. Machiavelli once warned that real detestation in war arises from the destruction of material inheritance, not the loss of one's parents.

The difference between killing soldiers and destroying the property of those who field them is critical, for it involves the ambiguous relationship between what constitutes true morality in war. However inexact the comparison, the difference between World Wars I and II sheds some light on the respective manner in which Grant and Sherman each fought the South—and the contrast is not, as might be expected, entirely to the detriment of Sherman. From 1914 to 1918, the Allies, Grant-like, waged a horrific war of annihilation in the trenches against the armies of autocracy that ultimately ruined their entire military, but left the populations and home territory of the Central Powers largely unscathed—and eager to find scapegoats. World War II followed a mere two decades later.

After World War II and the savage and systematic demolition of the German and Japanese landscape—far in excess of what even Sherman might have imagined or condoned—neither society warred again, and there has been in western Europe and Japan thus far a half century, not twenty years, of peace. No German or Japanese civilians after 1945 could ever underestimate the power of the British and American military, or think that their culture was betrayed rather than conquered, or that their own support for murderous regimes did not have consequences for their own persons and property.

Sherman would have approved of the carefully targeted bombing and enveloping strategy in the Gulf War that brought Iraq to its knees in hours at little cost in American lives—but he would have been appalled at the immorality of any negotiated settlement that left Saddam Hussein intact, and thus able to continue hostilities at a later date. We should remember that lesson when our leadership hints at postwar governments that include the murderous Taliban, or that we can overlook terrorists in nearby countries.

For Sherman, then, the attack on property and infrastructure was permissible, if the war was an ideological one against anarchy, treason, and slavery, and if it would lead to a permanent peace based on just principles. Those who argue that he was one with the modernist terrorist who indiscriminately attacks civilians fail to note that he did not kill civilians—"I do not war on women and children"—and he did not attack those who had not first attacked his own.

Fright, as a weapon to be employed in war by a democratic army, must be proportional, ideological, and rational. Sherman surely sought a proportional warfare: Southerners, who fought to preserve men as mere property, would have their own property destroyed. He was clearly ideological: those who would destroy Confederate property would do so as part of a larger effort of abolition that was not merely strategic, but ethical as well. There was a clear rationale to the March to the Sea: burning and looting would not be random, nor killing gratuitous, but rather ruin was to have a certain logic, as railways, public buildings, elite plantations—all the visible and often official infrastructure of a slave society—would be torched, but the meager houses of the poor and the persons themselves of the Confederacy would be left relatively untouched.

We must avoid, as much as humanly possible, the houses of the Afghani people. Yet we should be unmerciful against the homes of their leaders and the fixtures of the Taliban government—not merely to stop their murder, but to instruct the observant population of the real costs of tolerating such instigators of war. And the general chaos caused by our war-making must make all Afghanis aware of both the power of the United States and the general mess that even reluctant participation in such a murderous regime can bring down upon the general population.

In fact, much of Sherman's thinking is currently inherent in American military doctrine of the last two decades: despite our power, our forces usually react to the aggression of others, target enemy command and control and the property of the government and elite, and seek—in Iraq, Panama, and Afghanistan—to liberate residents from an oppressive regime. Yet often such attack, however precise, makes life miserable for an enemy citizenry and therefore prompts them to act against the authors of their calamity. The Afghanis, like the citizens of Georgia in their animus shown the plantationists, will come to blame the Taliban for the general bedlam brought on by the American counterattack.

Often Sherman's type of war is misunderstood and said to be itself terrorist or inhumane. In that regard, contrasts can be made between Robert E. Lee and Sherman. The former, who wrecked his army by sending thousands on frontal charges against an entrenched enemy and whose family owned slaves, enjoys the reputation of a reluctant, humane knight who battled for a cause—states' rights and the sanctity of Southern soil—other than slavery. The latter, who was careful to save his soldiers from annihilation and who freed thousands of slaves in Georgia, is too often seen as a murderous warrior who fought for a cause—federalism and the punishment of treason—other than freedom.

Lee crafted the wrong offensive strategy for an outmanned and outproduced South that led to horrendous casualties. Yet Sherman's marches drew naturally on the matériel and human surpluses of the North and so cracked the core of the Confederacy with few killed on either side. Lee wrongly thought the Union soldier would not fight as well as the Confederate; Sherman rightly guessed that the destruction of Southern property would topple the entire Confederacy. The one ordered thousands to their deaths when the cause was clearly lost; the other destroyed millions of dollars of property to hasten the end of bloodshed. Yet Sherman—who fought on the winning side, who

promised in the abstract death and terror, who was unkempt, garru-
lous, and blunt—is usually criticized. Lee—who embodies the Lost
Cause, who wrote of honor and sacrifice, and who was dapper, gen-
teel, and mannered—is canonized.

The lesson? By attacking the infrastructure of our enemies and
thereby saving lives in the long run, we must, as Machiavelli warned,
expect not to be lauded, but rather caricatured and even despised as
cruel. Sherman also had a keen sense of sociology. In his view, the rich
and landowning class of the South had instigated hostilities; yet more
often the poor free whites of the Confederacy, who did not own slaves,
were dying. In Sherman's view it was far more humane to attack the
property of those responsible for the conflict than to end the lives of
those who were not. Only that way could the entire population learn
the wages of supporting a reckless but impotent Confederate government.

Henry Hitchcock, an officer on Sherman's staff, summed up his
general's use of psychological warfare.

> Not we but their "leaders" and their own moral and physical
> cowardice three years ago are responsible. This Union and its
> Government must be sustained, at any and every cost; to sus-
> tain it, we must war upon and destroy the organized rebel
> forces,—must cut off their supplies, destroy their communica-
> tions, and show their white slaves (these people say themselves
> that they are so) their utter inability to resist the power of the
> U.S. To do this implies and requires these very sufferings, and
> having thus only the choice of evils—war now so terrible and
> successful that none can dream of rebellion hereafter, or ever-
> lasting war with all these evils magnified a hundred fold here-
> after—we have no other course to take.

What can we learn in the present age from General Sherman about
the waging of war? The real morality in war hinges not on damage
wrought but rather concerns the moral imperative to reduce the number of dead and so end the killing as quickly as possible. To accomplish
that goal an army must attack in overwhelming strength and be
imbued with a clear moral sense. The presence of sixty-two thousand
infantrymen in the heart of the South shocked the citizenry of the

Confederacy and prevented various forces under Generals Bragg, Wheeler, and Hardee from offering any defense. Yet the Army of the West wrought such cruel material damage because it believed its cause was just—the South had prompted the war and owned slaves while midwesterners were ending it and freeing the unfree.

In the present context, General Sherman would advise our military planners to use crushing force against our enemies in the Middle East, targeted especially against those who started the war, the personal assets of the terrorists, and the government and military infrastructure of the Taliban and Iraq. And he would urge that we must wage such a full-fledged war constantly with the refrain that an attacked United States was seeking to end terrorism and to overturn the political hierarchy of those guilty illegitimate governments. Cheering in the streets of Arab capitals and posters of bin Laden will disappear only when the ignorant understand the terrible costs of supporting the murderers of Americans. Only with a spiritual element to our battle can a humane society stomach the sheer devastation its army unleashes. "There is a soul to an army," Sherman wrote, "as well as to the individual man, and no general can accomplish the full work of his army unless he commands the soul of his men, as well as their bodies and legs."

Sherman also would be relieved that in our present crisis we are not fighting an adversary as formidable as the South, but rather an opponent from a military tradition that is not as terrifying as our own. In that regard, Sherman and his experience in the American Civil War also offer larger lessons about the Western world at war, which are also relevant in the present conflict that followed September 11, 2001.

We must remember that in the long history of European military practice, it is almost a truism that the chief military worry of a Western army for the last twenty-five hundred years was usually another Western army. Few Greeks were killed at Marathon (490 B.C.) or Plataea (479 B.C.) in the Persian Wars. Thousands died at the later collisions at Nemea and Coronea (394 B.C.), where Greek fought Greek during the Peloponnesian Wars. Alexander himself killed more Europeans in Asia than did the hundreds of thousands of Persians under Darius III. The Roman Civil Wars nearly ruined the republic in a way that even Hannibal had not.

Waterloo, the Somme, and Omaha Beach only confirm the holocaust that occurs when Westerner meets Westerner. The French,

Germans, and English suffered marginal losses in their brutal nineteenth-century colonial wars that resulted in the conquest of the entire continent of Africa. Yet the Crimean campaign (1854–6) and the Franco-Prussian war of 1870–1, both of relatively short duration, saw far more Europeans killed, with fatalities in the many thousands.

The South, of course, due to the presence of the plantation system and the ubiquity of chattel slavery, was not quite the North. Despite its elected congress and traditions of the American Revolution, its distortion of free agriculture and the reactionary nature of its institutions had robbed it of both a vibrant middle class and a climate conducive to research and technological dynamism on par with the North. That being said, the South nevertheless retained enough of the Western tradition to ensure that its armies were sufficiently deadly—highly disciplined, competently led, well organized, often superbly armed—to force Sherman to find another method of war other than the type Grant waged at Cold Harbor or the Wilderness. Sherman realized that Western armies, then, more often faced near annihilation not when pitted against Zulus, Aztecs, Chinese, or Native Americans, but when facing one another—such as in the horrific war between the Union and the Confederacy.

Why is that generally true? Why was the South a far deadlier adversary of the Federal government than had been the Seminoles, Black Hawk, or General Santa Anna? The Western way of war is deadly and as old as the agrarian Greeks of the early seventh century B.C. Its dominance is not haphazard or sporadic, but more or less consistent throughout the last twenty-five centuries, a manifestation of larger Western ideas about culture and politics. The West has achieved military dominance in a variety of ways that transcend mere superiority in weapons, and has nothing to do with morality or genes. The Western way of war is so lethal precisely because it is so unconstrained—shackled rarely by concerns of ritual, tradition, religion, or ethics, by anything other than military necessity. Western armies are often products of civic militarism or constitutional governments and thus are overseen by those outside religion and the military itself. The rare word "citizen" exists in the European vocabularies—Sherman's agrarians were no serfs.

Heavy infantry is also a particularly Western strength—not surprising when Western societies put a high premium on property, and land is often held by a wide stratum of society, such as in the North rather than in the Confederacy. Because free inquiry and rationalism are Western trademarks, European armies have usually marched to war with weapons either superior or at least equal to their adversaries, and have often been supplied far more lavishly through the Western marriage of capitalism, finance, and sophisticated logistics. By the same token, Europeans have been quick to alter tactics, steal foreign breakthroughs, and borrow inventions when in the marketplace of ideas their own traditional tactics and arms have been found wanting.

Western warring often is also an extension of the idea of state politics, rather than a mere effort to obtain territory, personal status, wealth, or revenge. Western militaries put a high premium on individualism, and they are subject to criticism and civilian complaint that often improve rather than erode their war-making ability. President Lincoln was an object of vituperation from both the press and his generals. The idea of annihilation, of head-to-head battle that destroys the enemy, seems a particularly Western concept largely unfamiliar to the ritualistic fighting and emphasis on deception and attrition found outside Europe—hence the greater acceptance of the traditional and quite costly tactics of Grant rather than those more unorthodox tactics of Sherman. There has never been anything quite like the samurai, Maoris, or Flower Wars in the West since the earliest erosion of the protocols of ancient Greek hoplite battle. Westerners, in short, long ago saw war as a method of doing what politics cannot, and thus are willing to obliterate rather than check or humiliate any who stand in their way.

At various periods in Western history the above menu has not always been found in its entirety. Ideas from consensual government to religious tolerance are often ideal rather than modal values. Throughout most of Western civilization there have been countless compromises, as what was attained proved less than what Western culture professed as the most desirable. The Crusaders were religious zealots. Many early European armies were monarchical with only occasional oversight by deliberative bodies. It is hard to see religion and politics as entirely separate in Cortés's small band. Not a phalangite in Alexander's army voted him general, much less king. During the sixth to ninth centuries A.D. there is little evidence that Western forces always enjoyed absolute technological superiority over their foes. German tribesmen were ostensibly as individualistic as Roman legionaries. The Confederacy was a slave society, where true agrarianism was rare.

Yet abstract ideas must often be seen in the context of their times: while Alexander's Macedonians were revolutionaries who had destroyed Greek liberty, there was no escaping their ties with the Hellenic tradition. And that shared heritage explains why soldiers in the phalanx, commanders in the fields, and generals at Alexander's table all voiced their ideas with a freedom unknown in the Achaemenid court at Persepolis. And while the Inquisition was an episode of Western fanaticism gone mad and at times unrestrained by political audit, the tally of its entire bloody course never matched the Aztec score of corpses in a mere four days of human sacrifice at the Great Temple to Huitzilopochtlin in 1487.

Even on the most controversial of issues like freedom, consensual government, and dissent we must judge Western failings not through the lenses of utopian perfectionism of the present, but rather in the context of the global landscape of the times. The essence of Western values is absolute and timeless, but concretely they are also evolutionary, being perfect neither at their birth nor in their adolescence. Slavery had distorted and ruined the Confederacy, but its shared American approach to government, free inquiry, and free speech nevertheless allowed it to field armies nearly comparable with those of the North—and to bring on its own destruction by a self-critical society that believed chattel slavery was abhorrent to the freedom and equality of Western civilization.

Of course, the intrinsic characteristics of Western civilization did not predetermine European success on every occasion. Rather, Western civilization gave a spectrum of advantages to its militaries that allowed them a much greater margin of error and tactical disadvantage—battlefield inexperience, soldierly cowardice, insufficient numbers, terrible generalship—than their adversaries. Luck, individual initiative and courage, the brilliance of a Hannibal or Crazy Horse, the sheer numbers of Zulu or Inca warriors all on occasion could nullify inherent Western military superiority. Yet rarely did these victories of a day affect the ultimate outcome of the war, as culture insidiously and inextricably manifested itself on the battlefield.

Sherman, who had seen the horror of Western warfare unleashed against itself early in the war at Shiloh (April 1862) and again at Kennesaw Mountain (June 1864), came to learn that head-on assaults against another Western power mean near suicide—a fate that would ruin the soul of his army and prevent it from being a moral force of reckoning. With enemies with effective Western weapons, sophisticated organization, and high discipline—and fighting on their home ground—Sherman knew that strategy and generalship had to evolve beyond what was transpiring in northern Virginia.

Like the later George S. Patton, who also understood well the lethality of his enemy, Sherman sought instead to craft a mobile type of war that avoided pitched battles, a war of envelopment, which the military strategist Liddell Hart once called the "indirect approach." His purpose, then, like ours presently in Afghanistan, was to find that elusive mechanism by which adversaries could be defeated most quickly with the least amount of lives lost on either side—while still conveying the essential lesson that the enemy had not merely been beaten but so humiliated that it would never again think of precipitating aggression.

In another context as well, we can also find solace from Sherman's war-making in the present war. Despite the unpredictability of our enemies and their murderous ability to strike our homeland—the World Trade Center was a far greater disaster than either Fort Sumter or Pearl Harbor, which both predicated the sacrifice of hundreds of thousands of Americans in battle—the Taliban, the terrorists, and their supporters in the Middle East cannot fabricate weapons such as ours. Their societies are either theocratic or autocratic and so give no freedom for unblinkered research, much less for the easy dissemination of knowledge or a system of true capitalism that allows private companies to profit from their ability to translate abstract research to the mass production of technologically sophisticated weapons.

The warriors of the Middle East share a distinguished military pedigree, but it is a different and less successful tradition of military discipline, one not centered on long adherence to drill, keeping in time, advance and retreat according to command, and group discipline. Their armies are not audited by civilians nor are their soldiers free to vote on the conditions of their own service. Most Middle Eastern economies are not open and so cannot supply men at war nearly as well as our own. These cultural fault lines—however controversial it may appear to suggest such radical differences—may seem subtle and often take time to become manifest, but in war a society's intrinsic values ultimately determine the very success or failure of its military. The present conflict is no exception.

The chief brake on a Western army is not merely another Western army but also at times our own humane traditions, which on occasion can question the very morality of our use of overwhelming force and therein impede its devastating use even in a very moral cause. Afraid to invade Germany and inflict greater suffering after November 1918, the Allies turned to Versailles—only to create the myth among German nationalists that they had been "stabbed in the back" by Jews and communists, and so never really lost the war at all. The Second World War and its millions of innocent dead were the harvests of that misguided utopianism twenty years earlier.

The grotesque carnage of Iraqi soldiers on the "Highway of Death" shocked our sensibilities, and led to calls to end the Gulf War—only to allow Saddam Hussein to live on to butcher thousands of innocents. Sherman taught us that such moderation in war is imbecility, and that smug moralizing before absolute victory is achieved—which he called "bottled piety"—in fact gets more, not fewer, killed.

If an army has the moral edge, and its soldiers, as Sherman proclaimed, are imbued with a "soul" that assures them that they are agents of righteous retribution and democratic justice, then Westerners can make war like no other people in the history of civilization. In the present conflict, if we adhere to our moral values, employ the unchecked power of our culture with confidence and without apology to achieve victory quickly and with a minimum of casualties, and seek to make the instigators of the war pay dearly and personally for their folly, then General Sherman would assure us that our ultimate victory will never be in doubt.

*Written on September 25; a shorter version, titled "America's New War,"
published in a special autumn issue of Military History Quarterly.*

8.

What If?

RETHINKING 1941 WITH EDWARD R. MURROW

What Should We Do?

BY EDWARD R. MURROW

WASHINGTON, D.C.

DECEMBER 8, 1941

PRESIDENT ROOSEVELT WILL call for a joint session of Congress today to discuss yesterday's bombing of Pearl Harbor and the reported loss of twenty-four hundred Americans. I can report that our commander-in-chief is calm and will not ask for a precipitous "outright" declaration of war against the Japanese, but instead leans toward a general consensus to "hunt down the perpetrators" of this act of "infamy."

Speaking for the Congress, Senator Arthur Vandenberg promised bipartisan support to "bring to justice" the Japanese pilots. Many believe that the "rogue" airmen may well have flown from Japanese warships. In response, Secretary of War Stimson is calling for "an international coalition to indict these cowardly purveyors of death," and will shortly ask the Japanese imperial government to hand over the suspected airman from the *Akagi* and *Kaga*—"and any more of these cruel fanatics who took off from ships involved in this dastardly act." Assistant Secretary Robert Patterson was said to have remarked, "Stimson is madder than hell—poor old Admiral Yamamato has a lot of explaining to do."

Secretary of State Cordell Hull, however, this morning cautioned the nation about such "jingoism." He warned, "The last thing we want is another *Maine* or *Lusitania*. We wouldn't want to start something like a Second World War and ruin the real progress in Japanese-American relations over the last few years." Hull himself is preparing for a long tour to consult our allies in South America, Africa, and colonial France: "If we get the world on board, and make them understand that this is not merely an aggressive act upon us, much less just an American problem, such a solid front may well deter further Japanese action."

Even as Hull prepares to depart, special envoy Harry Hopkins is calling for a general statement of concern from the League of Nations, condemning not only the most recent Japanese aggression, but also an earlier reported incident in Nanking, China. "If we can get an expression of outrage from the League, Japan may well find itself in an interesting pickle. We're looking for some strong League action of the type that followed the banditry in Ethiopia and Finland." Hopkins finished by emphasizing the rather limited nature of the one-day Pearl Harbor incursion, and suggesting such piecemeal attacks were themselves a direct result of past American restraint. "We did not rattle our sabers when they went into China. Had we listened to the alarmists then, we might well be seeing Japanese anger manifesting itself from the Philippines to Wake Island in the coming days."

Secretary of the Treasury Henry Morgenthau, Jr., a few hours ago reminded the nation of the current disturbing economic news. "Four million Americans are still out of work. Americans are not out of this Depression by any means. Are we to borrow money to build planes that we don't even know will fly?" The industrialist Henry Kaiser was no more optimistic: "There is simply no liquidity in these markets. We shouldn't even be considering rearming. It is not as if we are going to build a ship a day. Even launching a carrier every couple of years could put us back to 1932."

Military leaders, smarting over yesterday's losses, were no more ready for war. Even the usually colorful Admiral Halsey sounded a note of concern to this reporter. "Look, they have all the cards, not us. The bastards over there could give us a decade of war at least. Where do I get bases for my subs and flattops? Who gives me strips for the flyboys? This could be a new war with no rules. Believe me, brother, we ain't going to Midway or some place like that in six months and cut down to size the whole damn imperial fleet. It's just not going to happen." Admiral King was nearly as blunt. "Hell's bells, no one has ever conquered Japan since they kicked the Portuguese out. Do the American people really want to go over to that part of the world and fight those samurai madmen? The logistics are impossible. These people have been at war for years. I've seen these Zeros—you put a suicide basket case with a wish to die for the emperor in with a tank of gas, and you've got a guided rocket that will blow our ships out of the water." Colonel James Doolittle was even more cautious than the top brass when told of calls for potential early American counterattacks. "Swell—the last thing we need is to send in some hot-dogger to drop a few bombs for the press boys that cause no real damage and get our fellas killed in the bargain."

On the home front, prominent voices in the arts expressed far stronger reservations about possible American "revenge." Robert Maynard Hutchins of the University of Chicago explained to me that the Pearl Harbor incident cannot be separated from its larger cultural context. "We must guard against this absurd and ongoing moral absolutism on the part of the United States in seeing complex cultural differences in black and white terms of the Occident and the Orient. We have no monopoly on morality or justice."

His colleague Mortimer J. Adler elaborated: "Far too often we look at the world through Western lenses. But in Japanese eyes, this rather desperate attack is seen as a 'slap,' a lashing out of sorts to get the attention of the United States, really more of a desperate cry of the heart than anything else." Adler went on, "Japan has had a tradition of isolation from and distrust of Western civilization—rightly so in some respects, given everything from past European missionaries to racism, economic exploitation, and colonialism. If we inflame passions, they may well simply divorce themselves from the world community—or worse, set off a conflagration of pan-Asian hatred toward Occidentals that could last for generations. It seems to me Pearl Harbor is rather more of a case of Admiral Perry's chickens at long last coming home to roost."

Contacted at home, the noted naval historian Samuel Eliot Morison was pessimistic about the strategy involved in any U.S. response: "Good God, do they want us to fight the entire world—Germany, Italy, Hungry, Bulgaria, Romania, and now Japan? We lose twenty-four hundred sailors—less than an annual poliomyelitis outbreak—and then we start a World War II? I find these calls for mindless retaliation not only naive, but disturbing as well in their failure to take account of America's strategic impotence. That's a part of the world we know very little about."

Prominent American clergymen blasted the very idea of armed retaliation, calling instead for interfaith services and greater tolerance of Japanese religious beliefs. Cardinal Cushing warned against castigating the entire Japanese people for the actions of a few fanatics, adding that "Bushido, is, in fact, merely a variant of Shintoism, itself an age-old and misunderstood faith that is as humane as anything in Christian teaching." Cushing added, "There is nothing in Bushido, much less Shintoism, that is inherently bellicose or at all anti-Western. These few extremists are hardly representative of either public or religious opinion in Japan." Cushing concluded, "The Emperor himself is a pacifist, a Zen scholar in fact deeply devoted to entomology, with no interest at all in bloodshed. And so the better question might be posed: 'Why does so much of Asia hate us?'"

Well-known director John Ford reflected Hollywood's unease with the early rumors of war. "Hell, we are artists, not mouthpieces. What are we to do—join the Navy to make movies on government spec? Had we had more Japanese films available to the American people in the first place, we wouldn't have had this misunderstanding." A few Hollywood stars who were willing to speak on the record agreed. Jimmy Stewart called for a world conference of concerned actors and screenwriters. "There have been some great Japanese movies. We need to reach out to our brother actors over there. The last thing we need is a bunch of us would-be pilots storming over to Burbank to enlist." Clark Gable was adamant in his belief in keeping America from doing something "stupid," as he put it. "If you haven't heard lately: We're actors, artists really, not war-mongers. I'm sure that our Japanese counterparts feel the same way. We need to put away the B-17s and get the cameras rolling on both sides."

Celebrated veterans were especially angered about knee-jerk American anger. Alvin C. York, Medal of Honor winner and hero of the Great War, was reported as "madder than hell" at the "war scare." "We shouldn't fight in some jungle island just because the Japanese hate old man Rockefeller as much as we do." In an in-depth newsmaker interview, 81-year-old General John J. Pershing told Henry Luce of *Time* magazine, "I've made war before—long and hard. I've seen it. These sunshine sluggers talk a great game, but wait until our dead pile up. No, it is time to collect our thoughts and think like adults for a change. Lashing back is just what these extremists want us to do. If a war breaks out, then their mission is accomplished. I'd hate to see us playing into the hands of a few militarists who want to topple the moderates and the emperor. This ocean war with carriers is an entirely new challenge, nothing like we have ever seen before. Why get our boys killed only to make a few samurai martyrs?"

And so it is with confidence today that this reporter assures the American people and the world that sobriety, maturity, and prudence—not bombs—are the watchwords on the home front. Remember—our enemies can win only if they make us answer their violence with more needless violence.

Written on September 26 and published in National Review Online
on September 27.

9.

What Would Churchill Say?

THE PHONY SILENCE BEFORE THE STORMING

WE ARE ENTERING a surreal parenthesis, not unlike the brief but phony quiet of the "war" that characterized the French-German border between September 1939 and May 10, 1941. The destruction of the World Trade Center, the downing of four airliners, and the ravaging of the Pentagon—like the ruin of Poland in 1939—of course will not go away. Thousands of our countrymen are dead; we accept that the world can never be quite what it was.

So, like the French of 1940, we accept that war has been unleashed upon us. Yet the same counterfeit voices of good, but weak and therefore very dangerous men that arose in the false calm between the destruction of Poland and the blitzkrieg through the Ardennes— "Perhaps if we do not invade Germany . . ."; "Maybe if we redouble our border defenses . . ."; "Possibly moderates in Germany can make headway with Hitler . . ."—are still with us. Like the Greek city-states in the path of Xerxes' terror, or Athens in the shadow of Macedon, they wonder whether there is an escape from the ordeal ahead, through moderation and conciliation. There is none. The hesitancy of France led to the collapse of the last democracy on the mainland, and unparalleled killing of the innocent. Salamis, not envoys and ambassadors, halted Xerxes. Philip II was demanding not alliances or neutrality, but servitude.

But as the ghastly cloud over Manhattan thins, far too many of us hope for a reprieve that we really know shall not—and should not—come, cloaking that paralysis of resolve in the slogans of sophisticated enlightenment ("One could argue . . ."), religious tolerance ("Let us not . . ."), or occasional self-loathing ("It is because we . . ."). The voices of appeasement make themselves feel better by worrying more about purported racial profiling than about the fate of those who leaped into the great void from the Twin Towers—profiled for *their* murder by virtue of living in America. Pundits are now showing concern about European approval, not about the incineration of our infants in day-care centers. We are bombarded with images of the fanatical in Kabul and Islamabad; less common are words of outrage over our stewardesses whose throats were slit. Do our university presidents, anchormen, and theologians say of the Taliban, "What kind of people do they think we are?"

States that a few weeks ago harbored terrorist killers now cry that the operational name of our planned response, "Infinite Justice," is offensive to Muslim ears, and it is abruptly changed—even though the name reflected perfectly our American creed to accept responsibility, in the here and now, to right wrong to the bitter end. Our spokesman at the Department of State was asked inanely whether the Taliban were involved in the recent destruction of our abandoned embassy in Kabul—as if we, who have lost three thousand in our streets, should care much about an empty shell of a building or the motives of our enemies who torch it. The hesitant supreme NATO commander in Europe asks for greater proof of bin Laden's guilt, as if we, the offspring of Normandy and Okinawa, are to be reduced to mere barristers parrying at the Hague.

The voice of pained experts on the screen saturate us with so many worries: germs, small nuclear bombs, nerve gas, crop dusters, and hazardous waste from biological dumps, all of which may obliterate us in our sleep. Apparently, not a pundit is to be found who will recall a beleaguered Churchill's acceptance of the nature of the new war with his Nazi foe—"the latest refinements of science are linked with the cruelties of the Stone Age."

Military experts advise us that Afghanistan is both landlocked and mountainous. Are not caves there impenetrable? Will it not be soon snowing? Worse still, our foes are not traditional enemies and so immune from the laws of war of the ages! Do any of us shrug back, "No one can guarantee success in war, but only deserve it"? Other sirens beckon in the false melodies of Iranian, Syrian, or Sudanese friendship. Few leaders step forth to cut it off with, "We will have no truce or parley with you, or the grisly gang who do your wicked will. You do your worst—and we will do our best."

Rallies on our campuses, in our churches, and on our streets are calling for American restraint—seeking doubt within ourselves, and so with it perhaps escape from further ruin. The vocabulary of courage, victory, and triumph is not in our lexicon, but indeed is said to be more likely proof of brute savagery and ignorance. We have forgotten: "You ask, what is our policy? I will say: it is to wage war, by sea, land, and air, and with all our might. . . . You ask, what is our aim? I can answer in one word: victory. . . . Victory at all costs, victory in spite of all terror, victory however long and hard the road may be; for without victory there is no survival!"

Without mass funerals to remind us of our dead, three weeks later, some now worry whether our initial ultimatums were too obdurate. Perhaps the biological arsenal of Iraq has been put away? Or might not be used? Or was but a figment of our imagination? Or is none of our business? They forget that such momentary doubts are inevitable and human, but must be countered always by, "Never give in, never give in, never, never, never, never—in nothing, great or small, large or petty—never give in except to convictions of honor and good sense."

So we in this country have forgotten the essence of Churchillian humanity, itself the age-old definition that demands our sacrifice and courage to eliminate the evil that kills the innocent. We must act to end this scourge, without worry about the censure to come from the universities, the Europeans, the moderate Arab nations, and our media. Indeed, we must welcome it all, and always with confidence that these terrorists must fear us far more than we do them. We must be happy that it's now our task, not our children's nor their children's, to end this terror:

Do not let us speak of darker days; let us rather speak of sterner days. These are not dark days; these are great days—the greatest days our country has ever lived; and we must all thank God that we have been allowed, each of us according to our stations, to play a part in making these days memorable.

And so they are, and so we shall.

Written on September 29 and published in National Review Online *on October 1.*

II.

=====

October

(America strikes back, anthrax spores mailed to major media and Congress, U.S. Capitol partly shut down and evacuated; Northern Alliance not advancing on its enemies; Colin Powell visits Pakistan and speaks of "moderate Taliban"; U.S. Air Force bombing continues precision targeting of al-Qaeda command and control in the major cities)

WE WERE IN a war that did not feel like a war. In the three weeks after the September 11 attack, the United States slowly marshaled its forces in preparation for a military response against al-Qaeda and the Taliban in Afghanistan. Yet in the hiatus between September 11 and October 7, a number of Americans continued to argue that we should not respond at all, especially as the vehemence of the Taliban and the terrorists was broadcast around the world, replete with threats of more mayhem and thousands of American dead to come.

Academics, novelists, and social critics voiced more embarrassing condemnations of the United States' proposed retaliation, suggesting that America had either asked for or even deserved September 11—or at least now understood the wages of racism, colonialism, and economic exploitation among the Third World peoples. The longer America took to act in response, the more its detractors misinterpreted that necessary period of preparation as either moral reflection on our past wrongs or perhaps listlessness and uncertainty about the need to go to Afghanistan at all.

After the bombing began on October 7, such doubts about America's resolve dissolved—but only to be replaced by even more criticism from both the Left and the Right! The former talked of moral equivalence between September 11 and our air strikes in Afghanistan, more worried about collateral damage than the systematic and precise destruction of the command and control structures of the Taliban and al-Qaeda. The latter wanted more decisive results and near instantaneous victory, not understanding that the Pentagon was quite determined to destroy all enemy troops in the field—but only after it had first dismantled antiaircraft resistance and the logistical and military organization of the Taliban high command.

The themes of these ten October essays remained that Americans should ignore the increasingly shrill invective of its cultural elite, who had neither an understanding of their own country nor even rudimentary knowledge of military history. My only worry was that the stellar leadership of Mr. Bush and Mr. Rumsfeld was not yet appreciated for what it was—a courageous attempt to wage war six thousand miles away, to talk honestly about the costs involved, and to protect the innocent of Afghanistan as assiduously as to punish the mass murderers in their midst.

10.

On Gorgons and Furies

CIVILIZATION AND ITS DISCONTENTS

SADDAM ONCE PLEDGED to wage "the mother of all battles" and to leave "thousands of Americans dead in the sand." Even a few American pundits believed him—before his army was annihilated in four days. The terrorists in the Middle East and their Taliban sponsors in Afghanistan now promise to do all sorts of horrible things to us—from an unending jihad of terror, to murdering Americans on sight worldwide, to hints of gassing us in our schools and offices. We are told to be aware that our "new" enemies will be disguised, untraceable, unpredictable, and therefore nearly unstoppable.

This mythology of horror is hardly new and perhaps dates from the dawn of the Greek city-state. Classical folklore, both in art and literature, is full of brutal, terror-inducing creatures that practice every evil art of destruction.

Sirens—in the manner advised in the hijackers' manuals—masked their evil with sweet voices and smiles. Proteus, like bin Laden, appeared suddenly—but never in the same guise. Beastly Cyclopes and Amazons—just like the fundamentalists—did not build cities, write literature, or create technology. They instead preferred to murder against civilization.

What was the purpose of these scary creatures in the Greek mind?

The early myths conveyed to the city-state that civilization's struggle against wild hatred and fury—like our own against the present terrorists and their hosts—was a constant and always frightening one. Stymphalian Birds, like hijackers, dove out of nowhere. The many-necked Hydra shot out another ghastly head each time one was cut off. Foul, hit-and-run Harpies fed like parasites on their hosts. And the nearly invincible Nemean Lion was reputed to be impenetrable by the tools of conventional weaponry.

All these opponents—who symbolized the age-old evil that we once again see arrayed against us—played on the innate fears of comfortable citizens that there were primeval forces in the world that enjoyed chaos and killing, and that did not fight like the good hoplite soldiers of the polis. Disguise, stealth, bloody rhetoric, hideous new ways of murder, attacks on the innocent and unprepared, threats to use unspeakable methods of mass destruction can all, if we are not careful, turn us to stone in fear.

But arrayed against the precivilized Scylla, Echidna, and Charybdis, of course, are the fearless heroes of myth—Odysseus, Theseus, Perseus, Heracles, and others—who in art and literature reminded the new civilization of the city-state that culture could always defeat the untamed. Such figures as Theseus, slayer of the Minotaur, were enshrined as protectors of order through the tools of civilization—law, justice, reason, and technology. The Furies, Gorgons, and Cyclopes were hideous to behold, and their howls and shrieks worse to hear, but they were all eventually blinded, decapitated, or driven back into the dark through learning and courage. Perseus did not have to see Medusa to cut off her head.

There is also a rhetoric of war that can be as frightening as it is empty. Epaminondas, the Theban liberator, was lectured endlessly about the impossibility of marching into the heart of Sparta to free the Helots—in a land that had boasted of no invasion for "seven hundred years." In such a strong confine, "No Spartan woman would ever see the smoke of an enemy campfire," King Agesilaus bragged—shortly before his entire countryside went up in flames. "Oh, the ambitious man," the king later stammered of Epaminondas as he watched his own once vaunted army of professional killers, in their horrific dreadlocks and scarlet cloaks, cower inside the city.

On the eve of Normandy, Hitler and his generals boasted of the Waffen SS that such a singular division would push the "cowboys" into the sea—the same feared division that in a few weeks' time was incinerated by American GIs in the Falaise Gap. To paraphrase Churchill, "some cowboys." The sea of death, as it turned out, was not of water, but of flames.

I think some Americans are now fearful of the ordeal ahead, and not out of ideological concerns. How, after all, can progressives stomach mass murderers who treat women like animals, urge the killing of Jews on sight, behead innocents, and forbid religious or political tolerance? While the Vatican, the Harvard library, and the United Nations have not yet been blown apart, there is clearly no reason to believe that any of them are immune from these fundamentalists' hatred of non-Muslims, the Western rational tradition, or liberal internationalism.

Nor are those protesting really pacifists: Even the most "moral" now realize that ignoring evil—whether in Bosnia, Iraq, or Afghanistan—only gets women and children killed. The Vietnam-era cry of resistance, that "they are not attacking us here at home," is now irrelevant, and past restraint in confronting terrorism has only invited this disaster. Even the professedly peace-loving realize that the three thousand may be only a beginning, and that self-proclaimed nonresistance only fuels the arrogance of these killers—who act on the conviction that Americans are either cowardly or impotent.

And even critics of military action do not believe that our dead are a result of America's politics. They—and the world—know well that no country has saved more Muslims in the last twenty years—whether the Kuwaiti, Shiite, or Kurdish victims of Saddam; the Afghani enemies of Soviet Communism; the starving in Somalia; or the targeted in Bosnia and Kosovo. Make Israel or America disappear tomorrow, and the terrorists would only turn to murdering Westerners in Europe or Japan. India and Russia, both targets of these madmen, are not always strong American allies or sympathetic to our foreign policies.

Rather, many in America are hesitant because they are fearful of Gorgons and Harpies—in dread of a long, bitter struggle against the shrieking and beastly that will interrupt our daily routines, cost us more lives, and earn us more hatred. Fear—not the usual coffeehouse ideology, the abstract morality of the faculty lounge, or the easy five-minute guilt of the suburban affluent—is the real fuel of their protests.

This is understandable in an affluent democracy, which as the historian Thucydides tells us, is at first fickle and prone to self-doubt. Yet—as he also reminds us, of both classical Athens and Syracuse—democracies eventually prove the most resourceful and resolved in war, as they slowly marshal their enormous arsenal against the unfamiliar, and answer the mythology of terror with the reality of power.

In the trying months ahead, we should not listen to what the fundamentalist terrorists say, but instead watch what we do. Like all enemies of civilization, the primordial Taliban and the beastly supporters of bin Laden will soon fall. And perhaps best of all, at last—like Medusa and the Hydra—they too will grow mute.

Written on October 1 and published in National Review Online
on October 3.

II.

Cognitive Dissonance

WHAT YOU SEE AND WHAT YOU GET

WE ARE BOMBARDED by strange paradoxes that pop up on our television screens, and then disappear without a chance for proper reflection and gestation—only the contradiction, hypocrisy, and idiocy are left behind to enrage us. Analysts, pundits, and press officers offer the conventional wisdom du jour only to have it altered, confirmed, or ridiculed by a "late-breaking" flash, or by the throat-clearing of a more impressive grandee.

Are we sane or mad when we watch the Pakistani spokesman in Washington assure us of "continuing friendship" and "full support"—and then channel surf to her country's Taliban schools and mullahs promising death to Americans? Are terrorist states like Iraq, Syria, Libya, and Lebanon always, sometimes, or never sponsors of terrorism? Tragically, the only constant is that the memory of, grief for, and anger over our dead is fading, as our pundits give us every reason to do little, and little reason to do much.

Without a strong sense of national purpose—and the courage to act alone—option A is now suddenly "of course" B—but perhaps, tomorrow, either C or yet again A. Those in the prior administration—Mr. Christopher, Mr. Berger, Mr. Cohen, and Mr. Clinton himself—who did not act resolutely against a long series of terrorist bombings, now either explain why they did not act, or explain that they in fact did act—or explain why they did not act and why we should (or should not) act—or, at times, all four at once. Mr. Bush, Mr. Rumsfeld, Ms. Rice, and others have been admirable in this crisis so far, but they are up against formidable odds.

The high NATO command had made it clear for days that it wanted "evidence" of terrorist culpability, but then so do Pakistan, the

Taliban, Iraq, Iran—and Mr. bin Laden himself. Excepting the British, each day a European country takes its turn assuring us that it is helping, not helping, protesting, worried, or aiding mysteriously and stealthily, "in ways appropriate to the situation at hand." Yet the NATO command did not formally invoke Article Five for a joint response until nearly three weeks after thousands of innocents were vaporized. Perhaps, in 1950, had three thousand Germans been incinerated on the Warsaw Pact border, we could have asked for a twenty-one-day inquiry as Soviet tankers lunched into the coastal cafés of Normandy.

The European Union rhetoric of the last decade has turned many of our traditional allies into neutrals—and it is perhaps time that we should, with some regret, stop pressuring them and accept their decision. Germany, France, the Netherlands, Belgium, and others are more like Sweden and Switzerland than like military allies who will join ranks with their comrades-in-arms. NATO, dare we say it, has become a boutique alliance that requires no real sacrifice—unless it's to be American, and thus can be both decisive, and yet nuanced and criticized when successfully completed. Given the level of European assistance in hunting down and jailing the killers of Americans during the last two decades, it was indeed easier for a fundamentalist to cut a check in Brussels than it was for an American fighter to fly over France on its way to Libya.

Europe's hesitancy is paradoxical, when more muscular allies—Russia and India in particular—are so much more supportive. Like us, they are multiracial, secular, democratic, and nuclear—and with no illusions about the deadly purpose of Islamic fundamentalism. They are not shy about the need for action, and oddly are becoming more like us—and the kindred Europeans, less—as the war continues.

An Italian premier is lambasted by his European colleagues for suggesting that the culture of the West is superior to that of the Islamic world. Yet from his vantage point, the shores opposite Italy (past and present) are the more dangerous places, where fanaticism has turned to genocide in Algeria; Libya is a lunatocracy; and Egypt is unable to feed, protect, or govern itself. Europeans, the chastised leader seems to be suggesting, are not immigrating to the Muslim world.

Even more chaff clouds our domestic radar. Harvard University purportedly accepted over a million dollars from scions of the bin Laden family, whose ties with their bad-seed sibling are not always altogether broken; and we remember that Yale University not long ago rejected twenty times more from one of its own alumni to promote the study of Western Civilization. Saudi grandees lecture us on the inappropriateness of using their bases to kill murderers, yet in the aftermath of the slaughter immediately call in our authorities to help protect the bin Laden family inside the United States until it can be whisked safely away back home. Would that the princes worried more about the ghosts of three thousand than about the status of the estranged kin of a terrorist. But then Stalin purportedly scoffed that the death of one is a tragedy, the death of a million a statistic.

Our talking heads bring in Muslim moderates to explain to us yokels the differences between radical fundamentalism and Islam. But just as often the imams and even moderate Palestinians achieve precisely the opposite effect, by castigating Israel (usually ten seconds into the interview), warning us about racial profiling (fifteen seconds)—and rarely saying a word about the dead, or about the uniqueness of the United States in welcoming a self-critique impossible anywhere in the Arab world. Then they are thanked for their "insight," and go on to the next show.

Why are these images and pronouncements so contradictory, and so often infuriating? The ghastly events of September 11, of course, explain much of the chaos—more dead than in all American wars combined up to Shiloh. We are also stunned by the shadowy nature of our terrorist enemies, and surely worried about the volatility of the Middle East at large.

Yet much of our contradictory "yes, but . . ." language reflects more than just the uncertainty of these tragic days. Rather, we are seeing the last bitter wages of decades of the moral vapidity inherent in cultural relativism; conflict-resolution theory; and a general ignorance of history, whose result has been to leave us Americans—of all people!—quite afraid. More in government need to reply directly to critics here and abroad, and come to the aid of Mr. Bush and his stalwarts. Pericles, Lincoln, and Roosevelt (either one)—or Tony Blair—must single-mindedly remind us always of our dead—firemen like Michael Weinberg, Paddy Brown, Joseph Angelini, Gerard Schrang, Tarel Coleman, Joseph Gulleckson, José Guadalupe, and the hundreds more from Ladder 28 and Rescue 1—and the thousands more still whom they tried so desperately to save.

Press spokesmen must point out to the naysayers that we will use both special operations and conventional forces—because they are complementary, not antithetical, given the daring scope of our global response—whose methods are mysterious as their ends are not. Those in the State Department must make it clear, publicly, that allies lend assistance and neutrals do not, and that the choice is theirs, not ours, to either follow or get out of the way when we roll out. If history is any guide to the present, victory in battle alone—not pleading and obsequiousness—will bring us more allies than we need or desire.

Others should make it clear, in the new world after September 11, that if a country has a democracy, and is secular, and fights Islamic terrorism, it is most certainly to be welcomed to our cause. Perhaps one or two charged-up Trumans may "misspeak" on occasion, suggesting rudely that the active friendship of Russia and India is a good thing, and surely of more concern to us than whether Mr. Arafat donates blood, or whether the Iranian "parliament" gives us a polite admonition.

The American people are not saber-rattling, bloodthirsty, or hysterical. We do not want bombs tomorrow. But we do need help in bridging the abyss between what we know to be true and what we see and hear. Please, spokesmen, less counterfeit light and more heartfelt heat.

Written on October 3 and published in National Review Online
on October 5.

12.

What Made Them Do Their Duty?

FROM THE VERY first moments of the World Trade Center horror, the valor and élan of New York's firemen, together with that of the city's police and emergency forces, have transfixed the whole nation—especially us in rural America who rarely see the real Gotham. Danger was nothing to them, courage and honor everything. They responded instantly to the explosion and fire, all drawn to, rather than repelled by, the inferno—and without regard for their own safety or the consequences of their possible incineration upon their loved ones at home. We now know their last radio cries: "Move away from the towers! Everyone move away from the towers!" Silence. . . .

As the ghastly rubble gets turned over, we find their remains in clusters—four incinerated here, ten buried there, fourteen caught en masse in a stairwell, where they had guided the panicked down as they themselves ascended to their deaths: "All nonessential personnel move away from that building!" The antithesis, left unsaid, is obvious: "All necessary rescuers get into that building!"

So many of them disappeared—at least 388 firefighters—because in a heartbeat they chose to race into the flames and smoke rather than to hesitate and accept the obvious: that the towers were already death traps. In the tradition of all great American armies in battle, officers—47 lieutenants, 20 captains, and 21 chiefs—died alongside the rank and file, a heroic death requiring no prerequisite of class or color. Indeed, the magnitude of the terrorist-inflicted disaster rivaled that of a fierce battle, where the enemy overruns and annihilates an entire military unit—paramedics, a fire marshal, even the fire department's chaplain were engulfed. Remarkably, moments after the buildings collapsed, there were even more rescue workers on the scene than before. It is human to flee from a place of death; the firemen and the police were almost inhuman in mounting so quickly the rubble that buried their brethren.

As terrible as their loss was, however, we must never forget how successful the rescuers actually were. Nearly thirty thousand people escaped before the towers fell, in large part because the omnipresent cops and firefighters made sure that their own sense of calm and order guided the evacuation. Some of the saved made it out just seconds before thousands of tons buried their saviors on stairs and in hallways. Now, for these past few weeks, the nation has watched these brave men and women, joined by construction and sanitation workers, as they search for the victims, always overturning the debris and moving beams with care to avoid harming potential survivors or further violating the deceased. Finding one of their own dead, they carry him out on flag-draped stretchers, with ceremony and protocol. Then they return to the rubble, paying less attention to collapsing concrete, unexpected bursts of flame, and razor-sharp twisted steel than to their powerful sense of fraternal obligation.

It is impossible not to admire their selflessness. Inhaling what was once the World Trade Center, both human and inanimate, they do not bother to debate—as many fearful people have done in the wake of the attacks—what might be the best brand of gas mask to don. They are not calibrating their chances of survival in threatened future gas attacks, because they're already breathing a sort of awful gas in the here and now.

The rescuers' selflessness is always evident in their interactions with the press and media. As television crews shove cameras in their faces and microphones under their blackened chins, they respond with tact, worrying mostly that their Herculean efforts are not enough—that they won't bring the dead back to life. We catch an occasional "Good work, brother," or a "Don't worry, we are going to get everybody out," or a polite "We can't talk now, just work until it's over and we've brought them out."

Sometimes the contrast between the brave rescue workers and their occasionally hysterical observers among the chattering classes is glaring. *Nightline*'s Ted Koppel listens to the last radio transmissions of those caught in the collapses and asks: "Why were they so confused, why were the radios so bad?" We wince and sigh: "Because a million tons of concrete and steel were showering down on their heads!"

The rescuers' simple patriotism offers another favorable contrast with some of their elite observers. We do not hear from New York's heroic firemen and police any sophisticated nonsense that we brought the two towers crashing down upon ourselves because of our arrogance or imperial political ambitions. They do not tell us that we must change our sinful ways and abandon our friends. I don't think most of them give a damn what a Frenchman or a Palestinian says about our ordeal. Most seem to accept that a magnificent city such as theirs, in a nation as free and humane as their own, naturally invites the envy of lesser people and thus must be defended from those who hate what we are rather than anything we have done. Seeing the rescuers display their patriotism at Ground Zero, where they have carefully displayed American flags and patriotic slogans, swells one's own national pride.

These selfless, patriotic men and women project a physical presence that harks back to an earlier age—one largely unseen on the national scene for the last half-century. Muscular, tireless despite constant movement, a quiet confidence in corporeal strength—it is as if they stepped out of depression-era post-office murals or faded watercolors in long defunct magazines.

Their robust physicality seems less the product of the health club or plastic surgeon's office than of hard and dirty work. The younger workers look like—no, look better than—athletes, their biceps built not for play but for carrying hoses and scaling ladders. Their ongoing labor seems to magnify their physical presence; in comparison, the ripples and contours of professional athletes now look oddly artificial. Some working in the rubble—overweight, smoking, sweating profusely—hardly look fit, of course. But using ample bellies as wedges and levers against the stones and steel, they remind America that you can be tough as nails and still be deemed out of shape.

Even their unit names seem to belong to a different, older era— "Ladder 28," "Squad 41," "Rescue 1." They remind one of the first wave of torpedo bombers, wiped out nearly to the man at the Battle of Midway, whose planes, bearing names like "Torpedo 6" and "Scouting 8," drew fire from Japanese Zeros, so that U.S. dive bombers, flying above them, could attack unmolested the now vulnerable enemy carriers below. These days, we might have expected the nomenclature of the rescue units to be something like "Integrated Systems Protection" or

"Specialized Reaction and Control." That the unit names are so old-fashioned suggests that the rescue workers remain in some profound sense faithful to custom and tradition.

There is a lesson that the heroic dead and their courageous brethren at Ground Zero can offer to the elites and intellectuals who often look down on, or simply ignore, the concrete, physical world that forms the rescuers' daily milieu. What strikes many of us from outside New York who visit the city, after all, is how it all works. How do tons of water, food, and fuel enter the city every day, along with millions of commuters? Where do the sewage, trash, and litter all go? And in such cramped confines, how do people not kill and maim one another by the hour?

Now we have proof of what we've suspected all along: that "regular" New Yorkers like these, showing enormous versatility, make it all work. The concrete canyons of the city have not enervated their audacity, strength, and cunning, but have sharpened them in ways we could scarcely imagine. Any of us on America's farms or in its factories or mines who thought New Yorkers soft now realize how mistaken we were. The rescuers, it turns out, could easily drive tractors, ride horses, or dig in mines, if their duty was not to brave flames and catch criminals.

Indeed, many of the rescuers exemplify a Hellenic balance. These firemen and cops, like the Greeks, innately understand that muscles matched with mind are essential to our collective flourishing and safety. This balance, I think, underlies the steady confidence that the surviving rescuers show when they speak of responding to the September 11 attack. Their voices remain calm, never frightened; they are not crying out blindly for revenge for their brothers. They talk—often incisively—of a slow, growing, and enduring response that accords with their own very American sense of fairness, righteous indignation, and humanity: "They will pay for this; you'll see."

I would not wish to meet people such as these in battle. Yet I think the Taliban and their henchmen face in our military forces just such people. Everywhere, we hear warnings to be cautious and afraid, but I think it is our enemies, not us, who have real cause for worry, for until now they have struck only at the innocent and unaware. Now they must confront the spiritual kin of the rescuers.

Brave, selfless, patriotic, strong, and versatile—no wonder these public servants seem to bring out the best in those who cross their paths. Where do such marvelous people come from? Doubtless part of the answer has to do with the clannish ties of many of the rescuers, who, like farmers and miners, often feel more comfortable living among their own (frequently near their parents) and working along-side siblings and cousins. A striking number of them were Catholic. One Staten Island Catholic high school lost 23 alumni on September 11—about half of them cops or firemen. Such benevolent tribalism—that one should not be a walking and transient résumé but find worth instead among family, community, and a grandfather's profession—can be a powerful force for good, whatever its potential limitations. Military historians tell us, for example, that the key to group cohesiveness and fighting spirit in any good army is the regimental system, based on the idea that soldiers—and these firefighters and cops are surely that—battle better together when arrayed alongside neighbors and friends in a common purpose.

The existence of these virtuous men and women, however, also owes much to the universal genius of American—or rather Western—civilization. We are seeing in this tragedy and in these firemen and police, alive and dead, the flesh and bones of our entire culture laid bare: what it means to be both American and Western at the moment of our peril and greatest need. Consider the ease with which the workers operate the huge cranes and bulldozers that remove the World Trade Center rubble—and consider the machines themselves. Only a civilization like that of the West, steeped in the rationalist tradition and protected by freedom of inquiry, could invent and use such remarkable equipment. The busy activity at Ground Zero reminds us how the Hoover Dam arose so speedily, how in World War II the wrecked Yorktown was made as good as new in mere hours, and why both earthquakes and hurricanes fail to level our cities permanently.

The rescuers are also free men and women, exhibiting all the associational skills that have made civil society so vibrant in Western history. The rescue workers do not first look to central government authority before plunging into their daily toil. Ingenuity, improvisation, and spontaneity are everywhere—the wonderful fruits of a free society. In addition, the police who ring the site owe allegiance to civilians and elected officials, not self-proclaimed authorities who hang and hector as they see fit. Our enemies brag of the brutal order of the chopped hand and stoned face: let them come to New York and see how much better and more humane free guardians are than thugs obeying the ravings of a mendicant fanatic.

Could New York's free rescuers be any more different from the city's attackers? New York's suicidal enemies demand adherence to their religious creed and are more likely to be of a regimented mind and even hue. The firemen and cops, conversely, are of all colors and faiths. The names of the dead—Michael Weinberg, Manuel Mojica, Paddy Brown, Joseph Angelini, Gerald Schrang, Tarel Coleman—sound scripted from corny World War II movies. Yet the diversity is not corny but real—far more real than Hollywood fantasies or the resentful multiculturalism of the politicized campus. By all accounts, these men worked in relative harmony alongside one another even as they expressed pride in their ethnic heritage—a fertile, and particularly American, tension of the universal and the particular.

We are discovering, ultimately, the West's powerful advantage of having three, rather than two, classes—the critical presence in society of men and women who are neither terribly rich nor abjectly poor, who own property yet struggle mightily to acquire and keep it. This middle class is not the norm of the world, either today or in the past, which was and is likely to remain pyramidal: a small elite tottering at the peak, dictating to an impoverished and restless mass below, as one now finds in Afghanistan and Iraq. The independent and resourceful of New York are what we would expect of a hallowed tradition that goes back to the Greeks, whose civilization arose on the backs of the mesoi—the "middle ones," who were neither rich nor poor, neither dispossessed nor royalty. As property-owning, voting citizens, the mesoi created and sustained our culture, which explains why their descendants, on their own initiative, rushed into the flames and now find and care for our dead—and will quickly rebuild what the terrorists destroyed.

Make no mistake: a horrific catastrophe has struck New York. A trillion dollars has vanished from its markets, and repairing damage to the city's structures will cost at least $40 billion. The loss of human treasure is incalculable. And like it or not, we are in a real war. But the firefighters, police, and other rescue workers have proven an invaluable asset. Their heroic conduct in the present crisis will change the nature of New York, teaching many in the city's vast offices that hefty salaries don't mean much if one does not help one's kin and do so with honor and courage. What has gone on in the rubble should be as reassuring a sight for our friends as it is ominous for our foes.

Written on October 5 and published in the autumn issue of City Journal.

13.

Tragedy or Therapy?

DEFINING OURSELVES

AT THE UNIVERSITIES, throughout the national media, in our suburbs—and perhaps, unfortunately, inside the State Department—there are very dangerous ideas floating around about Mr. bin Laden and this present war. We would do well to cast them aside and look to our past.

War for most of the past twenty-five hundred years of Western Civilization was seen as a tragedy innate to the human condition—a time of human plague when, as the historian Herodotus said, fathers bury sons, rather than sons fathers. In other words, killing humans over disagreements should not happen among civilized people. But it did and so was "a curse from Zeus," the poet Hesiod concluded.

Conflict does and will always break out—and very frequently so—because we are human and thus not always rational. War is "the father, the king of us all" the philosopher Heraclitus lamented. Even the utopian Plato agreed: "War is always existing by nature between every Greek city-state." How galling and hurtful to us moderns that Plato, of all people, once called peace, not war, the real "parenthesis"! Warfare could be terrifying ("a thing of fear" the poet Pindar summed up)—but not therefore unnatural or necessarily evil.

No, the rub was particular wars, not war itself. While all tragic, any of them could be evil—or good—depending on the cause, the nature of the fighting, and the ultimate costs and results. The defense against Persian attack in 480 B.C., as the playwright Aeschylus (who chose as his epigram mention of his service at Marathon, not his dramas) says, was "glorious." Yet the theme of Thucydides' history of the internecine

Peloponnesian wars was folly and senseless butchery. Likewise, there is a language of freedom and liberty associated with the Greeks' naval victory at Salamis, but not so with the slaughter at the battle of Gaugamela—Alexander the Great's destruction of the Persian army in Mesopotamia that wrecked Darius III's empire and replaced eastern despots with Macedonian autocrats.

If war was innate, and its morality defined by particular circumstances, fighting was also not necessarily explained by prior exploitation—or even legitimate grievance. Nor did aggression have to arise from poverty or inequality. States, like people, can be envious—and even rude and pushy. And if they can get away with things, they most surely will. Thucydides says they battle out of "honor, fear, and self-interest." How odd to think that the Japanese and Germans were not starving in 1941, but rather were proud peoples who wanted those they deemed inferior and weak to serve them.

To the Greeks, such bad guys also fought mostly over tangible things—more land, more subjects, more loot. Wars were a sort of acquisition, Aristotle said. Bullies, whether out of vanity or a desire for power and recognition, took things from other people unless they were stopped. And if they were to be halted, citizens—among them good, kind, and well-read men like Socrates, Sophocles, Thucydides, and Demosthenes—fought to protect their freedom and to save the innocent.

In this classical paradigm, the present crisis, I think, looks something like this: The United States, being a strong and wealthy society, invites envy because of the success of its restless culture of freedom, democracy, self-critique, secular rationalism, and open markets. That we are often to be hated—and periodically to be challenged by those who want our power, riches, or influence—is to be listened to, more often regretted, but always expected. Our past indulgence of bin Laden did not bring us respect, much less sympathy. Rather, our forbearance invited ever more contempt and audacity on his part—and more dead as the bitter wages of our self-righteous morality and tragic miscalculation.

The enemies of free speech and intolerance—Germany Nazism, Italian fascism, Japanese militarism, Stalinist Communism, or Islamic fundamentalism—will always attack us for what we are, rather than what we have done. Only our moral response—not our status as fighters per se—determines whether our war is just and necessary. If, like the Athenians, we butcher neutral Melians for no good cause, then our war is evil and we should lose. But if we fight to preserve freedom like the Greeks at Thermopylae and the GIs at Normandy Beach, then war is the right and indeed the only thing we can do. Caught in such a tragedy, where efforts at reason and humanity fall on the deaf ears of killers, we must go to war for our survival and to prove to our enemies that their defeat will serve as a harsh teacher—at least for a generation or two—that it is wrong and very dangerous to blow up three thousand civilians in the streets of our cities.

That depressing view of human nature and conflict is rarely any longer with us. It was not merely the advent of Christianity that ended it; centuries ago the Sermon on the Mount fell by the wayside to the idea of "just war"—once a beleaguered West realized that pacifism meant suicide. More likely, the 20th century and the horror of the two world wars—Verdun, the Somme, Hiroshima—put an end to the tragic view of war. Yet, such numbing losses—and our arrogance—caused us to miss the lesson of both world wars. The calamity of sixty million dead was not only because we went to war, but also because we were naive and deemed weak by our enemies well before 1914 and 1939. At the time, real resolve could have stopped Prussian militarism and Nazism before millions of blameless perished.

The deviant offspring of the Enlightenment—Marxists and Freudians—gave birth to even more pernicious social sciences that sought to "prove" to us that war was always evil and therefore—with help from Ph.D.s—surely preventable. Indeed, during the International Year of Peace in 1986 a global commission of experts concluded that war was unnatural and humans themselves unwarlike! Unfortunately, innocent people get killed by that kind of naive thinking. We are now convinced that war always results from real, rather than perceived, grievances—mostly the poverty arising out of the usual sins of colonialism, imperialism, racism, sexism, et cetera. In response, dialogue and mediation that might work on the campus or over the suburban fence have been elevated to the grand science of "conflict resolution" theory, a sort of marriage counseling or small-claims court taken to the global level. But unfortunately among nations there are no police, no legal writs and court summonses that can be enforced.

Rich and smug Westerners simply could not accept the idea that more civilians in the twentieth century were killed by Hitler, Stalin, and Mao off, than on, the battlefield. How depressing to suggest that the Khmer Rouge, the Hutus, and the Serbians went on killing when left alone—and quit only when either satiated or stopped.

In our new moral calculus, bin Laden figures to be no Xerxes or Tojo. And he is not even an inherently evil man who hates us for our clout and our influence. Far too few of us believe that he wishes to strut over a united Middle East under his brand of medieval Islam that makes decadent Westerners cower in fear. Instead, we insist that he is either confused (call in Freud) or has legitimate grievances (read Marx), and so we must find answers within us, not him—Western importation of Arab oil? Land stolen from the Palestinians? Decadent democracy and capitalism? Jewish-American women walking in the land of Mecca? Puppet Arab governments? Take your pick—he has cited them all.

The tragic Greeks would make ready the 101st Airborne, but we must chitchat with him (thus Reverend Jackson), fathom him (our professors and novelists), or accommodate him (the Clinton State Department). In this age of our greatest learning, wealth, and pride, we see war as "Zeus's curse." Our sophisticated tell us not to descend into "savagery"; that prayer, talk, or money might prevail. But if we deem ourselves too smart, too moral—or too soft—to stop killers, then we have become real accomplices to evil through inaction. Generations slaughtered in Europe, incinerated Jews, massacred Russians and Chinese, and the bleached bones of Cambodians are proof enough of that.

Bin Laden knows all this—hence his boasts that we are cowardly and decadent. Yet, for the moment, he is still puzzled. And perhaps, just perhaps, he is even afraid: people are fleeing Afghanistan; Pakistan has suddenly proved a most fickle host; his co-conspirators, the Taliban, suddenly are not so defiant; and jihad is falling on so many deaf ears. Does this new American rhetoric of war mean, bin Laden wonders, that there are still Greek moralists in the land of Wal-Mart and Britney Spears? Are there still men like Lincoln and Roosevelt, with stern Grants and Pattons as their great captains, whose creed is victory and whose terms are only unconditional surrender?

Mr. bin Laden—for the first time in his life—is now unsure whether we are a tragic or therapeutic society. We too shall find out shortly in the momentous days ahead.

Written on October 7 and published in National Review Online
on October 9.

14.

War on All Fronts

MILITARY, DIPLOMATIC,
PHILOSOPHICAL, CULTURAL

I. Military

THE GENERAL OUTLINES of the campaign in Afghanistan are now becoming evident: air strikes on selected Taliban and terrorist leadership, along with attacks against air defense and their conventional assets, to aid indigenous forces in their motorized assaults against the cities. Our on-the-ground reconnaissance and special operations—thanks to the advances in technology of the last decade—may well make these missions far more destructive than even what we witnessed in the Gulf War, perhaps resulting in a precipitous collapse in Taliban resistance in weeks or even days, rather than the predicted months or years. We were warned of "thousands to be killed" in Iraq, and instead lost a few dozen to actual hostile fire. Pompey, under the Lex Gabinia of 67 B.C., was given an *imperium* for three years to rid the Mediterranean of pirates; he destroyed them in three months. Overconfidence is the supposed bane of all armies, but in fact, wise generals more often deliberately downplay their chances of success in the dawn of battle.

Tanks and artillery, we must remember, are not obsolete in Afghanistan; at some point, such American conventional forces may need to help direct and organize resistance movements that move out of the hills and onto the plains—if only to ensure that a particular local thug or warlord does not hijack the temporary unity of the resistance. While our Defense Department has been adroit at emphasizing the unconventional nature of this conflict, we are in fact seeing just how effective the symphony of conventional (planes, carriers, submarines, destroyers) and special operations forces actually is. Some traditional armored units on the ground will also be critical in guarding our smaller teams from any sudden movement from Iran, or a precipitous change in government in Pakistan—as well as readying operations for action in Iraq.

Commandos and air strikes will win the Afghani phase of the war against terrorism, but large battle groups are also critical in showing and using American muscle. We must remember that Pakistan is now neutral, and Iran wary—not out of sympathy for our dead or in moral support of our cause, but out of fear that the United States is acting unpredictably and most out of character from its behavior of the past eight years. The most visible signs of this new resolution are our ships and planes—symbols of confidence not lost on the American people themselves, who will never know the full story of our efforts at stealth and ruse on the ground. Terrorists and mullahs will fear our commandos, but Iraq and Iran must be reminded of the conventional strength of the United States they saw in Libya rather than in Somalia. With a frightening presence in the area now, our future campaigns against other terrorist hosts may become somewhat easier. Neither Saddam, Assad, Khadafi, nor the Iranian mullahs wish to lose billions of dollars of planes, armor, and bases to sustained American air and naval strikes—or to see that followed by an arms blockade and embargo.

Comparisons with past war-making are commonplace. Perhaps we should emphasize the similarity of our present struggle with the masterful American action in the Pacific during World War II. Then, too, we had enormous logistical problems: vast and daunting landscapes, savage and often suicidal enemies, propagandists to threaten us with a vast racial war of Orient versus Occident, and few friends with any real power. Nimitz and MacArthur nevertheless saw even the first tiny steps clearly as evolutionary and ending in Tokyo, as paired boxing gloves of alternating American battle groups advanced from one island to the next. We should see Iraq and its sympathizers as our fathers saw the Gilberts, Marshalls, Mariannas, and Carolines—with one of our task forces fighting while the other, in reserve, prepares the next strike. Once our enemies understand the nonnegotiable logic of our sequential strategy, they may well decide wisdom to be the better part of valor, kill or expel their terrorists, and close down their bases. In this regard, just as we learned of General Schwarzkopf in the Gulf, so too should the American people soon be introduced to our theater commanders in the Middle East.

II. Diplomatic

THE VOCAL SUPPORT of allies is, of course, critical to our success. Yet the United States finds itself militarily unsurpassed in a manner civilization has not seen since the Rome of the first to third centuries A.D.—and quite unlike even its own singular position during the two World Wars. Quite simply, there is no other friend or rival that really can help us, so great has the imbalance in the world's militaries grown in our favor. Allies, who pledge support now in the adrenaline rush of the first bombs, will bow out when the critical issue of Iraq arises in the next few weeks. We should not expect or welcome their armed assistance, but should demand, as the price of their neutrality, at least public signs of support.

Again, the coalition (is there not a better name?) is a critical, but largely cosmetic, entity—and a means, not the end in itself. That must remain the single-minded destruction of terrorist havens that have helped kill *our* women and children. We can excuse the relative inaction of the Europeans with praise of NATO, but only on the condition that they not fire up their vast cultural engines of cynical demagogy to denigrate the efforts of America. And it is one thing to entice a powerful ally like Russia with sympathy for their similar problems with fundamentalism—quite another to do much of anything to win over a suspect Iran.

III. Philosophical

OUR PUBLIC PRONOUNCEMENTS so far have been both judicious and politic, especially in the repeated emphasis that ours is no war against either Islam or the Arab world in general. But just as critical, here and abroad, must be the constant refrain of our poor dead. Only that way will our allies fathom our single-mindedness, and our enemies at last realize that Americans are not merely a just, but also an angry and avenging, power. Rumors that a B-52 had its nose cone painted with "NYPD" are a good start. There must be much more.

In every great struggle, proclamations of intent, purpose, and values emerge when even the mere hint of victory is in the air—whether they be Lincoln's Emancipation Proclamation or Roosevelt's declaration of the formation of the United Nations. Within the year, President Bush should establish a formal American doctrine of military principle. The Bush Doctrine should supplant the Powell manifesto, and thus state unequivocally that a terrorist attack on the citizens or the shores of the United States is defined as an act of war, and will bring immediate retaliation of all our forces, without qualification, against any state that hosts, aids, or comforts the perpetrators. This is no small commitment, and may in the future raise real risks, involving nuclear rogue states like North Korea or perhaps even changed governments in Pakistan or South Africa. But the Bush Doctrine will warn the world—and Americans here at home—of the seriousness of the present danger and the audacity of our response. Only that way can our children someday sleep in peace.

At the same time, our president must also craft something more recognizably humane and visionary—akin to Roosevelt's enunciation of the Four Freedoms, even as it is less utopian than Wilson's Fourteen Points—a creed that will send a strong message of American purpose to "moderate" Arab governments in the aftermath of this crisis. The United States should declare that it supports the right of all Islamic peoples to self-determination through consensual government, and, indeed, we shall work for the gradual evolution of democracy in countries where the impoverished have no voice or freedom. Failing to do so in Kuwait may have been as critical an error as stopping before Baghdad.

Such unsophisticated idealism also offers real peril: Fundamentalists may well be elected and replace autocrats professedly sympathetic to America. But such reform offers the only chance to avoid repetitions of the present disaster in which corrupt Westernized strongmen buy off indigenous criticism, by allowing their fundamentalists to vent popular outrage against us rather than them. These illegitimate governments have a free press only in the sense that they are free to damn America.

In this regard, we must recognize that much of America's energy policy is a concern of the Department of Defense. Can we at last realize that cheap imported oil from corrupt Saudi fundamentalists is not really cheap at all, but rather the real fuel funding the killers of our innocent? So many moral anomalies arise from our shortsighted energy policies! Our Defense and State Departments lecture us ad nauseam on the "special relationship" we have with Saudi Arabia, yet no government—through its autocracy, hypocrisy, and misogyny—is more inherently repugnant to the American people. Rarely in our history has a foreign country enjoyed so little popular, yet so much official, American support.

IV. Cultural

OUR VISIONARIES MUST be far clearer and more eloquent about the nature of our struggle. In their understandable efforts to say what we are *not* doing—fighting Islam or provoking Arab peoples—they have failed utterly to voice what we *are* doing: preserving Western civilization and its uniquely tolerant and humane traditions of freedom, consensual government, disinterested inquiry, and religious and political tolerance. In this regard, we must especially distinguish, in the manner of Roosevelt and Churchill, the historic ties between Great Britain and America—something either ridiculed or forgotten in the current fashion for multiculturalism.

Our institutions are shaped by the British inheritance of the classical tradition. The English Enlightenment, far more so than the French, tempers and moderates our ongoing evolution toward greater equality. And had it not been for British resistance from 1939 through 1941, the United States may have well lost millions in World War II. It is time our leaders explained these intellectual bonds and shared sacrifices to a new generation of largely ignorant Americans, who are perhaps either dumbfounded by or else completely oblivious to the singular loyalty of Great Britain.

Finally, Americans must answer the Islamic world bluntly, and with pride rather than reticence, about why we support and always will protect the Israelis. Our sympathy is not attributable to some mythical Jewish lobby, a CIA plot to put down Islam, or a worldwide conspiracy of Zionists; it is simply because they are the Middle Eastern state most like ourselves in their commitment to a free society based on the rule of law and the consent of the governed. Our special relationship with Israel is open equally to any Islamic country that accepts the idea of democracy and the essence of freedom. We must, as a nation, cease the apologetic tone we have developed with the Arab world, and make it clear that their ministers who hector us are not legitimate without elections, their spokesmen are not journalists without a free press, and their intellectuals are not credible without liberty. The right to admonish Americans on questions of morality is not an entitlement, but something earned only through a shared commitment to constitutional government.

This war really is on all fronts, as we are told. Our leaders need to remind friends and enemies alike that we are as confident in our values and ideas as we are in our carriers and commandos.

Written on October 9 and published in National Review Online
on October 12.

15.

Truth and Consequences

SPEAKING THE LANGUAGE OF TRUTH

ONE OF THE first casualties of war is language. The historian Thucydides told us that in the cauldron of killing, where emotion trumps reason, words lose their meaning: so in the Middle East extremists become known to the mobs as "soft" even as executioners are seen as "heroes." Crowds hector the reckless, incendiary Mr. Arafat for being too moderate as they chant in praise for the mass murderer bin Laden.

But there is also a different type of linguistic distortion in the West—the opposite phenomenon of a deflation in vocabulary. Our distortion of meaning derives not from the excess, but rather the complete absence, of emotion. We Americans embrace euphemism at all costs—the wages of a culture that demands the preservation of material comfort at the price of real conviction, denies the acceptance of evil, and in its arrogance believes that it can reinvent the nature of man through either state intervention or the lure of pseudo-science.

We see such an insidious ruin of words everywhere. The news agency Reuters objects to the use of "terrorists." Americans in turn fumble over the nuances of "fundamentalist." In fact, by any historical definition both bin Laden's followers and the Taliban are fascists. They believe in the innate superiority of a fanatical elite—violent devotees of a perverted medieval Islam—and are willing to torture, jail, and kill any who disagree. Women, homosexuals, and non-Muslims are all dehumanized as their innate and natural inferiors.

These fascists are not fundamentalists like Jerry Falwell, nor even extremists like those of Earth First, in that they are not merely intolerant, zealous, and occasionally dangerous. Rather, the fascists now residing in Afghanistan seek to spread their creed through the *mass* killing of innocents and the desire of "conquest" at the national level. Fortunately, our president and Mr. Rumsfeld, in their embrace of a moral vocabulary to describe these perpetrators of mass murder as "evil," and "liars," are the rare moralists. In their candor and diction, they radiate leadership in forcing us to accept the unpleasant, and for now are ready to incur ridicule from the self-satisfied and cynical.

By the same token our media seeks desperately to avoid the word "war." Far better that we are caught up in a "crisis," a "struggle," or more rarely a "conflict." But by any fair historical measure when three thousand innocents have been butchered in a time of peace by enemies of our very civilization—in addition $100 billion of material losses, more still in economic dislocation, and our symbols of American internationalism, military power, and finance blown apart—then, by God, we are in a war. The catalysts of every war in American history—Lexington, Concord, Fort Sumter, the sinking of the *Lusitania,* Pearl Harbor, and the invasion of Kuwait—all cost us far less killed— and more often soldiers, rather than women and children. Our "enemy"—itself a word in rare usage—at least has few doubts of the stakes involved in their battle against America, as they wave posters of jets crashing into towers and convey promises of germs and nukes on the horizon.

Yet perhaps we feel the employment of the word "war" might suggest a finality of sorts: Will our tranquility then be forever interrupted? Are we really then traitors to the Enlightenment in resorting to brute violence? In a "war" are we the moral equivalents of our enemies? And so we find it more comfortable to reinvent words to mask reality. "War," after all, brings such unwholesome baggage, the entire nineteenth-century lexicon of "treasonous" and "evil," or their antitheses "patriotic" and "moral"—or even worse terminology like "defeat" and "victory" or "surrender" and "triumph." Imagine a Dan Rather or Peter Jennings reporting that America seeks the defeat and surrender of its enemies in its commitment to victory and the triumph over evil.

There are real consequences for a society that has lost the value of its language. In a "crisis" rather than a "war," bombing killers who attacked and murdered our families and vow to continue until stopped is simply the ethical equivalent to ramming airliners into office buildings. "Terrorists" must be given a trial by a jury, but "fascists" conjure up the scary image of the SS, who murdered American prisoners and so received no mercy from GIs at the Battle of the Bulge. And with the rejection of the word "evil," a free society of voters is not all that different from a regime that kills its own.

Our euphemism seeks to reassure Americans that by not provoking our enemies we might not further endanger our lives or risk our careful self-image as superior creatures of reason. Falsity in expression is so much easier than the brutality of truth. Hardworking people slaughtered at their desks are not "incinerated" or "vaporized" and so to be "avenged" or "remembered" (as in "Remember Pearl Harbor"), but are now "lost" or "gone." "Rubble" and "debris" suggest an absence of corpses, limbs, teeth, and skin. Without funerals, without visual reminders of their deaths or mention of the circumstances of their killing, our sanitized language has nearly allowed our dead literally to "disappear."

States that are hostile to the United States—their crowds cheering the killers of our children, state media inflaming hatred of our people, and autocracies turning their own internal civil dissent against America—are now deemed "moderate" in that they are not openly hosting our enemies or killing us. Such language is not always reactive, but helps to govern events. Instead of lecturing the Saudis or Egyptians on the need to allow their citizens to vote and speak freely, we instead promise right at this minute to revisit the sore of the West Bank—and in the process convey the idea that there are rewards for the butchery of New Yorkers.

Our enemies use the inflated rhetoric of distortion while we, mirror-imaging them in falsity, avoid the reasoned lexicon of truth. If they are premodern, so we are postmodern. Thus we seek to wonder why we are "hated," instead of firmly and candidly reminding Islam that America the last two decades has been the protector of Muslims. Do we dare bark back at the Palestinians that the real killers of Muslims the last thirty years have been other Muslims and atheists?—whether in the horrific Iran-Iraq War, the Russian assault on Afghanistan, the Jordanian liquidation of Palestinians, the extinction of whole villages in Lebanon by Syria, and the Iraqi murder of Shiites, Kurds, and Kuwaitis? Arab Muslims, not us, sent missiles into the streets of Iran, gassed their own people, polluted the sands of Kuwait, killed Afghanis, and tortured their own citizens.

If we are to restore moral purpose in this country and end the era of cynicism and nihilism, then we must stand for something in this war. And we can only begin to do so and thereby regain a sense of who we are, when our spokesmen speak the language of truth. And when they do so, they should be pleased rather than ashamed that it is not pleasant to everyone.

Written on October 15 and published in National Review Online *on October 17.*

16.

The Time Machine

A PARODY

NEWSFLASH! APRIL 1, 1942
AMERICA STRIKES BACK!
Lieutenant Colonel James H. Doolittle's Sixteen Bombers
Take Off from Hornet to Bomb Tokyo!

•

~~Read the National News Roundup of American Reactions~~
to the Marvelous Doolittle Raid!

ABC's **Peter Jennings** *offered the following commentary from prelimi-nary reports filtering in from Nationalist forces inside China.*

IT IS NOT all clear to Americans tonight that Colonel Doolittle and his crews always enjoyed clear visual bombing over Tokyo. Clouds and antiaircraft firing—some of the surviving pilots are reporting to our Chinese sources—may have caused "weaving," made still worse by pilot panic or inattention. Yet all sixteen crews, ABC News has been told, were under strict orders by Colonel Doolittle to drop their bomb loads despite clear and advanced warnings of inclement weather, resulting in significant but undisclosed collateral damage. Japanese sources tell ABC News that perhaps fifty civilians were killed and an undisclosed number of them were wounded.

Whether Admiral King was aware of this "drop, don't verify" order—or, in fact, gave it himself—is something we are now investi-gating. Would it not be ironic that four months after we were sur-prised and suffered noncombatant deaths at Pearl Harbor, American warplanes in a similar fashion bombed unexpectedly and indiscriminately—resulting in a similar or even much greater loss of civilian life? Yet another—but perhaps not the last—of the ironies of this, America's most perplexing and in some sense paradoxical war.

Stanley Fish, *dean of the College of Liberal Arts and Sciences at the University of Illinois at Chicago, cautioned against seeing the raid in terms of moral retribution.*

WE MUST REALIZE that one man's freedom fighter is another's terrorist. We construct Doolittle as a brave hero, but to the men and women he bombed he was a mere terrorist. There can be no independent standard for determining which of many rival interpretations of this raid is the true one.

What we must not do is to fall back on some absurd notion of absolute and enduring values like truth, freedom, and democracy, but rather we can and should invoke the particular lived values that unite us and inform the institutions we cherish and wish to defend—which, of course, are neither absolute nor enduring, at least I don't think they are. Which is not to say that Chicago under the Japanese would not be necessarily a different place from what it is now, inasmuch as Japanese imperial lived values and cherished institutions could in theory by some sort of objective standard be different, as for example in my ability—or my children's at some future time—to make this statement freely.

Philip Wilcox Jr., *former U.S. ambassador-at-large for counterterrorism in the Clinton administration, cautioned about initial American enthusiasm over a dramatic military effort that he described as little more than a catharsis for public outrage and demands for action.*

UNTIL THIS RASH response, we were at a critical lull in a precious four months of reasoned sobriety, a sort of equilibrium where Pearl Harbor could be seen in terms of a response to our own prior indifference—or in fact hostility—to the legitimate aspirations of the Japanese people. But with Mr. Doolittle's theatrics we are entering a cycle of violence, where the root causes of this conflict will not be addressed by bombing in some sort of endless tit-for-tat. Such ill-planned strikes have never solved anything, but only encouraged yet another rejoinder. The United States must realize that, notwithstanding our great power, indeed because of it, we cannot dictate respect and cooperation. The bombing will make war overt, and we can only wonder about the effect of collateral damage on attitudes of those in the streets of Tokyo toward America. Bombing will not eliminate the ideology of Japanese militarism nor its often inchoate and diffuse operations. We must not commit the fallacy of treating past Japanese terrorism as pure evil in a vacuum.

*The **Reverend Jesse Jackson** was interviewed at the Pan-Am terminal in JFK airport in New York. In light of the unexpected and unannounced bombing, there was a great deal of confusion surrounding his planned peace trip to Tokyo. Jackson pleaded for "hands across the Pacific" to stop the "madness," and concluded:*

STOP THE GUNS and save our sons. Keep peace alive and don't let the planes dive. Don't be in fearo of the Zero or Emperor Hiro. Let our planes drop more for the poor, and make less of a mess. Now is a time not to Doo-Little, but Doo-lots. Talk truth to power, and don't cower.

***Oliver Stone**, noted film director, pointed out the significance of the prior Pearl Harbor raid:*

WE HAVE FAILED completely to understand Pearl Harbor. That attack was pure chaos, and chaos is energy. All great changes have come from people or events that were initially misunderstood, and seemed frightening. But Doolittle? His bombing had none of the Japanese verve; it was redundant, silly, unimaginative, predictable, hardly chaotic at all—completely unspectacular.

Ted Koppel of ABC's Nightline questioned the purpose and method of the American attack:

AM I CORRECT in saying that the B-25s could take off from the Hornet, but in fact could not land there on return? And did the attack in truth depart prematurely from what appears to be a single carrier, with only one other in reserve? And are not B-25s land-based bombers that are poorly suited for operations from the rolling deck of a carrier? I find all this difficult to accept—and we await clarification from Mr. Doolittle himself. Is our desire for revenge such—there seems to be very little effort at targeting key industries in Japan—that we in effect sent our airmen on what appears tantamount to a suicide raid? And did Colonel Doolittle really promise, as was reported, to crash his plane and crew into a target should his own bomber become disabled? And is either such proposed ramming or indiscriminate bombing now the official policy of the Roosevelt administration? And if so, why and on whose orders? Tonight the raid has clearly left more questions raised than answered.

Former national security adviser **Sandy Berger** *put the Doolittle raid in a larger strategic perspective:*

IT IS CONSISTENT with our own administration's past policy of reciprocal action, albeit with a sort of reckless escalation that brings with it the acknowledgment of greater risks and potential for destabilization in that most critical part of the world. Our relationship with the Japanese is sort of like that arcade game with the stick and the moles. Every time they pop up like they did at Pearl Harbor, we are going to knock them down a little bit. After they get a little sore, they will know the rules of the game, and keep well within inside parameters that we can live with.

Susan Sontag, *acclaimed novelist, called for Americans to write Congress:*

DO WE CALL this courage—itself a morally neutral idea? Whose courage—theirs or ours, the pilots or the bombed? Flags on houses? Burlesque and sexist art on the nose of bombers? A frenzied society that has abandoned self-reflection and given itself over to the logic of war? Is anyone in America listening? Is there a sane person left at this hour thinking of the children who were incinerated by this carpet bombing? These were not rose petals raining down upon the innocent of Japan, but rather postcards of American death. I cannot accept the moral equivalence of an attack on our soldiers at Pearl Harbor with a desperate lashing out against Tokyo. The blood of Japanese women and children is on our hands. Who is the real April Fool?

Oprah Winfrey, *syndicated talk-show host, pleaded with the American people not to adopt the politics of hate:*

AMERICA NEEDS TO know exactly WHO Mr. Doolittle was bombing and WHY. Does anyone in this country UNDERSTAND Bushido? Do you realize it has everything to do with family and tradition, and very LITTLE to do with war? Do we understand that *our* Japanese brothers and sisters in Tokyo are just like *us*—that there is a Red Cross in Japan, yes, and a Boy Scouts as well as Little Leagues? Is there anyone in our book club that has not read some haiku?

Christopher Hitchens, *columnist and noted social critic, sounded a rare note of support:*

WE ARE IN a war with evil. This was a very symbolic and much needed raid in the first real offensive against fascist aggression in the Pacific. And we should congratulate these brave American pilots for risking their lives to stop the sort of wide-scale Japanese butchery of the innocent that has been going on in Asia for years. Bravo, Colonel Doolittle.

Contacted at Columbia University, **Edward Said** *analyzed the larger cultural forces propelling what he called the "Doolittle dialectic."*

THE RAID ONLY clarifies what many of us have suspected about the American intent in this so-called war—a sort of surrogate and quite desperate defense of European colonialism and nineteenth-century hegemony. Are we, in fact, with this act of aerial piracy not proxies for French and British imperialism? Among many Western colonialists there is a deep and abiding—may I say fear and hatred?—of what they have construed the Other into as the "Oriental." If we are to continue to lash out like some wounded predator when we take a blow—to some, no doubt, well warranted and much needed—we should not be surprised in the following days to see a coalescence of sorts throughout the Asian world. People of color in Manila, Nanking, and Seoul will not be cheering this desperate act of misplaced braggadocio; indeed, they may well seek an alternative construction of resistance, a Co-Prosperity Sphere of sorts to facilitate solidarity against Western economic exploitation and now military aggression.

Gerry Spence, *celebrated trial lawyer and best-selling author, warned of unforeseen legal ramifications to come:*

IN THEORY, AS much as it might disturb Americans, this act makes Mr. Doolittle legally culpable in a number of most unfortunate but fascinating ways. An indictment, a preliminary hearing, a disinterested jury, and a judge from a neutral country—yes, indeed, all this is necessary if we are going to accept the principle of equal justice. There will be a need for prudent and experienced American jurists—perhaps compensated by League of Nations Funds—to step up to the international docket of justice. I can envision a World Court at which the Japanese pilots at Pearl Harbor and those who followed Doolittle will equally stand trial as perpetrators of death from the air. Of course, there must be culpability as well in the civil sense. And the families of the fifty killed by Doolittle have a perfect right, a legal right, through proper legal representation, to press their wrongful death suits in American courts.

*Former president **Bill Clinton**, speaking at a corporate retreat, offered an immediate statement of unqualified support:*

IT IS ABSOLUTELY critical—and I want to focus on this point like a beam of light—that we back the president. There was no other moral choice for Americans. We must not ask whether we struck too soon, whether there were Japanese envoys on the way to America at the time the order was given, whether the causes of this war were in part due to this administration's earlier inattention to the region, whether there was a chance at creating a neutral zone in the Pacific that respected the legitimate aspirations of the Japanese people, whether four months of reflection after Pearl Harbor rashly gave way to fury, whether . . .

***Jerry Falwell**, president of Liberty Baptist College, sought to place the raid in a very complex and nuanced religious context:*

AREN'T BOMBS TO be expected for a society that rejected God? After all, Japan turned its back on God long ago when they killed and expelled our courageous Christian missionaries. Perhaps Colonel Doolittle's bombs will do what God's typhoons and earthquakes have not. I just pray to God for the Japanese people now to wake up and accept Biblical scripture.

***Dick Morris**, former political adviser to President Clinton, analyzed the domestic ramifications of the raid:*

THIS WAS IN fact a brilliant stroke!—and a harbinger of things to come. President Roosevelt knew, as few others have grasped, the psychological and political effects of planes silhouetted against Mount Fiji. Think of those visuals! I can envision—and here I am quite willing to be considered a lunatic prophet—subsequent raids, perhaps in less than three years, in which literally thousands of newly crafted gigantic multiengine bombers—now perhaps already on the drawing boards, B-22s, 27s, 29s or such—torch Japanese cities with deadly new incendiary explosives.

And there's more. Once the "Doolittle Factor" comes into play, there may well be some terrible weapons on the horizon that will unleash the power of the cosmos—all of it posing huge political risks for any president bold enough to play a wild card from a full deck.

When told of the largely negative America reactions, a bewildered **Colonel Doolittle** *reportedly was terse in his reply to his critics:*

MY GOD! WHAT planet are these nuts from?

Written on October 16 and published in National Review Online
on October 18.

17.

If This Be War

A TIME FOR CHOOSING

NO AMERICAN WISHES to contemplate the idea of war—the horrific circumstances in which our country could lose many of its most precious citizens in a brutal effort to kill other humans. War is tragic and it is unfair, and we must weigh very carefully any decision that results in our own being killed in efforts (far away) to kill others. Yet sadly, killing is what we have suffered, and war is what has been unleashed upon us; therefore a number of very difficult, but inescapable, consequences must naturally follow.

Postwar Governments

JUST AS WE would never have allowed a Goering, Rosenberg, or even Speer to join a postbellum coalition in conquered Germany, or General Tojo and his warlords to help reconcile factions in Japan in September 1945, or the North Korean Communists to share in a unified pan-Korean government, so too the very idea of the murderous Taliban taking part in the reconstruction efforts in Kabul is morally reprehensible and absurd. We cannot ask our young men and women to risk death to eliminate the Taliban, only later to allow them to enjoy the powers of government. If we bury Americans killed in Afghanistan, and then allow the mullahs of the Taliban to forget the past, we will have profaned the sacrifice and memory of our own dead. In this regard, the adamant condemnation of proposed Taliban inclusion by both Russia and India is to be held in higher regard than what has been offered so far from Europe and the United Nations—or some members of our own State Department.

Belligerents

IF THIS WERE a war, we would not hesitate to end the evil in Iraq, where there is a history of germs brewed, missiles stockpiled, and the use of poison gas. We can insist on U.N. inspections of all suspect facilities in Iraq, and ask Baghdad to surrender its arsenal. When those reasonable proposals are rejected—as they will be—we should prepare to end the reign of terror of Saddam Hussein. Only that way can we correct the blunder of the last day of the Gulf War and turn Iraq from an autocracy to a democracy—a rebirth that might make a greater impression on Saudi Arabia and its ilk than did the prior nightmare.

Such a campaign is fraught with risks—crumbling coalitions, vulnerable flanks, logistical nightmares, depletion and scattering of our stretched-thin forces, the specter of tactical nuclear and germ warfare against our troops, more terrorism at home, domestic dissension, European repugnance, and a complete absence of allies. But if we are at war, if we wish to avenge our dead and ensure the safety of our children, we have no real choice, even as our eventual victory is not in doubt.

True, air power can wreck the Iraq military, but a ground invasion, aided by indigenous resistance movements from the current no-fly zones, is essential. The real lesson of the Gulf War was not merely that coalitions were critical to our success, but equally that by bringing aboard an assortment of dubious allies that were not critical for victory, we failed to go to Baghdad—and made no demands for Kuwait's medieval and cowardly government-in-exile to promise its citizens the eventual hope of consensual government. After the events of September 11, allowing Iraq to continue its dark work as before would be like not invading Italy in our war against Germany, or seeking to ignore Pearl Harbor while trying to marshal our desperately unprepared army against Hitler. There was a logic of sorts to both, but national purpose and common morality made us go after all three, and at once.

War Leaders and Their Language

IF WE WERE really at war, our national lexicon would reflect that seriousness of purpose. Americans would be told to brace for setbacks but always be assured of victory. The candor and resolve of Bush, Cheney, and Rumsfeld would not raise eyebrows—if this were really war. Stability in the Middle East is to be hoped for. We all pray for good relations with the Islamic peoples in dozens of countries—as our past aid to them against Communism, Iraqi fascism, and Serbian genocide attests. Americans wish the war to be short and without civilian casualties. We hope the elimination of terrorism will bring greater understanding of Islam and closer relations with Muslims in general. But right now those considerations—if we be at war—are secondary to victory and the abject defeat of our enemies: bin Laden's terrorists, the Taliban government, Iraq, and enclaves in Syria, Lebanon, Somalia, the Sudan, and the Philippines.

General Sherman—perhaps the most slandered and misunderstood figure in American history—accepted that his marches through Georgia would result in lasting negative public relations. But he also knew he was dismantling the infrastructure of a slave society at its heart, humiliating those who had called for his destruction, and—by his very audacity—killing few and losing less. At the beginning of his march, Sherman was told he would end up like Napoleon in Russia; a week later, those same plantation owners were begging him instead "to go over to the South Carolinians who started it." In war, reasoned and sober men like Halleck, Marshall, Eisenhower, Bradley, and Mark Clark are necessary to craft the organization of war, to marshal the powers of resistance, and occasionally to rein in the more mercurial and dangerous in our midst. But they do not, in themselves, bring us victory.

The defeat of our enemies in the dirt and carnage of war is accomplished by a different kind of men, themselves unsavory and often scary in their bluster and seriousness—the likes of Grant, Sherman, Patton, King, Halsey, LeMay, and a host of others still more uncouth. They speak differently, act differently, and think differently from most of us, but in war they prove to be our salvation, for they understand best its brutal essence—that real humanity in such an inhuman state of affairs is to use *massive* force to end the killing *as quickly as possible.* Men such as George S. Patton expect to offend us with their vocabulary, scare us with their assurance, and be relieved or discredited when we no longer need them. Thanks to them, in the luxury of victory and peace we can pretend we never really wanted to be (their) war-makers at all. But now we have not yet achieved either victory or peace—and so we need the ghost of Patton more than ever.

Neutrals and Not-So-Neutrals

IF WE ARE really to be at war, it might be wise to worry more about bringing battle to our enemies wherever we find them, than about warnings from neutrals, near-hostile governments, and frenzied but organized protest groups in Western countries. Muslim associations in European nations were cheering at the news of three thousand American dead; posters of bin Laden continue to blanket the streets of the Middle East; funds for his killers are traced to banks in the Gulf— surely, in times of war, such open hostility means something. Our forefathers in World War II did not worry much about what the Spanish, the Turks, or those in Argentina felt about our war with Germany. They assumed that many of their elites were hostile to the Allies, that their governments would intervene to aid the Axis if victory was assured—and that only our annihilation of Nazism would keep them out of the war and in fear of us.

So, too, only resolute action and victory in Afghanistan and against Iraq and other terrorist enclaves will ultimately silence the hateful crowds, and convince the Palestinians, Egypt, Syria, and Saudi Arabia to change their ways—both to cease their direct aid to terrorists, and to stop transforming domestic dissent into nationalist fury against us. It is disingenuous to say that those of the Islamic media simply enjoy a free climate of critique like our own, when their governments encourage criticism of us, but *not* of the real, indigenous causes of their own misery. Promises of largesse, coalition building, and assurances of our measured response and moderation are perhaps salutary in the present morass. But only victory will impress upon those who have funded the terrorists the need to stay neutral, get out of our way, and pray that in our systematic campaign against our enemies we do not at last turn our righteous anger against them.

Concern for Our Enemy

IF BY CHANCE we were really to be at war—when, right now, Americans are parachuting into the dark to stop the killers responsible for the Trade Center attacks—then we would look upon those who seek to restrain U.S. retaliation in its proper wartime context. The director of the Muslim Public Affairs Council of Los Angeles, for example, wants greater disclosure from the White House about the details of the

campaign, hinting that only fears of backlash prevent that organization from calling on America to *cease* the bombing altogether.

If we forget that the disclosure of such information would endanger the lives of American servicemen; *if* we pass on their misdirected
emphasis away from the slaughter of thousands of Americans, to
worry instead about the regime that helped kill them; *if* we ignore that
all of the killers, and nearly all of those in custody by the FBI either for
past bombings or for complicity with the present slaughter, are from
the Middle East; *if* we choose not to mention that self-proclaimed
Islamic fundamentalists operated freely within the American Muslim
community and were sometimes aided through so-called Islamic
charities—even then, we are still left with the disturbing fact that *in a
time of war,* the Muslim Public Affairs Council is considering calling
for an end to U.S. retaliation in Afghanistan. Indeed, the Council on
American-Islamic Relations has already done essentially that by
demanding an immediate end to the bombing that is directed at the
terrorist bases and Taliban military—and is critical to reducing casualties among American ground forces.

We, of course, are a free and tolerant society, where expression of
dissent is crucial to our national fabric. But good sense, and some
shred of the old idea of patriotism, might at least caution against such
petitions when we are at war against Islamic fundamentalists. Muslim
organizations must not emulate the German-American groups of the
late 1930s that criticized U.S. policy toward Nazi Germany. Once the
firing started—as it has now—it would have been difficult to stomach
German-American organizations organizing for a halt to B-17 raids
over Berlin, or expressing angst about civilian casualties as Patton
crossed the Rhine.

The Abyss

WE ARE AT the precipice of a war we did not seek. We can grimly
cross over it, confident in our resolve, more concerned about our poor
dead than the hatred of enemies or the worries of fickle neutrals,
assured that our cause is just, and reliant on the fierce men of our military who seek no quarter and need no allies in their dour task. Or we
can fall into the abyss, the well-known darkness of self-loathing, identity politics, fashionable but cheap anti-Americanism, ostentatious

guilt, aristocratic pacifism, and a convenient foreign policy that puts a higher premium on material comfort than on the security of our citizens and the advancement of our ideals.

If we really are at war, let us perhaps have pity upon our doomed enemies. But after what we suffered on September 11, if we are not at war, then we should have pity upon ourselves for what we have become.

Written on October 21 and published in National Review Online
on October 23.

18.

Class War

DIVIDED WE STAND

THOSE IN THE media seemed startled to see Richard Gere and Senator Clinton roundly booed at a recent benefit concert for the victims of September 11. Gere clearly earned his opprobrium, by smugly lecturing his audience—among them relatives and close friends of the dead—about the immorality of their desire to punish the murderers. Mrs. Clinton may have been hissed because the politics of her husband's administration projected national weakness and timidity, which prompted these attacks. Or perhaps concertgoers remembered some of her harebrained pronouncements about her own purported victimhood during the health-care debate, when she was bothered by angry callers. Or maybe New Yorkers in general were just fed up with her past coziness with Palestinian leaders.

Or was it that the crowd believed that Gere and Clinton live in a different world from their own?

There is a growing class division in this country over the war. Of course, 90 percent of us, of all classes, at least for now profess support for strong military action. Yet at least a tenth of the country—a very influential tenth in the media, the university, politics, foundations, churches, and the arts—is adamantly and vocally at odds with most Americans. Why is this so?

It is often not a divide between Democrats and Republicans. Nor does the abyss always separate the wealthy from the poor. Most strikingly, the fault line pits a utopian cultural elite against the working middle class. On campuses, especially public universities such as the California State University system, one feels the tension constantly. The tenured, well-educated, and relatively affluent among the faculty are adamantly against the military response in Afghanistan. Yet the students—mostly children of the working class of every conceivable ethnic background—almost uniformly support our troops.

Similarly, I watch the well-heeled upper echelon on television chastising our government and then see my twin brother—with decrepit pickup truck, fighting the lowest agricultural prices since the Great Depression, losing an ancestral small farm to the bank— proudly driving in and out with a tattered flag flying from his truck antenna. Recent immigrants in Selma, my hometown—which is now nearly 85 percent Mexican-American—have plastered fresh American decals over faded Mexican flags. Yet when I come to work, professors, who have done far better in America, suggest that our classes should now read Edward Said to "understand" the crisis "in its proper prospective." Those who are not thriving in America seem incensed by attacks on their country, while the beneficiaries of this wonderful system of freedom and capitalism are cranky—like angry puppies who gnaw and chew at their mother's ample teats.

The usual explanations about the sociology of dissent do not quite make sense anymore. So far, those who are fighting in Afghanistan— mostly highly trained pilots and special-forces operatives—are not from among the unwashed poor. The affluent Left, then, is not opposed to action because the less-privileged are dying in droves. Is it because the better-educated are more sensitive to world opinion? To the nuances of Islam? To the "Other" in Afghanistan, who are not male WASPs? To the vagaries of the European press? Perhaps.

Perhaps not. Rather, I think fashionable anti-Americanism and pacifism have now become completely aristocratic pursuits, the dividends of limited experience with the muscular classes and the indulgence such studied distance breeds. Our pampered critics may be as clever as Odysseus, but they have lost his nerve, strength, and sense of morality. And so they have neither the ability nor desire to ram a hot stake into the eye of the savage Cyclops to save their comrades.

In contrast, those who toil with their hands for a tenuous living, who become unemployed frequently and work two jobs, who take out loans for their kids to go to college at public universities, and who do real things like grow food, put out fires, and arrest felons have a very practical view of humankind—not all that different from the pessimistic assessment of the old hard-as-nails veteran Thucydides himself. Because they see brutality daily, understand how hard it is to survive and raise a family in the arena of national competition, and know too well what man is capable of at his rawest, they do not in their own lives enjoy the luxury of seeing awful people as "ignorant" in the abstract, rather than evil in the concrete.

If a neighbor steals communal irrigation water, the farmer knows his grapes will not come to harvest until he stops the miscreant himself. The tile-setter calibrates the purchase of his kid's books by how many tiles he sets on his arthritic knees, the roofer by how many shingles his ruined back can withstand, the carpenter by how many hours of nailing a week he can scrounge up, the realtor by how well he hustles to sell houses. Men and women such as these—the descendants of the *mesoi* who founded the Greek city-state—tell the uncouth at movie theaters to "shut up," and square off against bullies at Little League parks, so the rest of us can enjoy the movie or game in peace.

Not so with the elite media, the professorate, the corporate establishment, and many in education and the arts. They rarely work with their hands or meet those who do. Arguments, if settled at all, are settled by committee and consultation—not fisticuffs and two-by-fours—or maybe by corporate pink slips, with orders to clear out the desk in two hours. Insults among our elite critics invite sarcasm and irony, never a knuckle sandwich. For many, there is the lifetime employment of tenure, and summers out of the classroom. Quite simply, in America, in this its greatest age of freedom and affluence, we have created an entire leisured class who were not always born into great wealth, but who nevertheless have obtained an easy sinecure without worry and danger. They have completely lost sight of the fireworks when good and evil enter the realm of muscle and sinew.

Our aristocrats are convinced that the Taliban and bin Laden are akin to an angry news producer, a supercilious dean, or perhaps a high school vice principal run amok—pushy types who can be reasoned with or flattered, or, barring that, paid off, out-argued, petitioned, or ignored. Theirs is the arrogance of the Enlightenment, fueled by the ease of American materialism, which alike suggest that their nation is too good, too sophisticated, too wealthy, and too modern ever to stoop to fight in the gutter with thirteenth-century terrorists over a mere three thousand dead.

Cannot the hateful gaze of fascists in the Middle East—like those of the crazed road warriors on the freeway, or wild-eyed thugs on the

train home—be simply avoided? Or reported to the authorities? Or—
in extremis—reasoned with in polite give-and-take? Would a man or
woman with ample free time, a title, and a nice car and house—America's critics circa 2001—risk all that to tangle with a psychopath who
has nothing to lose? And over what? An insult? A little money? Or perhaps your life?

The firemen and policemen in the audience know how to deal with
bin Laden because they have seen something like him every day, and
protect those who have not from his ilk. They suspect that Richard
Gere and Senator Clinton not only know little about real evil—much
less how to deal with it—but most certainly, in safety, will sometimes
scoff at those who do.

Written on October 23 and published in National Review Online
on October 26.

19.

Ripples of Battle

FANTASIES GIVE WAY TO REALITY

IF WAR IS the powder keg of history, then battle is the match. Years, decades, and sometimes centuries can all be altered in hours at places like Salamis, the Teutoberger Wald, Adrianople, Waterloo, the Somme, or Pearl Harbor—when thousands are killed, and even more bodies and minds maimed. Even though the dead at the World Trade Center were not predominantly male, young, in uniform, and at battle, the horror of September 11 marks a similar fault line in the history of our people.

Ostensibly we can calibrate our losses. But there will be ramifications far beyond the death and destruction that we now see and hear, as shock waves from those minutes at the World Trade Center and Pentagon reverberate for years to come in ways we can now scarcely imagine.

Before Shiloh, Ulysses S. Grant believed that the Civil War would be ended by "one great battle." Afterwards—there were more casualties on April 6–7, 1862, than in all of America's wars to that time—a few prescient generals on both sides knew that rifles and canister shots made the courage of frontal charges suicidal. In response to the carnage on the Tennessee River, a previously "crazy" Sherman would go on to think the once unthinkable—like the March to the Sea. Just as generals woke up on April 8 to a new world, so we have as well. Gone is the old idea of easy retaliation through the cruise missile, and with it the fear of losing a single American life to protect freedom and the helpless. Like it or not, when three thousand innocents are butchered in our streets—and their killers unpunished and promising far more to come—some very deadly things to save our progeny will be discussed, well beyond the fighting now going on in Afghanistan.

In peace and affluence, we have shuddered with revulsion at Hiroshima, but forget what suicidal fanaticism at Okinawa had weeks earlier taught Americans of that age—2,000 kamikaze attacks, 34 ships sunk, 368 damaged, more than 12,000 American dead, 35,000 more wounded, along with 100,000 Japanese killed and another 100,000 civilian casualties, all in hand-to-hand fighting to take an island minuscule in comparison to the far better defended and armed Japanese mainland.

But such black days of history not only reinvent what is thought militarily possible and allowable, but radically realign politics as well. Before Thermopylae, the Spartans were considered an insular, if not bizarre people. Yet once Leonidas and his three hundred fell for Greek freedom, for a half-century his countrymen were looked upon as the real stalwarts of Greece. The American dead, in the manner that the Thermopylae three hundred once galvanized the Greeks, will resonate with our troops in the Middle East and unite the country under a moral imperative not seen in the last half-century.

After the cheering in the streets on news of our dead on September 11 in so many Arab countries, I do not think many Americans will ever again see Yasser Arafat as a real peacemaker, the medieval yet ultramodern sheiks of Saudi Arabia as friendly—or even some of our NATO allies as real comrades in arms. Neither our diplomats nor our strategists have yet quite grasped that the world has been turned upside down—that Russia is a more powerful and friendly country than Saudi Arabia, that India might be a better recipient of American military aid than Egypt, and that the Middle East is not on the rise against the West, but more isolated, impotent, and dependent than ever before. The three thousand dead in an instant have replaced past fantasies with reality.

Culture is not immune to the ripples of battle. The accelerators of Modernism were Verdun and the Somme. Perhaps the present brand of Postmodernism was born in France after the inexplicable and humiliating German romp through the Ardennes in 1940. The crater in New York at the very epicenter of American arts and letters will have a similar, if not more profound, effect. With a rubble pile instead of the World Trade Center on the skyline, it will be very difficult a few blocks away at the nexus of American culture to suggest that facts are mere historical fictions or that reality is but a contextual expression of power—or that feces on canvas and urine jars best capture the ordeal of the human condition. Not that such art and literature born out of cynicism and nihilism will vanish as we proceed with this war and the inevitable losses, blunders, and paradoxes to come. Not that such ideas won't continue to filter down in pernicious ways to places like Fresno, where grammar-school teachers are not to teach the "dominant" story of any one group. They will not—at least for a time. But most people, desperate for transcendence and something real—and perhaps even beautiful—amid catastrophe and recovery, will now gradually grow uninterested in the clever, but empty, games of the glib and bored. We have thousands of dead, after all, to mourn, the threat of still more lethal attacks, and a war in their memory to win—and our art, literature, and history will reflect that.

Pacifists shamed us into thinking that all wars were bad, relativism convinced us that we are no different from our enemies, conflict resolution and peace studies hectored us that there was no such thing as a moral armed struggle of good against evil, and academic specialists preached there was too much complexity in the Middle East ever to act decisively. September 11 and the struggle we are now witnessing have returned us to the classical view of war as a tragic fact inherent to humans that transcends culture when evil exists unchallenged. We may rediscover that it is not wars per se that are always terrible, but the people—Hitler, Tojo, Stalin, and bin Laden—who start them. And we may also learn from the fighting now going on between our own soldiers from the middle classes arrayed against so many of these affluent and educated terrorists that wars can often arise not out of real, but rather perceived, grievances. In response, the way in which Americans look at defense spending, immigration, foreign aid and alliances, domestic security—and war itself—will be altered for decades by September 11.

The sight of airliners obliterating people and the wave of fury it has aroused have also brought back moral seriousness. A current popular memoir of Bill Ayers that recounts with nostalgia the life of a campus terrorist of the 1960s now seems not cute, but grotesque. After witnessing the heroism at the World Trade Center, we are more likely to think of all the poor blue-collar policemen whom the present-day professor's friends once wished to dismember, rather than sympathize over moca and latte with his professed zeal and upscale idealism. The nightmare of battle does not reinvent the way people think and act, as much as remind them of enduring truths long forgotten and deemed trite in the luxury of peace. War, the historian Thucydides wrote, really is "a violent teacher." And the present one is no exception.

Just as September 1, 1939, shattered sympathy for fascism and discredited appeasement, so September 11 will sound a death knell to easy and fashionable anti-Americanism. Some on our campuses have been teaching some very silly and scary things these last decades. In the weeks ahead the American people may see and hear them firsthand in protests—and they will not enjoy the slogans of these aristocratic and tenured elites while our more industrious classes on their behalf are battling fascism a world away. What will we make of demonstrations to stop Americans from punishing murdering terrorists and their fascist hosts, cruel men who now boast of having vaporized civilian men, women, and children—with pledges of more to come? After the calamity of September it will be impossible to convince our citizens that America caused or deserved this from principled opponents who despise women, kill gays, destroy the venerable monuments of culture, and torture religious and political dissidents—and still manage to wager on the global stock market and compare the prices of tuition at American universities.

Battles even of an hour or two can also transform more stealthily the lives of thousands of ordinary folk well apart from the grand cosmology of politics, war, and culture. Among the grieving in New York and Washington there are right now undiscovered brave and courageous souls who will vow to remember their fallen in all that they do and say for the duration of their lives. And these tens of thousands of writers, poets, and actors to come may do and say quite a lot that will shape the world ahead in art, literature, and culture. If the past is any guide to the future, we shall see their influence soon enough at shops, on television, and in bookstores for decades hence—and with it the knowledge that the voices of the battlefield dead can still speak among us.

Written on October 27 and published in National Review Online
on October 29.

III.

November

(Taliban cracks; al-Qaeda forces flee; beginning of Ramadan; fall of Mazar-i-Sharif and Kabul; uprising at Kunduz prison and death of American CIA agent; three Americans die in mistaken bombing; siege of Kandahar)

JUST AS THE early lull of October was suddenly broken by the bombing against Afghanistan, so too the apparent stalemate in the initial month's fighting until November 9 was abruptly ended with the wholesale collapse of the Taliban. Yet few Americans appreciated how effectively their military in a space of a few days had utterly wrecked thousands of terrorists and their supporters. Instead new controversies arose almost as quickly as the old ones faded.

Was bin Laden dead, and did it matter? Had the very nature of war changed with the amazing successes of the American air force and its special-operations operatives on the ground? How should we deal with the thousands of prisoners now falling into our hands? Was Iraq next---or should we cease hostilities with victory achieved in Afghanistan? Were military tribunals or civilian courts the proper way to try the captured terrorists?

In general throughout these November essays the same themes remain constant: the laws of war are absolute, time-honored, and unchanging, despite radical transformations in technology and tactics. Critics, not having learned from the embarrassment of September and October, now lost their remaining credibility as the victories of November further discredited nearly all their skepticism about either the morality or progress of the war. And instead of widespread starvation and random violence in the streets of the major captured cities, relief efforts expanded, while steps toward a government of reconciliation progressed.

20.

War Talk

IF ONE TALKS at campuses or on the radio in support of the current American military response, the staccato of both hostile questions and the questioners themselves often blurs into a depressing pattern. What follows is a mélange from the dozens of actual inquiries I have encountered since September 11, along with the more or less standard replies.

The Pacifist

(The question is rarely presented as a question, but rather as a quite heated and very unpacifistic rant—with ample references to little-known foundations, books, and the questioner's own high-minded efforts and programs.)

Q. Violence begets violence. What did war ever solve? Do we have to reply in kind—to get down to their level? Haven't we learned more than "an eye for an eye" in the last thousand years? You cannot bomb in my name.

A. Violence can, in fact, often breed an endless circle of violence (note Northern Ireland)—but only if there is no clear moral consensus, and it is practiced solely in equal measure. But overwhelming violence in response to great evil, while tragic, is not therein evil. Such a military response constitutes real humanity and bravery because it is not rhetorical or cheap, and stops the killing on the part of the killers. Those who work in peril twenty hours a day on carriers and behind enemy lines on the ground did not ask for this war, but they are nonetheless fighting to ensure that their own children and those of others to come do not have to make the sacrifices they are now so bravely enduring.

War—whether to end slavery, to ruin the Nazi death camps, or to dismantle the Japanese military—has in fact ended great evil inflicted on millions. And if we don't reply now—as we didn't to Hitler after Czechoslovakia, the Italians in Ethiopia, or the Japanese in Nanking— murder unchecked goes on to kill millions. Ask the Cambodians, Bosnians, or Tutus. We have learned from the last twenty-five hundred years that human nature is unchanging and that the well-intentioned efforts to disarm and outlaw war are dangerous—and that such utopian pacifism is always at someone else's expense: usually those poorer, less educated, and not so "sophisticated" as yourself.

Can you please tell me what you would have advocated on December 8, 1941? And if we cannot in your name bomb the source of our terror, can our domestic forces at least use deadly force here at home to protect civilians from more crashing airliners and suicide bombers?

The Voice of Moral Equivalence

(Like the pacifist, the moralist offers no realistic plan of action to deal with September 11, but wishes to force you to concede that you are in fact a murderer like the Taliban.)

Q. They bomb us; we bomb them. They kill children; now we kill children. So what is the difference between them and us?

A. Quite a lot. First, we do know that our innocent were murdered, but we do not know how many Afghani citizens have been killed—either due to misplaced American bombs or to Taliban shells falling back among their citizens or to Taliban executions and terrorism against their own people. We do know that it is the deliberate policy of the Taliban to put their combatants among mosques, hospitals, and schools to ensure their survival, out of the expectation that Americans, unlike themselves, would not deliberately inflict collateral damage. If our enemies know that difference, why do not some of our own citizens, such as yourself?

For the sake of argument, let us assume that more than one hundred noncombatant Afghanis have so far been killed. The dead, of course, are the dead, and their loss is tragic. But there is a difference, a moral difference, between deliberately targeting civilians in peace and deliberately attempting to avoid them in war—especially at the risk of endangering the lives of our own pilots. And just wars have never been waged with 100 percent moral perfection, but rather—as against Germany or Japan, for example—with the full knowledge that innocents die in order that the mass murder by their governments be stopped, and in the expectation that their own lives, and those of their children, will not in the future be sacrificed as victims of or abettors to their own government's evil.

The Europeanist

(The questioner is soft-spoken and sometimes condescending, typically highly educated, well-traveled abroad, and a denizen of either coast. In a live setting, clapping usually follows his question.)

Q. This is more of the senseless retaliation that is typical of American unilateralism. After Kyoto and Durban, why should Americans expect European support?

A. Well, the three thousand dead are ours, not Europe's. And we, not they, must take care of our own—as we, not they, see fit. Still, although it took twenty-one days to invoke NATO's Article Five, in theory Europeans and Americans are not mere friends but military allies, sworn as such under treaty. The terrorists struck the United States first, but not necessarily last—and might equally have hit the Louvre (cf. the destruction of the great Buddha in Afghanistan), the Vatican (cf. their deadly rhetoric about non-Muslims, the murders in Pakistan of Christians, and murmurs of plots against the pope), or the Eiffel Tower (as we now know was once planned). Without a long climate of permissiveness in Europe for terrorists, much of the present carnage would have been impossible. We in America were naive and foolish, but those in Europe were far more knowingly and deliberately lax. The shores of the southern Mediterranean and what lies far across the Aegean are much closer to Europe than America—and most in Europe now recognize that far better than we. If anything, as our military continues to blast apart the enemy, small flotillas of European ships will join the fray before it ends.

The Anti-Americanist

(Full of all sorts of false knowledge, strange, but unsupported and fasci-
nating, "facts" and conspiracy theories; usually his voice breaks into
pained stammering by the fourth minute of the question, which can be
summarized by the following.)

**Q. Why don't you admit that this is just more of the same impe-
rialism, and that we have killed millions all over the globe in places
like Iraq, Serbia, Panama, Grenada, and Haiti?**

A. U.N. sanctions hurt Iraq, but not nearly as much as did its own
government, which built palaces and bought weapons while its
people—according to Iraqi "journalists"—went without. Those who
preferred to act militarily and unilaterally against Saddam Hussein,
rather than by sanctions with the U.N. against the Iraqi people, would
have incurred even greater animus from you. How odd that we were
told to work with the U.N. to obtain embargoes, and then, after they
were implemented, they were dubbed "U.S." sanctions. Hussein's
attacks with nuclear and biological weapons, if they reach fruition, are
indiscriminate and will not distinguish you from me; the fact that we
are American, free, and relatively affluent makes us the same target in
his eyes.

The bombing in Serbia—against Christian butchers of Muslims—
saved hundreds of thousands, as even our European critics now
admit. Hundreds, not millions, were lost through American intervention in and around the Caribbean. Despite our past unpredictable
policy and sometimes poor planning, most in Panama, Grenada, and
Haiti confess that they enjoy life now more than they did under the
tyrannies we replaced.

The Military Alarmist

(Usually half-educated, he has culled the Internet for bits and pieces
about Alexander the Great and the Soviet invasion of Afghanistan.)

**Q. Afghanistan has swallowed up dozens of armies—do we really
want another Vietnam?**

A. In fact, Alexander the Great and the British alike were eventually successful there, and at last defeated far greater armies with their

own very small forces far from home. The Russians gave up because they sought, insanely, to replace Islam with atheism—and yet after a decade quit only due to sophisticated American support to their enemies, and their own collapsing society at home. How strange that, before the bombing started, we were told that Afghanistan was too formidable to attack—and then after we obliterated much of the command-and-control structure of the Taliban we are now "bullying" an "asset-poor" country. That Afghanistan might be more difficult than the Gulf War hardly makes it Vietnam. In fact, so successful and brilliant have been our war-makers in the last decade that we now define a three-week war—with hundreds, if not more likely thousands, of enemy dead, and fewer than five of ours—as "protracted."

The Islamist

(Usually a visitor from the Middle East who mentions Israel in the first ten seconds of a very, very, very, long nonquestion, ending with . . .)

Q. America just won't leave Islam alone. You Americans should quit intervening throughout the world to hurt Muslim nations!

A. The great killers of Muslims these last decades have been other Muslims—whether in Iraq, Iran, Jordan and Palestine, or Lebanon. Indigenous theocracy, homegrown statism, and traditional autocracy—not Israel or the United States—have impoverished the masses of the Middle East. The United States has intervened out of its own self-interest, but also with the result that Muslims have been helped, rather than hurt—in Kuwait, among the backwaters of Iraq, in Afghanistan, Somalia, Kosovo, and Bosnia. Our great fault is that we have supported illegitimate regimes, out of an understandable fear that their overthrow might produce something like the past reign of terror in Iran and Algeria, rather than Jeffersonian democracy—or that a real consensual government might turn socialist and confiscate American investments. Still, promotion of democracy in Iraq and Afghanistan may be our only chance of salvaging a viable Middle East policy—and thereby thwarting the fundamentalists, as well as the corrupt and illegitimate Arab moderates who are alike now enemies of democracy. Israel has about as much to do with the poverty in Cairo or the undernourished babies in Baghdad as does life on Mars. What exactly is your question?

The Advocate of the Palestinians

(Usually on a student visa, he raises the word "Israel" after second two, and thereafter every third second, until minute five of the question. Questioner usually announces that he is a moderate, but then proceeds to prove by voice and tone that he in fact is hardly moderate at all. He also ends with . . .)

Q. The events of September 11 are very sad, BUT only to be expected given the American bombs Israel uses to kill Palestinian children. Why are you surprised?

A. I'm not surprised, but for reasons far different from your own. American restraint and timidity, not recklessness, got us into this mess. Bin Laden, like Saddam Hussein, only mentions the Palestinians when he is desperate and near defeat. Israel—unlike its opponents—is quite able to craft its own guns and planes without our help. We deplore the killing, and in the past have supported the concept of a Palestinian state that has reasonable borders and that pledges nonviolence toward Israel; in fact, we provide over $100 million a year to Mr. Arafat and twenty times that to Mr. Mubarak, despite the animus shown America in their state-controlled papers.

But we are not stupid either. Despite American prompting, Palestine is not a democracy; it has no free judiciary, nor any history of protecting human rights. It waged its first three wars not to free the West Bank, but to destroy Israel. And we remember Mr. Arafat's past alliance with Saddam Hussein and the present cheering in the streets of the West Bank at the news of our dead—not unlike the similar jubilation there a decade ago at the rumors that the Iraqi SCUDs landing in Tel Aviv were laden with gas. We are humans, not gods, and—like you, in fact—have a long memory. If you dislike us so, perhaps, by mutual agreement, for a year or two Americans will promise not to visit Palestine and you should not visit us. And finally, could we carry on this conversation in safety inside Palestine?

The Frightened

(Often refers to kids, suburbs, work—as if he or she alone has such concerns.)

Q. If we have the Twin Towers and anthrax now, what can we expect when we kill bin Laden or invade Iraq—nuclear bombs and smallpox in our streets and schools? How can we stop this nightmare?

A. In fact, we can, if we wish, envision all sorts of nightmares. But the anthrax was postmarked contemporaneously with the World Trade Center ruination, not after our response in Afghanistan. The enemy is going to do what it desires until it is stopped by us. Past policies of accommodation and moderation, not strong responses, have endangered our children. In every war there is always the unpredictable, but close analysis of our actions since September 11 suggests that few Americans have died and many of our enemies have and will. Kabul is a far more dangerous place than Washington, D.C., and will become even bleaker still.

Not a soul believed, in December 1941, that not a soul four years thence would claim to be a Nazi or Japanese militarist. Yet by 1945, not a soul bragged to be either—and so it will be with the Taliban and the bin Ladens, whose fate is already sealed. Such past revolutionary change in the hearts of millions was not accomplished by therapy, or by expressions of fear and guilt, but by military force, joined with humanitarian aid to the humiliated, misled, and soundly defeated. After December 1941, there was never again an attack on the homeland of the United States—but quite a lot on Germany, Italy, and Japan. By any standard of military history, our armed forces are doing a superb job under the most trying of conditions. Our edgy critics are clamoring for more movement, yet our observant enemies in the Middle East are as we speak quietly hoping that such a terrible arsenal, and the brave professionals who run it, are not turned loose against them.

The Academic

(Usually a professor of English, sometimes of political science or government, in his/her mid-fifties—their long questions require a very short answer.)

Q. Like some bull in a china shop, you charge into, as it were, some in fact quite complex issues of culture, race, class, and gender in the Middle East that simply cannot be resolved by brute military force used in a very unsophisticated, unfocused, and I must say frightening way that we saw only too well in Vietnam. We have foolishly spent much of the world's sympathy accrued after September 11 in just the sort of unnecessary saber-rattling you so recklessly advocate. I have argued at length elsewhere that the United States must take very seriously complaints coming in from almost every corner of the Islamic world regarding its treatment of Muslims, from Palestine to Iraq to Saudi Arabia, and its predictable inability to hear the voices of those who by any reasonable definition are genuinely oppressed.

All too often we offer only the worst of our culture to those in dire need of basic necessities; if we must intervene in the internal affairs of others—something in itself extremely problematic, and which I remain very troubled by—it would be far better to craft a second Marshall Plan with no strings attached than to rain down bombs on children. September 11 was an unfortunate event, for which proper criminal and judicial measures—albeit with special care to prevent the ominous onset of a police state—must be addressed; but simply lashing out at suspected sympathetic governments will only compound the problem, and leave a legacy of hatred and impoverishment that will last for generations. By your logic we should bomb the havens of Boston or Frankfurt, where in fact terrorists were known to have lived quite safely.

A. Bin Laden would agree with almost everything you have said.

The Oil Conspirator

(Prefaces questions with odd bits of information about redwoods, the ozone layer, and far-distant pipelines with strange names.)

Q. I see that you deliberately chose not to tell the audience that Cheney and Bush are oil executives. Do you know anything about the oil in Afghanistan? Or why we are really in Saudi Arabia?

A. I know about as much about the oil in Afghanistan as I do about all the purported oil that was "really" in Vietnam during the Tet Offensive. If our government has cozied up to corrupt oil producers like the sheiks in the Gulf, it was not to give Mr. Bush and Mr. Cheney impressive stock portfolios, but rather to provide cheap electricity and gas for the likes of you and me. A principled position of disengagement from the Middle East would require you, in a significant way, to extricate yourself from our current power guzzling world—laptops, SUVs, plane tickets, and vacations abroad—or to support coastal drilling off Santa Barbara and in the Arctic Circle, or to explain how hydrogen, solar rays, strong breezes, or batteries can power our cars, power plants, and aircraft this year. If our policy was solely designed to protect cheap oil, then we would not be responding in the Middle East at all—as, in fact, a number of isolationists and oilmen have advocated.

The Ignoramus

(Most often a student activist, and the most interesting of all the questioners, since he reveals instantaneously the erosion of the American educational system during the last three decades—arrogance coupled with ignorance proving a fatal combination.)

Q. Why don't you mention that the United States killed two million babies in Iran last year?

A. Wrong country, wrong number, wrong year—wrong planet.

Written on November 1 and published in National Review Online on November 2.

21.

The Dogs of War

LESSONS OF THE TWENTIETH CENTURY

Cry, "Havoc!" and let slip the dogs of war.
SHAKESPEARE, JULIUS CAESAR III.i.270

THE TRAGEDY OF war is that the unthinkable soon becomes the accepted. Yet those who expect the macabre from their bloodthirsty enemies and are not awed by it—but rather are grim and ready to answer every manifestation of evil with overwhelming force while still pledged to a moral cause—usually prevail. Such is the case now with America.

We were rather startled, after Pearl Harbor, that Hitler would suddenly declare war on the United States. Blinkered Americans woke up on December 8 to discover that all of Europe united under fascism was now every bit as determined as Japan to wipe us out. Few thought that cannonballs over Fort Sumter in but four years would lead to battles like Shiloh, Antietam, and Cold Harbor; ironclads and repeating rifles; Lincoln assassinated; and six hundred thousand dead. In the Gulf War, no pundit predicted that the purportedly battle-hardened army of Saddam Hussein would collapse within one hundred hours—despite missiles raining down on Israel and the Kuwaiti oil fields afire. When the dogs of war slip loose, accurate prognosis is almost impossible; the surreal becomes the typical.

Before Marathon, the Greeks had purportedly been afraid even to look on the Persians—yet once they charged head-on at that battle and slaughtered them, Herodotus would say that a "destructive madness" had taken hold of them. Saddam Hussein learned that neither the threat of poison gas attacks on Tel Aviv nor ecoterrorism in the oil fields could stop American armored divisions from destroying his military. Not his terror but only American naïveté in the guise of realpolitik saved his regime.

In this present war, we must brace for the unthinkable. The government in Pakistan could crumble. A few nuclear weapons could conceivably fall into the hands of renegade officers sympathetic to the Taliban, or be smuggled out and sold. Far worse germs may reach our inner chambers of government. A cornered Saddam may well send missiles again into Israel; the oil fields might again be set on fire. There could be splits in the Saudi royal family and terrorists' attempts to take over that government. Tens of thousands of fundamentalists may flee Pakistan to join the Taliban (promises, promises . . .). There may be stored caches of Stinger missiles waiting for our low-level helicopter attacks. Americans may be targeted in every country in the Middle East and beyond. Indeed, we may see appalling things in this Götterdämmerung that few can imagine—but then the vaporization of three thousand of our dear citizens, and the toppling of our landmarks, were themselves rather unimaginable. Two kilotons of destructive power dropped into downtown New York City at a time of peace is not to be forgotten.

I would not wish to fight the United States—either militarily, politically, or culturally. For every threat, our history teaches us that Americans offer not just a rejoinder, but the specter of a devastating answer of a magnitude almost inconceivable to those now chanting and threatening in the streets of the Middle East. Do they have any idea of what sort of dangerous people we really are? Do they understand the history of the names of those ships now off their coasts, like the USS *Peleliu* or *Enterprise,* or the pedigree of the 82nd or 101st Airborne?

The Saudis' princes tease us with polite lectures about our errant policies, more obliquely suggesting that our bombing may lose "friends" among the moderate states. Yet America, unlike Saudi Arabia, has not merely the veneer of modern civilization, but is its wellspring. In a real war, despite severe dislocation, we can survive, as in the past, without Saudi oil. The royal family and the faux-culture of the Gulf cannot. Fifteen of their citizens helped to murder three thousand unsuspecting Americans in a time of peace—a single wing of American fighters could end their entire regime in a few days of war.

Such are the frightening and horrendous realities that lurk beneath the unspoken surface when the dogs of war are unleashed. Battle indeed is the ultimate nightmare because accustomed rhetoric recedes before the truth of abject military power, and so the more the United States is shrilly hectored, in still more stark contrast loom the silhouettes of aircraft carrier groups and B-52s.

We are warned by the media that Americans might be blown up and shot abroad, but a simple and quite legal change in our own immigration policy can—if need be—expel all those visitors on visas from all suspect countries of the Middle East, and so, besides offering us increased protection, in a real war deny to thousands the access to American education and Western technology that so many crave (and yet apparently hate) all at once. So one of the great tragedies of the present war is not merely that Americans will be targets in the Arab world (most will discover that they can live without seeing the Pyramids or flying a fighter jet out of a Saudi Arabian hangar), but that an entire generation of Middle Easterners will be under a veil of suspicion in Western countries. Life for an Egyptian scientist on leave in Berlin, or a Saudi tourist with a camera in Los Angeles, or a visiting Lebanese businessman with binoculars on the bay in Boston for years hence—*terribile dictu*—will not quite be the same. All this sadness and unfairness was unleashed not by us, but by Mr. bin Laden, who is canonized by millions in the Muslim world. Yes, he is lionized by millions, but the next few years will prove that no one in the last century has done so much to harm so many of the Arab world.

When the dogs are unleashed, there may be more catastrophes to come—none of them our own. We are told that the entire Muslim world may turn on us—a ghastly thought, no doubt, but hardly as scary as a united Europe aroused or a suddenly angered China, which have real military capabilities. The fact is that the most potent countries in the world—Japan, Russia, and India—are not mere neutrals, but are daily becoming incensed at Islamic fundamentalists and enacting policies whose natural evolution can only end in the isolation of the radical Muslim world.

A once snapping and American-snarling Europe is hunting out terrorists as never before and beginning to talk again of "the West." The really bizarre specter after September 11 is not that the moderate Muslim world threatens to fall to the side of the fundamentalists, but that the leisured and sophisticated of Europe are now suddenly talking as if they were seamen at Lepanto. The truth is that bin Laden, the Taliban, and the shrieking fundamentalists in the Arab capitals may have united hundreds of thousands against America, but in the process their dogs of war have turned billions of the world against them—a global community that they sorely need but that, if the truth must be brutally confessed, in scientific or economic terms, sadly does not need them at all.

After the unprovoked murder of thousands of Americans, the governments in Saudi Arabia, Pakistan, Palestine, Iraq, and Iran should not lecture us about either our policies or morality, but rather should fear that they themselves are on the edge of a frightening precipice. For the first time in a half-century, America has the unity and resolve to act as a nation rather than being paralyzed as a loose affiliation of squabbling tribes, interests, and cultures. And America has discovered in its renaissance that it has the military power to end hostile militaries, the moral anger to confront corrupt governments, the cultural dynamism to ostracize bellicose societies—and, after the horrors of September and October, is nearing the recklessness not to care.

Moderates in the Middle East must draw *us* back from the brink to protect themselves, not us. They must distance themselves far more forcefully from those who sanction the murders of thousands of Americans. They should not fund or sponsor radicals on our own shores. Millions of Americans on Halloween night viewed on C-SPAN perhaps the most ghoulish expression of unadulterated hatred ever telecast in American history. Live from the National Press Club, the New Black Panther Party and their Islamic allies in America—Imam Abdul Alim Musa, Imam Mohammed Asi, Imam Abdel Razzag al Raggad, and others of the various mosques in the Washington, D.C., area—cheered on the Taliban, venting racist, anti-Semitic (and subversive) propaganda in a time of war. These prime-time hate-mongers blamed Jewish agents for the September 11 bombing, and were clearly not unhappy at the deaths of thousands of Americans. Surely similar incendiary groups, like the foul Ku Klux Klan, would not be given free time on public television in a time of war. The transcript alone of that disgusting spectacle before the era of Vietnam would have qualified as evidence for treason and sedition under the classical definitions found in Article III of the Constitution.

There is a growing chorus of rarely-heard-from Americans between the two coasts—one little known by fundamentalists in the Middle East, or their agents in our capital—that has had enough of all this. They are reaching a state of fury over thousands of our dead, constant germ scares, bomb threats, screaming imams on public television slandering our dead, sneering caveats from puffed-up academics, and lectures from corrupt governments mixed with veiled threats. So most Americans have sadly accepted that the dogs of war have indeed slipped loose, and their anger, as I can discern it from this central California farm, can be summarized by something like, "Hell, enough is enough—let's get to it and not stop until the whole damn thing is over with!" That crescendo, which elites decry as "unilateralism" and worse, is actually similar to the mood of resolve and desperation of December 8, 1941, when we didn't worry much about anything other than annihilating our enemies, and letting neutrals, allies, threatening enemies, and our own critics sort it all out and live with the aftershocks.

Reviled by those in the Middle East, caricatured on campuses at home, and second-guessed by pundits of every persuasion, our military and its leadership—by any military standard of the past—have been rather brilliant in waging a war of unprecedented logistical challenges against an elusive enemy. In less than a month, America has devastated an evil government more than six thousand miles distant at a loss of fewer than five dead! Its planes roam freely over enemy skies; its opponents are either ensconced in caves, hiding among mosques, or striking out by the pathetic spectacles of public executions, threats to poison the food of their own hungry, and the shanghaiing of reluctant conscripts. Rarely has such a boasting adversary proved to be both so craven and so foul. Critics of our progress, in the aftermath of the Gulf War and Kosovo, and in ignorance of military history, have judged past miraculous and rare victories as typical rather than as exceptional in the long story of battle, and so have weirdly defined success only as instantaneous triumph, rather than real achievement over months—or a few years—of hard fighting.

Remember—those who promised us a generation of suicide bombers three weeks ago are lurking incognito among women on buses. Unlike after the unexpected attacks on Pearl Harbor or the invasion of South Korea, it has not taken the United States six months to regroup and attack, but only a few days. What is maddening to our enemies is not that we are bombing with untold devastation, but that we are bombing with care to avoid the innocent and to target the guilty, and all the while are trying to feed the hungry—and with far more success than failure.

If we have learned anything from the twentieth century, it is that the braggadocio of fascism is not the same as the brawn of democracy—and that the evil and weak should not attack the strongest and better. Bin Laden and his supporters have let slip the dogs of war; history teaches us that they more often turn on and devour their masters. We must be patient and let the dogs reach their fury.

Written on November 4 and published in National Review Online *on November 6.*

22.

Heads, They Win

TAILS, WE LOSE

WE ALL RECALL that when Saddam Hussein's weapons of mass destruction were not being eliminated as prescribed in the armistice agreements, moderate Arab governments, our own State Department in both Republican and Democratic administrations, and those on the Left and Right opposed unilateral military action to take out his missiles, germs, and stored nuclear material. Instead we were directed to the U.N. Yet once international sanctions began to have some moderate effect, the Iraqis nevertheless continued splurging on their elite, stealthily purchasing weapons, and broadcasting on CNN pictures of purportedly starving children. At that point, the initials "U.N." were insidiously replaced with "U.S.," and we incurred the world's blame for "U.S. sanctions" that "killed babies"—but without the benefit at least of ridding Iraq of the mechanisms for killing us. Of course, had we used force to blow up Iraq's ordnance of mass destruction by sustained air strikes, in 1992 or 1993, we would have been roundly denounced as interventionists and crude unilateralists, insensitive to the nuances of the Muslim world.

Pundits here and abroad wax on about how we "created bin Laden" and then "abandoned Afghanistan." They should look at histories of the Soviet invasion written during the 1980s. Most accounts, after outlining Russian atrocities, are bugle calls for U.S. action and castigation of the slow American aid to the "freedom fighters." Soviet mines disguised as dolls and toys were said to have been dropped from the sky. Prisoners were tortured, and carpet-bombing of entire villages, we were told, made it imperative to help these brave but outclassed patriots. The media saturated our screens with images of flintlocks against attack helicopters, piety pitted against atheism. And so Stinger missiles, sophisticated automatic weapons, and mobile artillery followed, sensationalized by Dan Rather and others caught up in the zeal of helping the seemingly helpless. Most military historians agree that such heavy machine guns, rocket launchers, and the Stingers turned certain Muslim defeat in 1983 into virtual stalemate by 1985. However, what once was seen as principled assistance to indigenous underdogs now is reinvented as cynical CIA machinations—"chickens coming home to roost."

Of course, had we done nothing to help the Afghanis, we would then have been scolded that we were amoral Kissingerians, who did not think dying children in Afghanistan were worth confronting the wrath of the Soviet Union. Had we stayed on to create democracy we would have been dubbed naive liberal "nation-builders," interventionists intent on idealistic secularism in a fundamentalist society. And so we pulled out our military assistance, kept giving millions of dollars in food aid, and accepted the charge that we had "ignored" our "friends," all the while "giving aid to the Taliban."

Most Americans agree that supporting corrupt autocracies and medieval theocracies, such as Kuwait and Saudi Arabia, is against our long-term interests and must stop. But we also realize that such countries supply not only our imported oil, but the world's as well. And so, between a rock and a hard place, we are not sure something far worse—like the evil in Algeria, Afghanistan, and Iran—might not take the sheiks' place. Yet now we are told that bin Laden might, in fact, have some legitimate grievance, because his constituencies have not had the freedom to vote and speak. That may well be so, but it does not follow that bin Laden himself would ever have sanctioned freedom or democracy, as we've seen from the Taliban gangsters. Of course, had we mandated elections in the Middle East, had bin Laden's thugs swept to victory, and then destroyed nascent democratic machinery and taken over the oil to buy frightful weapons—we would now be told by an aroused world that we were naive, foolish, or culturally blinkered.

For much of September we were reminded, through historical fictions, that attacks against Afghanistan meant suicide—with no real study of Alexander the Great's career, the Third Anglo-Afghani war, or the true situation during the Soviet occupation of 1980–82. Then, after our initial strategic air strikes and near-annihilation of the Taliban's traditional military assets, talking heads sarcastically referred to an absence of real targets, while critics overseas agonized that a sophisticated modern air force was simply pounding those who could not fight back. Now, weeks later, the harpies have reversed course and castigated our military for not doing enough. By this logic, we should expect in the future that when we are successful in the use of overwhelming force, we will be dubbed bullies of an outclassed foe—and that, when we suffer reverses, we will be pounced on for naively blundering into a quagmire.

For years, PBS documentaries like *American Jihad* demonstrated that real supporters of anti-American terrorists reside in the United States. Anyone who has taught on American campuses in the last twenty years has been struck by the occasional vehemence of foreign students from the Middle East who quite bluntly lecture their professors on American foreign policy, spicing their remarks with open hopes of destroying Israel and expressed tolerance for terrorist groups. On Halloween night, live from the National Press Club, we saw more of it. The FBI has known that Islamic "charities" were often conduits for cash transfers to terrorists. And the State Department surely was aware that known leaders of murderous groups like Hamas, Islamic Jihad, and others openly raised money among Muslim groups, community mosques, and student organizations on campus.

Yes, we know all that, and so are now told that our intelligence agencies are inept, naive, and worse, for not spotting the hijackers in advance. But we also surely suspect that, had any government watchdog agency swept down on America's universities, mosques, Islamic leagues, and Muslim charities—to expel agitators hostile to the United States, to infiltrate such groups, or to wiretap—they would have met with a storm of protest. The Islamic-American community would have quickly mobilized the considerable arsenal of our politically correct media; universities; the legal professions; and local, state, and national government to allege ethnic stereotyping, racial profiling, religious intolerance, Islamophobia, and all the usual -isms and -ologies we have become acquainted with.

We have been aware for years of what the Taliban was doing to millions of women: arbitrary executions, gender apartheid, daily degradation, child abuse, whipping, and sexual mutilation. Afghanistan violated every consideration of civilized life—from desecrating cemeteries to book burning and cultural vandalism—and was at odds with a number of United Nations pronouncements on human rights. Indeed, the Taliban was every bit as diabolical as the racist regime in South Africa and, had it had the resources of Serbia, as genocidal as the outlaws in Belgrade. Yet if the United States had taken prompt action, cut off all travel to Afghanistan and Pakistan, frozen their assets, embargoed their trade, and treated both as rogue nations (such as Cuba or North Korea), a storm of protest would have arisen both here and abroad. Moderates in the Arab world would have lectured the United States on our insensitivity toward Islam, while cultural relativists and anthropologists would have bleated the usual mantras of "Who is to say what always is normal?" "Are we always any better ourselves?" and "This is just a part of their culture very different from our own." Feminists who damned the Taliban would have damned American military interventionism and bellicosity just as much.

Much of the hypocrisy, of course, is simply what a great power expects from the envious and inferior—as Pericles reminded his Athenian audience in the first book of Thucydides' history. But a great deal of the paradox is the sad wages of the times, and reflects our own troubling uncertainty about morality—and our allegiance to what is relative and of the moment, rather than to what is absolute and of the ages. This new species of upscale and pampered terrorist hates America for a variety of complex reasons. He despises, of course, his own attraction toward our ease and liberality. He recognizes that our freedom and affluence spur on his appetites more than Islam can repress them.

But just as important, these terrorists realize that there is an easy aristocratic guilt within many comfortable Americans, who are apologetic about their culture. Few, when pressed by critics, are able or willing to defend their values and way of life when a simple "I'm sorry" or "It's our government, not me" will ease the tension. And in this hesitance, our new enemies sense both decadence and weakness. Rather than appreciating Americans' self-confidence or simple manners when we accept rebuke so politely, our enemies despise us all the more, simply because they can—and can so easily, and without rejoinder.

September 11 has taught Americans that we need to return to being the confident moral force we once were, and fast—to act resolutely and to follow principle. We must expect, but ultimately ignore, the carping; be polite, but forgo the apologies; and let our critics, not us, worry only about the tension and hurt that follows.

Written on November 7 and published in National Review Online
on November 9.

23

More an Okinawa Than a Vietnam?

LESSONS IN WAR

FROM APRIL 1 to mid-June, 1945, we fought die-hard enemies well entrenched in vast caves stocked with telephone switchboards, tanks, artillery, and mortars. The enemy, while adopting European arms and military organization, had completely rejected Western pluralism, freedom, and tolerance as "weak" and "corrupt," and instead fortified its military with the fanatical religion of "Bushido," a crackpot and deviant Buddhist fundamentalism that sought to marry emperor-worship with a medieval warrior code to produce a purportedly unstoppable new type of high-tech samurai warrior. The fanatics' goal was to rid the Pacific of Occidentals, and let China, Korea, southeast Asia, and the Pacific Islands "join" an "Oriental" alliance, orchestrated from Tokyo as an exploitive empire passed off as the "Greater Co-Prosperity Sphere." Sound familiar?

American soldiers were thousands of miles distant from our shores, closer to the enemy mainland than to friendly bases. As an ally, we had only Britain—who did her best, but could not offer much in our hour of crisis. The enemy shanghaied local civilians into their army, filled them full of lies about Americans, and turned them loose against us either to charge as suicide bombers, or often to commit mass suicide themselves. Soldiers hid in civilian houses, hospitals, even tombs of the dead to avoid our bombers—which were never successful in finding the Japanese high command, but hit a lot of civilians trying. Fanatics like General Isamu Cho and Mitsuru Ushijima boasted of no surrender, rejected all efforts at armistice, and vowed to take as many Americans as possible with them. Crude propaganda leaflets and radio broadcasts promised horrific deaths to Americans and portrayed them as cowardly killers who would rape and murder innocent civilians—more than one hundred thousand natives of the island would eventually be casualties. The Japanese leadership itself, in the manner of ancient warlords, believed Americans were decadent and soft. Indeed, without the overwhelming firepower of the United States—purportedly to be neutralized on Okinawa by offensive suicide attacks on ships, and the defense of caves and concrete bunkers—the generals swore that few of the stinking Americans could ever stand up to Japanese soldiers in battle.

Suicide bombers were everywhere. Kamikazes ("The Divine Wind") dove unexpectedly from cloud cover; eventually they would fly almost 2,000 sorties and sink 34 American ships. They hit another 368 craft. The Japanese unleashed previously unknown and quite bizarre new weapons to terrify Americans, such as the human guided rocket (*ohka*), the crash boat (*Shinto*), the suicide midget submarines (*koryu* and *kairyu*), and the *fukuryu* or human mines.

The wounded and dead were wired with explosives; holes in the ground opened up to pour forth small squads of charging Japanese suicide machine-gunners at the rear of American troops. Despite days of preliminary bombing, it was soon discovered, to the Marines' dismay, that few defenders on Okinawa were killed in their fortified and hidden bunkers. Meanwhile, Japanese suicide gliders attacked Marine airfields while kamikazes from Japan dove onto carriers at sea. Americans met every challenge, but victory proved costly—and far more deadly—than planners had anticipated.

Nearly everything, from bullets to toilet paper, had to be flown in. The weather was cold at night, and during the day wet and muddy— the terrain full of poisonous snakes, razor-sharp coral, and dense underbrush. Hundreds of GIs suffered from exposure and tropical diseases. Americans at home, gladdened by news of the European armistice in early May, gradually seemed to lose interest in the protracted fighting in Okinawa. They were more worried about rumors of a wider war in which millions of Americans would be asked to storm the Japanese mainland at the end of the year.

When "Operation Iceberg" was completed by June 22, twelve thousand Americans were dead—including the ranking American general in charge of the entire operation, Simón Bolivar Buckner. Thirty-five thousand more were wounded, along with one hundred thousand Japanese killed and another one hundred thousand civilian casualties.

What can we learn from Okinawa? First, the "good" news: In less than three months Americans captured the largest group of islands off the Japanese mainland, destroyed an entire Japanese army, and obtained a base of operations that would doom future enemy naval and air resistance—and were ready to move on to the next objective of Japan herself. American GIs and Marines—among those killed on May 19 at Sugar Loaf Hill was my namesake Victor Hanson of the 6th Marine Division—fought brilliantly, and proved as savage and brave as their desperate Japanese counterparts. And we should remember that the Japanese on Okinawa were far fiercer adversaries than the Taliban. Once the conquered Okinawans themselves learned the true nature of American troops, they became friendly and many welcomed liberation from the Japanese—there was almost no terror in the aftermath of the American victory. Okinawa today enjoys democratic government, as a part of the Japanese nation.

All that being said, the strategy at Okinawa must stand also as an object lesson of what not to do in war. The bombing, both from land-based squadrons and carrier planes, was far too brief, and not effective in penetrating thick fortifications. The ground commanders were far too eager to precipitate operations, and used little imagination in their approaches. Pockets of fortified resistance were not isolated and repeatedly shelled and bombed, but instead almost immediately stormed. And once the fighting turned hand-to-hand, General Buckner rejected the advice of four seasoned subordinates who wished to outflank the deadly Shuri-Yonabaru Line through amphibious landings to the rear. Too much of the fighting on Okinawa resembled World War I: on the ground, mass against mass, machine guns dueling with rifles and mortars, the entrenched enemy gaining enormous advantages against an open and exposed attacker. American soldiers had trouble distinguishing hostiles from neutrals, especially when the fighting reached settled areas.

One final ripple from Okinawa? After the bloodletting, the American military was reluctant ever again to fight such a Japanese-style battle, and looked desperately for ways to avoid such mass carnage in the promised invasion of Japan to come. The mainland, after all, offered a battlefield ten times as large, with twenty times the number of combatants, in the midst of millions more of armed civilians. And so American planners, stunned by the tens of thousands of casualties at Okinawa, found their answers at Hiroshima and Nagasaki.

Ground troops are necessary in Afghanistan—and no doubt elsewhere, in the multifaceted campaigns to come. And we Americans should not be shy in using thousands of them very soon. But to avoid the carnage of Okinawa, let us at least give our planes a little more time to hit the Taliban forces to cut off all their supplies, and to ensure that their solders become hungry and cold in the snow, before sending American troops into the battle. We should ignore the passive-aggressive admonitions of our fretting allies and the carping Muslim world over bombing during Ramadan, and instead ensure that the enemy is further pulverized before our conventional forces enter the fray. A few more days or even weeks of bombing—as during the Gulf War—may enrage some in the Middle East, but in the long run, patience will save American lives, which are far more important than our enemies' feelings. In historical terms, the strategy of continued attrition of adversaries without loss of one's own assets is wise—not flawed, nor cowardly.

With far more accurate and deadly preliminary bombing than that of World War II, our infantry can soon win on the ground—within a similar three-month period, but without the losses of Okinawa. Frontal assaults against entrenched Taliban lines should be avoided in favor of flank attacks and envelopments, and a sustained propaganda program must reach civilians to convince them to kill or at least to oppose those hiding among them, rather than us. Street fighting in villages and towns should be largely left to the resistance, who can use our forward bases and firepower stationed outside the metropolitan centers to regroup and reorganize.

Our military, which knows a great deal about the ordeal of Okinawa, is planning precisely this right now. But we, who do not, must give them some time—and more of our composure and support.

Written on November 10 and published in National Review Online
on November 13.

24

Five Not-So-Easy Pieces

THE WORLD ANEW

IF THE WORLD abroad has been turned upside down, so it has here at home as well. Moral equivalence, cultural relativism, and anti-Westernism on the cheap have been discredited as the conceited indulgence of the affluent and bored. Our critics have not been principled in their moral censure of the military response, but rather shallow, ethically bankrupt, and dead wrong; the poor in Kabul amid the bombs seem to like what we have done far more than do the wealthy and comfortable of Berkeley, Madison, and Cambridge in their faculty lounges. In truth, throughout this crisis the predictable protesters have had real trouble hitting the keys to the usual five easy pieces of fashionable anti-Americanism. Some, like Oliver Stone, Susan Sontag, and Alice Walker, have tried, but they sounded so shrill and dissonant—and silly—that the rest of the symphony simply threw away their usual sheet music, and have now quit playing altogether. Why is this so?

I. Fascism—Not Socialism

WE ARE FIGHTING fascists, not Communists or Leftists. If it proved difficult to mobilize public opinion during the Cold War, against the mass murdering of the Soviet Union and of Mao's China, it was often because of the Communists' propaganda about egalitarianism and concern for the working classes. Those embarrassed by the genocide and gratuitous killing by Stalin, Mao, or the North Vietnamese grimaced, but perhaps felt that to make the omelet of a class, race, and gender paradise, one simply had to break a few reactionary, capitalist eggs. Communism, after all, professed to use force only to force others to justice. Decades ago, thousands of naive young college students—in safety and leisure and far from the gulag—hung North Vietnamese flags in their dorm rooms because they fell for the lie that Ho Chi Minh was a Jeffersonian, or that his theft of the Western nomenclature of "republic" and "liberty" really meant elections and freedom— rather than a totalitarian police state to jail, kill, and exile millions.

But the Taliban and the terrorists? They offered no such rhetoric and so started bad, and will end worse. The Taliban and their hench-men will kill you at home, not shatter your idealism thousands of miles away. It is hard to make these creepy torturers—who kill homo-sexuals, debase women, murder the learned, and root out the bones of infidels in their graves—into real reformers. These murderers are no different from Nazis in their hatred of Jews, similar to jackbooted book-burners in their destruction of cultural icons, and near identical to the Gestapo in their hunt for the nonbelievers in hiding. So it is nearly impossible for America's feminists, gay activists, progressive Christians, and connoisseurs of art to sympathize with these savage enemies of civilization.

II. Jews—Not Just Israel

IT IS FASHIONABLE on campus, and in elite circles, to damn Israel and promote the Palestinian cause. But the Taliban and bin Laden? They and their American supporters are simply too much to stom-ach—for their rhetoric is not political and principled, but anti-Semitic, racist, and lunatic. Unlike most of their Palestinian supporters, they slander not even with the term "Zionists," but openly with the word "Jews"—I suppose in theory that must mean everyone from Jerry Seinfeld to Barbra Streisand. The domestic agents of the Taliban—on national television and in prime time, no less—openly spread lies that Jewish agents had destroyed the World Trade Center, and fled the building minutes before the crash to sell off their airline stocks. That invective was surely a loathsome example of what we know as "hate speech"; and if "words matter," then we haven't heard voices of revulsion like this since Radio Berlin in the 1930s. So it is hard for America's usual critics of our policy in the Middle East to enter the fray, when these monsters, in the manner of Hitler, are not merely frothing to incinerate Israel, but really do wish to murder Jews in general.

III. Us—Not You

CULTURAL UTOPIANISM, MORE than political revolution, was the great arena of Leftist energy in the 1980s and 1990s. But the Taliban and the terrorists have discredited nearly all of it. African-Americans are said to be overwhelmingly in support of antiterrorism racial profiling—the purportedly odious idea that an easily identifiable group might be given special police scrutiny if its members statistically violated particular laws at particular places not otherwise commensurate with its own proportion of the general population. When nineteen of nineteen killers are from the Middle East, young, male, and self-described Islamic fundamentalists, things apparently do change. College deans and trial lawyers alike on planes feel uneasy when three or four men from the Arab world board in groups. As terrorist threats increase, very few from the ACLU or Earth First on planes are staring at Norwegians or Vietnamese.

But it is not just that even the liberal and progressive feel apprehensive among young males from the Middle East on planes; those now shouting in the Arab street see us too in monolithic terms, as a group rather than as individuals. It was once reassuring to the Left that at least our enemies could spot sympathetic voices in our midst. The Vietcong welcomed solidarity with Jane Fonda and Bill Ayers. Fidel Castro made it clear that he could distinguish good from bad Americans—say, a Noam Chomsky from William Buckley—as did Mr. Arafat. But the Taliban and their ilk? They apparently hate Dan Rather as much as Rush Limbaugh. Their supporters even boo the cosmopolitan French as much as they do the hick Americans. They kill alike immigrants in lunchrooms at the bottom of the Twin Towers, and the Wall Street grandees atop with the power views. Indeed, I think should Eleanor Smeal and Gloria Steinem visit Afghanistan, the Taliban in their caves might cut them off at their first stanza of "Race, class, gender . . ." instead to cover them in *burqas* and with special dispensation, sell them off as the fifth and sixth wives of bin Laden.

IV. Here—Not There

THE ANTIWAR MOVEMENT told us in past conflicts—Vietnam, Grenada, Panama, Iraq, and Bosnia—that we had the choice not to use force. After all, did any of these nations or tribes attack the United

States? In all these cases, critics pointed to the real culprits of interventionism: colonialism, racism, and the military-industrial complex— and ridiculed any notion that our mission could end totalitarianism, misery, murder, or even genocide. No, we were in Vietnam for oil and pride, in Grenada to squeeze Cuba, in Panama for the canal, in Iraq for yet more oil, in Bosnia because we just liked to bomb. But the Taliban? There are more than three thousand dead in our streets, germs at one time or another have shut down the chief buildings of our government, and nearly a million Americans are out of work. Civilians, not soldiers, have been killed, at home, not abroad, in peace, not at war. Bin Laden's mass murder is not a repartee or a desperate slap from the oppressed, but a calculated, massive act of war—with more purportedly on the way. How do you play that piece as interventionism abroad?

IV. The Top and Middle—Not Just the Bottom

THE LEFT TELLS us that America's wars grind up our own poor, as the engine of racism, class exploitation, and gender discrimination puts the most vulnerable on the front lines to fight and die for the affluent and privileged to the rear. Yet Afghanistan is not as easy to mischaracterize as was Vietnam. Our bombers are professional pilots, pros in their late twenties and thirties—to use an odious term, perhaps "overrepresented" by white males—who brave hostile fire and know their capture can mean certain death or worse.

The dead so far are civilians of every class, many of them the captains of industry at the top floors of the Pentagon and the World Trade Center. Germs blow into not only the noses of our working poor but also those of the upper echelon. Class struggle and the mantra of racism, sexism, and colonialism are not melodies but cacophonies after the mass murder by the spoiled multimillionaire bin Laden. Can it really be that the man who incinerated Puerto Rican immigrants, working-class Asians, single mothers, gay art dealers, and African-American shopkeepers was himself a polygamist, a pampered brat who grew up in affluence with an occasional bored top-dipping into the eddies of Western "decadence," a fop of sorts who has siblings in the Ivy League, who likes his watches expensive, his cell phones crisp, and his photogenic side prominent in his tacky infomercial videos, replete with Flintstones-like backdrops?

Like the fairy tale of the naked emperor, we in America these past few weeks have seen a few pathetic pianists playing what we are told were the same old melodies, but the pieces have produced no sound. And so we in the audience are at last learning that those onstage were never musicians—and there was never really any music—at all.

Written on November 14 and published in National Review Online *on November 16.*

25.

They're Back!

EIGHT THOUSAND ACCUSED AL-QAEDA TERRORISTS TO GO ON TRIAL TOMORROW—BEST AND BRIGHTEST ORGANIZE DEFENSE

A parody.

ASSOCIATED PRESS
ISLAMABAD, PAKISTAN
MAY 1, 2002

A STELLAR AMERICAN legal team is readying briefs for tomorrow's opening arguments in the trial of eight thousand purported al-Qaeda defendants on charges of conspiracy to commit bodily harm, in association with the World Trade Center and Pentagon bombings of September 11, 2001.

Change of Venue?

AT THE VERY outset, noted criminal defense attorney Gerry Spence—retained by the Saudi Arabian government as an impartial outside observer—sounded a note of caution about any chance of a fair hearing in Islamabad. "We must move these trials outta here yesterday. There's an American air base in Afghanistan now, and we hear hourly the booms of American planes overhead—intimidation, anyone? If we can't get to Baghdad or Mecca, I'll opt for Detroit, and pronto. And we'll move to separate all these trials. After all, there are at least five thousand courtrooms in Michigan alone. And I want a full accounting of the conditions of our clients' confinement. I mean, eight thousand still in makeshift tents and caves? What kind of inhuman prisons are we talking about? And Lunchables instead of traditional rice and lamb? Is that cruel and unusual punishment or what?"

Dream Team II?

NATION OF ISLAM interests have apparently retained Johnnie L. Cochran Jr. to coordinate the defense of those accused from the Sudan and Somalia. "This is a classic rush-to-judgment racial-profiling case, and it stinks to high heaven. The G-men made a decision months ago that the "al-Qaeda 8K" were guilty, and now they can't lose face by admitting there is not a shred of evidence. But if the prints don't stick, you gotta acquit."

Cochran went on, "And where are the North Africans on the juries? I'd like to see some brothers too from Ethiopia and Nigeria. Lord, I've got security people with me right now over here from the D.C. mosques and the New Black Panthers, and they're all ready to serve. No way we're going to get a fair trial without Mohammedans of color. This is the worst transgression of justice since the Holocaust."

Purportedly struggling with legal problems of his own, celebrated defense counsel F. Lee Bailey was nevertheless reported to be close to obtaining a visa, in hopes of flying into Islamabad later this week to direct the Syrian cross-examination of government witnesses.

"I plan to get Rumsfeld on the stand," Bailey announced when reached in Florida by phone. "Oh, yeah, baby, I'll go *mano a mano* big-time with him—one old soldier to another—to see if his planes have been killing my clients without a trial."

Bailey gave some hint of his colorfully combative style: "I want Rummy to look F. Lee Bailey in the eye, man-to-man, and tell the world that we were not attacking anyone without a warrant. Let's see if he has the cojones to go one on one with me—under oath—and spill his guts that he in fact bombed without a single court order. Without a single one!"

Unidentified parties in Lebanon have reportedly retained noted appellate expert Barry Scheck, fresh from his American lecture tour on the sanctity of DNA evidence in capital punishment cases. Scheck acknowledged, however, that in this particular instance, the government's acquisition of DNA evidence from the TT (Twin Towers) was quite unusually and "hopelessly" contaminated. But even more important, Scheck asserted, was the critical, yet unanswered, question of "visual video distortion."

"VVD is an entirely new field. Only a handful of experts from SA (Scheck Associates) know that perhaps as many as four or five per every six billion video transmissions—even more common an occurrence in live-video linkages from caves—are simply inaccurate due to DD (digital disruption). At least four or five—maybe even as high as six—mind you out of a mere six billion! And that's a conservative figure, with an error rate of less than 1 percent. The military GQ hasn't got a clue that its entire video evidence in this trial is VVD unsound. Seismologists of the ASA, geographers from the AAG, and electrical engineers at UL are all prepared to testify under oath that there is a distinct mathematical possibility that Mr. bin Laden's purported videos were garbled in transmission. In fact, due to VVD and some DD blowback, these VCR reproductions may well not represent, at least in their present fragmented state, those words which OBL actually spoke. SA has obtained at least three or four reliable al-Qaeda witnesses who were present during the initial filming, and they all will swear under oath that OBL never made reference to any of the events at TT on 9/11."

The trial phase will be a mere "formality," concluded Harvard legal professor Alan Dershowitz, who is coordinating the expected appeal phases of the proceedings for the Egyptian and Kuwaiti accused. "We'll get all this back into the civilian courts and into America, where it belongs. I think three thousand of the Egyptian defendants will shortly see their charges either dropped or reduced to misdemeanor assault charges. The other eleven hundred under threat of reckless endangerment convictions are even less of a worry—all hearsay and coerced confessions. I doubt whether more than a half-dozen felony conspiracy indictments ever reach a jury. This was simply not a capital punishment case. If the government had been watching my analysis on *Geraldo*, this case would never even have gone to trial."

Cultural Icons to Play Critical Role?

FORMER PRESIDENT CLINTON, reached while delivering an inspirational speech in Malibu, California, at first seemed hesitant about his reported upcoming role in the trials. While legally barred from appearing formally as counsel in some federal courts, the ex-president nevertheless hinted that he has been retained by the Palestinian defendants—and may appear as an expert but "hostile" witness to the military's case.

"I'll be offering more a historical perspective than anything else," Clinton volunteered. "I've been reading a lot lately. You know, I've discovered that you cannot understand the Twin Towers without some knowledge of Sherman's Sentinels. And we simply cannot call the eight thousand accused 'terrorists' without reference to Wounded Knee. Did you know that Crusaders burned civilians in Jerusalem, no less? We Americans use the word 'terrorist' a lot—but much of its real meaning depends on just how you define that suffix '-ist.'"

The popular American telejurist Judge Judy has been asked by prominent Islamic clerics in Cairo to monitor the international jurists' ability to navigate between Western law and the *sharia*. "I'm ready when they are," Judge Judy remarked. "I'm here to translate court to Koran, but I tell ya—if there's going to be a *burqa* then this gal's going berserka."

Cultural critic Edward Said was purportedly leading a stone-throwing demonstration outside the U.S. military detention center. "Where are the trials of U.S. combatants?" Said shouted over the noise. "An American pilot sears a peasant with napalm and he is constructed as a virtual hero—a freedom fighter below replies with a flintlock and he is delegitimized as a terrorist?"

Said added: "This entire case is little more than the distortion that characteristically emanates from the edifice of control, in which the 'Other,' through the fictive discourse of jurisprudence, is fictionalized into a near-subhuman entity to reassure his oppressors that the purported tools of civilization can maintain disequilibrium in the access to power."

ACLU Wish List?

NADINE STROSSEN OF the ACLU hinted at a series of sequential motions for dismissal, and promised extensive fund-raising to help ensure that enough legal representation was on the ground in Islamabad—at least through the expected first five years of in-court appeals. Steven Shapiro, national legal director of the ACLU, issued a terse press release: "This is a travesty of American justice that can only deprive some eight thousand accused of any reasonable chance at a fair trial." An ACLU media guide accompanied Shapiro's strong condemnation:

1. *Documents have been poorly translated.* Arabic is a rich language with a variety of dialects. Yet the U.S. military has assumed—to the possible detriment of thousands of defendants—that patois as rich and diverse as Kuwaiti and Egyptian and Lebanese can be rendered into simple Arabic. And if the formal documents are unreliable, there is even more concern about the quality of the seventy-five hundred in-court translators who are both inexperienced and underpaid. We are in the process right now of discovering that very few of the accused were read their Miranda rights in the proper dialects of their native languages.

2. *An untold number of the defendants may not be eighteen.* No proof exists that they are of legal age to be tried as adults in felony trials. At least two thousand cases must immediately be referred to juvenile courts.

3. *The question of mental soundness has been entirely neglected.* Even the meager preliminary pool of three hundred psychiatrists estimates that four thousand defendants alone may be suffering from bipolar disorder, neurosis, and chronic depression. Bin Laden himself had a documented history of child abuse, parental neglect, and mental suffering. The effect of polygamy on childhood adjustment in mass-murderers is still not fully understood in the West—though a logical criterion for dismissal.

4. *The quality of legal representation remains in serious question.* While the wealthier of the accused have had access to impressive American representation, we suggest that perhaps as many as two thousand in detention will be no more than wards of the court. And despite the presence of the twelve thousand public defenders in Islamabad, few are seasoned enough to handle capital cases of this magnitude.

5. *We believe that even the present forty-five hundred counselors and mental-health workers are hardly sufficient even to begin to deal with the*

confirmed cases of PTSS (Post-Traumatic Stress Syndrome). Thousands of the defendants were under constant bombardment for weeks, and remain in a virtual catatonic state. We shall be filing friends-of-the-court briefs to seek somewhere between thirty-eight hundred and forty-two hundred postponements, of from six to ten years, until proper mental health can be restored.

6. *At least thirty-five hundred of the accused were assigned extra-ordinarily unreasonable bail.* As a result, none have seen their families for weeks and, in some cases, even months. There is no documented history that any of these unfortunates has had any past record of violating conditions of parole. We want them released immediately.

Outcome Uncertain?

AN APPARENTLY SHAKY Robert Shapiro, who has increasingly taken a secondary role in the defense of the Hamas and Hezbollah accused, sounded a rare note of apprehension—just hours before the trial was scheduled to commence. "I'm a little disturbed about some of the occasional anti-Semitism I'm hearing from one or two of my defendants—and all dealt from the bottom of the deck, no less."

However, chief co-prosecutors for the U.S. military legal corps, Marcia Clark and Christopher Darden, reassured Americans about the ultimate verdict. "Oh, no, no, no—we're not worried at all. We are convinced that we can try and win all these cases in Islamabad. I have confidence that the Pakistani man in the street will stand up to the plate and put these eight thousand away for a long, long time to come."

Written on November 15 and published in National Review Online
on November 20.

26.

The Time Is Now

SOME CONSTANTS GUIDE US IN
OUR PRESENT DILEMMA

WHEN WE ARE finally victorious in Afghanistan, should we confront the next nightmarish regime in Iraq—a thugocracy that we know, now and in the past, has fostered terrorism, created frightful weapons of destruction, and murdered its own and thousands of others? Or rather do we seek triumph only in Afghanistan, and then go home to delegate the "global war on terrorism" to the stealthy work of the FBI and CIA?

Does military history advise us that armies on the verge of victory should press their luck and move on to destroy utterly their crippled enemies—or cease with the triumph at hand and consolidate success? In the past, have conquering forces who failed to finish off tottering adversaries thrown away their hard-won achievements by letting wounded beasts escape—only to have them return angrier and stronger? Or is it the rule that overzealous and victory-drunk armies, like the Panzers rolling on to Stalingrad ("no enemies ahead, no supplies behind"), fritter away gains by pressing their luck too far, and so find themselves overextended, outnumbered, without allies, and far from home? The long story of war can provide examples to support either audacity or conservatism, but close examination suggests there are some constants that may guide us in our present dilemma. We can all agree, of course, that overconfident victors, without either a clear moral edge or real military superiority, often are deluded by transitory moments of battlefield triumph and so fall into false notions of invincibility.

Don't Go On?

PERSIA PUT DOWN the Ionian revolt at the battle of Lade, destroyed Miletus (494 B.C.)—and then wrongly surmised that Greeks across the Aegean were as weak as those in Asia Minor. When a cocky Darius went on to invade Marathon, he learned the true mettle of Athenian hoplites and shortly sailed home in defeat—a precursor of the greater Persian catastrophe to come a decade later at Salamis and Plataea. Clearly Persians were neither stronger nor more moral than the mainland Greeks, and paid a frightful price to learn that bitter lesson far from home and without friends.

Similarly, Athens during the murderous Peloponnesian War gathered the wrong messages from the armistice of 421–415 B.C. and foolishly interpreted reprieve as victory, and so pressed on to disaster in Sicily (415–413 B.C.)—losing forty thousand men and most of their fleet, and prompting nearly all of the Greek world, Sicily, and Persia to join Sparta in finishing off Pericles' once grand empire.

Don't Stop Now?

YET HISTORY HAS plenty of examples where timidity, not audacity, has destroyed momentum—and with it any chance of eventual victory. Historians disagree over the counterfactual suppositions of the Second Punic War (218–201 B.C.), but most concede that had Hannibal marched on Rome after the destruction of the legions at Cannae, the Republic may well have met his terms—so Maharbal's stern rebuke to his commander: "You know how to win a battle, Hannibal, but not how to use your victory." More than one hundred thousand legionaries had fallen at the disasters in Trebia, Trasimene, and Cannae—and one final push a few more miles more to Rome might have put the Carthaginians in the forum. Within twenty-four months, however, the relieved and ever resilient Romans ensured that there were more legions than Carthaginian mercenaries—and that the last battle of the war at Zama would take place near Carthage, not in Italy.

After December 7, 1941, had Admiral Nagumo's Japanese fleet steamed for another two weeks off Hawaii, all the while repeatedly bombing Pearl Harbor, destroying critical fuel depots, hunting down the two sole aircraft carriers in the Pacific, and incinerating the port facilities—before moving on to the West Coast to attack San Francisco and Los Angeles—America may have been on the defensive well into 1944. Instead, Admiral Yamamoto awoke a sleeping giant and pulled back east, proving that the only thing worse than attacking an unsuspecting and militarily superior adversary is not destroying it in its lair with the first strike.

Such examples hinge mostly on questions that are purely military and thus more easily explicable: bullies like Persia or imperial Athens often find themselves despised, outnumbered, and not as strong as they thought—even as weaker aggressive states like Carthage or Japan should have finished what they started before their very brief window of opportunity closed for good.

A Different Paradigm

YET, MORE RELEVANT to our present war are instances where democratic armies, with a moral cause and overwhelmingly superior force, faced a reeling foe. Quite simply, the history of aroused militaries of consensual governments makes up a different sort of category altogether—and suggests that we must press on to the bitter end to Iraq and beyond. After Sherman's swath through Georgia, an exuberant Grant asked his subordinate to bring his army by sea to join him in Virginia. Lincoln too was relieved that Sherman had reached Savannah in safety and had no desire to see sixty-five thousand precious Union troops continue to tramp incommunicado through the heart of the Confederacy. But Sherman? He saw Georgia only as "a beginning," realizing that once he had created a marvelous army and a new way of war, and was nearer to, not more distant from, the heart of secession, it made no sense to quit. Had Sherman ceased at Savannah, the war might have dragged on for another year, the Confederacy interpreting his respite on the coast as much needed sanctuary for a tired and exhausted army rather than the lull before the storm to come.

After the sea victory of Lepanto, the victorious combined armadas of Spain and the Italian states awoke on October 8, 1571, to gaze out at a wrecked Ottoman fleet, the Mediterranean entirely empty of enemy ships, and Greece and eastern Europe ready for liberation. Instead, timid Western admirals, thankful for a miraculous victory, and seeing their triumph due to God's will rather than innate strength, rowed home. Within two years, Christian unity was lost for good. The

Republic of Venice, Spain, and the Papal States returned to their intrigue and squabbling. New Ottoman galleys were launched on the seas, and the iron hand of Turkish retaliation ensured a Muslim Balkans for another twenty-five decades. The sultan was not wrong when he sighed in relief that his beard "had only been trimmed, not cut off."

Patton, a firebrand at the head of a huge democratic army of vengeance, shared a fate sometimes more like the captains at Lepanto than the uncontrollable Sherman. At the Falaise Gap in August 1944, he begged his superiors to close the salient and exterminate the tens of thousands of trapped Panzers. A confused Omar Bradley (purportedly preferring a "soft shoulder to a broken neck"), fearful of German pressure, let entire enemy divisions escape the tightening noose— some of those Nazis who would go east, be reequipped on the other side of the Rhine, and reappear at the Battle of the Bulge to help kill thousands of Americans.

Nor was such hesitance only a question of tactical catastrophe. In April 1945, Patton rolled into Eastern Europe, at the head of the largest and most lethal army in American history, bent on liberating Prague and perhaps all of Czechoslovakia from crumbling German armies. Instead, he was ordered to halt. Prague fell to the Russians, and a half-century of communist misery followed. As Patton put it: a war that had begun to free Eastern Europe from totalitarianism had ended with totalitarianism amid the ruins that Hitler evacuated.

Such decisions to press on are never easy. An unrestrained Patton might have caused "incidents" with the Russians, incurred "unneeded" dead from fanatical German resistance, and "offended" diplomats who had sketched out zones of occupation. Yet the ultimate verdict of his cessation was unmistakable: a militarily superior force in an effort to save millions from fascism had allowed millions to fall to communism—in the process sending a message to the Russians that we were accommodating and reasonable rather than idealistic, unpredictable, and overwhelmingly powerful.

Lessons of the Gulf War

OVER THREE YEARS ago, in *The Soul of Battle*, I wrote of the American decision not to end the reign of terror of Saddam Hussein in January 1991 that "the cessation of the American advance in the Gulf War and the negotiated armistice that followed were the greatest American military blunders since Vietnam." Nothing that has transpired in the nearly four years since has altered my views. We had the clear momentum and a preponderance of force. We enjoyed moral purpose, and we possessed commanders and soldiers on the ground who had the desire and ability to storm Baghdad. Yet fearful of postbellum power vacuums, jittery allies, regional instability, further costs in treasure and lives—of every fear other than absolute victory—we, like republican Venice, let a bleeding enemy limp away to nurse its wounds and grudges, and a fraudulent government to return to Kuwait. And so we are still paying dearly for our ignorance of history.

That reluctance to topple a dictator was seen by Iraq not as magnanimity but as timidity. Allies of the region professed relief in public at our sobriety, gnashing their teeth in private at our naïveté. We were told in the short run that we were saving lives and money, but not advised in the long duration that far greater costs of both must be paid. Professing worry not about oil, but rather about morality, our forbearance caused far more Shiite and Kurdish blood to be spilled than what was saved in Kuwait. Pictures of the "Highway of Death" where Iraqi killers were killed shocked a nation—even as scenes of far more numerous butchered and starving innocent civilians in the weeks that followed went largely unnoticed. Such are the sad and immoral wages of leniency when what is moral and doable is left undone.

The Intersection of History

IN THE MONTHS ahead, the same questions that obsessed Hannibal, Don Juan, Sherman, Patton, and Schwartzkopf and their superiors shall haunt us once more. At first glance, the voices of moderation will argue for caution. Indeed, we can anticipate their judicious reasoning in advance: the Europeans will turn on us, the Muslim world may explode, nuclear and biological terror may be unleashed, the world's oil may light up, our campuses may seethe, a glib press may snarl and third-guess, our treasury will go broke, our youth may be killed, and our forces surely will be overstretched.

Yes, we know them all and they all must be ignored. Mr. Powell, a decent and experienced man—who wrongly cautioned restraint after the Marine disaster in Lebanon; advised more negotiations with Serbia; tragically urged cessation, rather than an advance to Baghdad; and most recently suggested a governing coalition to include ex-Taliban mullahs and a pan-Islamic force of occupation—will be eloquent about what we cannot and must not do. But if history is any guide to the present, we should remember that we are unusually strong and clearly in the right; that our enemies in Iraq are evil, in the wrong and inherently weak—and that victory, if we press on, will be seen as a catalyst of good, our tentativeness dubbed weakness and worse.

If we wish to end terror, in the coming months we should turn to Iraq. If we turn to Iraq, we should be resigned to go it alone. If we attack alone, we should seek absolute victory; if we obtain victory, we should institute a constitutional government; if we promote legitimacy, we will see a gradual end to terror. Great forces of change are now on the move that may well reinvent the world as we have known it. We did not ask for such a revolution, but we are now the riders of this apocalypse—and have so discovered that we can be agents for, not obstacles to, this renaissance of freedom in the making that could turn millions of enemies into friends, both in and outside of the Muslim world. We must see this perilous mission through to its ultimate end—if for no other reason than to ensure that those in the World Trade Center and Pentagon did not die in vain.

The removal of fascism in Afghanistan and Iraq, with the implementation of legitimate governments in its wake—a far easier task than the metamorphosis of Russia and Eastern Europe—will require sacrifice coupled with military skill and brilliant diplomacy. And so Mr. Powell, ironically of all Americans, now has the best opportunity to ignore the tired voices of orthodoxy and consensus, and instead in a quite new role to use his abilities at war and peace to engineer a revolutionary course—one that will place him and his country in the vortex of history. Overwhelming military victories in both Afghanistan and Iraq—as was true of Germany and Japan in 1946—could turn havens of terror into allies, where millions in the streets of Kabul and Baghdad will see us more as honest brokers of democratic reform rather than cynical purveyors of self-interest. If they wish then to elect themselves into the slavery of Islamic republics, so be it—but at least we can say that we fought for legitimacy—and they, not us, ruined their countries. And after the sorry record of Iran and the Taliban, it is just as likely that they will not be willing to vote those nightmares upon themselves.

A freed and democratic Iraq will help clean out the rotting tentacles of terrorism that thrash about still, but also fire an even more ominous and unexpected shot across the bow to our corrupt and illegitimate "friends" in the Gulf, Egypt, and the Middle East—who, we are learning, were never really our friends at all. In an otherwise brilliant campaign in 1990–1991, we made two tragic mistakes—stopping before Baghdad and allowing a medieval and repressive Kuwaiti government to return to power. At the eleventh hour, we now can still do much to correct both by ending fascism, promoting democracy, and proving to the world that we are as highly principled as we are downright scary.

Written on November 19 and published in National Review Online
on November 22.

27.

A Voice from the Past

GENERAL THUCYDIDES SPEAKS ABOUT THE WAR

LAST NIGHT I had the pleasure of consulting with an obscure ex-general. Now retired (under somewhat dubious circumstances), he is currently hard at work on his first book—a rambling and rather academic account of a long-forgotten war. Although Lt. Gen. Thucydides is in poor health, near seventy, and desperate to finish his work, he agreed to take some time out to talk for a few minutes about his views on the current conflict. His tone was formal, almost grim—yet also philosophical.

Question: Why is it those crowds in the Muslim world rush the streets to promise us death, and yet now the same firebrands have suddenly retreated into the shadows on the news of our power and mercy?

Thucydides: Hope and greed, the one leading and the other following, the one conceiving the attempt, the other suggesting the facility of succeeding, cause the widest ruin. [3.45]. Their judgment was based more upon blind wishing than upon any sound prevision. For it is a habit of mankind to entrust to careless hope what they long for, and to use arbitrary reason to thrust aside what they do not fancy. [4.108]

Question: So, we shouldn't take all that shouting too seriously? Is that what you're saying—that it is based on false dreams and empty hope, not real power?

Thucydides: Hope is danger's comforter and it may be indulged by those who have abundant resources—if not without loss, at all events without ruin. But its nature is to be extravagant: those who go so far as to put their all upon the venture see it in its true colors only when they are ruined. [5.103]

Question: And do you think that human unpredictability, which you describe, also explains the fickleness here at home, when critics, Left and Right, damned our initial bombing efforts—and yet now are eager to praise our sudden victories?

Thucydides: One must support the national resolve even in the case of reverse, or forfeit all credit for their wisdom in the event of success. For sometimes the course of things is as arbitrary as the plans of men; this is why we usually blame chance for whatever does not happen as we expected. [1.140]

Question: Okay, but many say that we Americans are now too eager to go to war. Don't pacifists have a point that we are the moral equivalent of our enemies when we retaliate with force?

Thucydides: For those, of course, who have a free choice in the matter and whose fortunes are not at stake, war is the greatest of follies. But if the only choice is between submission with loss of independence, and danger with the hope of preserving that independence—in such a case it is he who will not accept the risk that deserves the blame, not he who will. [2.62]

Question: So we are going to be in a real war?

Thucydides: It must be thoroughly understood that war is a necessity, and that the more readily we accept it, the less will be the ardor of our opponents. [1.144]

Question: But, General, you must concede that after Vietnam and now the disaster in New York, there is a growing fear that we might not prevail, but instead provoke even greater terror. The Taliban sounded pretty dangerous, after all, and there's still Iraq and all the rest.

Thucydides: One must confront enemies not merely with spirit but with disdain. Confidence—indeed a blissful ignorance—can reside even in a coward's breast, but disdain is the privilege of those who, like us, have been assured by reflection of their superiority to their adversary. Where the chances of war are the same, knowledge fortifies courage by the contempt that is its consequence. Its trust is placed not in hope, which is the prop of the desperate, but in judgment grounded upon existing resources, whose anticipations are more to be depended upon. [2.63]

Question: I guess what you're saying, General, is that Americans should remember that B-52s and the Rangers have a better track record than the Taliban? On another matter—why do you think that bin Laden and his terrorists were so ignorant of American society, at least in the sense that they believed they could repeatedly get away with killing Americans, win prestige, and gain concessions—without eventually incurring the destructive wrath of the United States?

Thucydides: Their own prosperity could not dissuade them from affronting danger; but blindly confident in the future, and full of hopes beyond their power though not beyond their ambition, they declared war and made their decision to prefer might to right. Their attacks were determined not by provocation but by the moment which seemed propitious. [3.39]

Question: The hijackers were relatively educated and affluent, as was bin Laden himself. So their desire for power doesn't seem to arise out of economic exploitation, colonialism, or real need, does it?

Thucydides: Fear was the principal motive, though honor and self-interest afterwards came in. [1.75]

Question: So bin Laden and his associates were nothing new, but old-fashioned bullies who mocked our restraint? Let me ask you for a minute to just imagine—in a moment of candor— what the terrorists and the Taliban would have said of us before September 11.

Thucydides: "You are alone inactive, and defend yourselves not by doing anything but by looking as if you would do something; you alone wait till the power of an enemy is becoming twice its original size, instead of crushing it in its infancy." [1.69]

Question: Are you saying that they hit us because they got away with it in the past and had hopes for further success?

Thucydides: Fortune helps delusion, and by the unexpected aid that she sometimes lends, tempts men to venture with inferior means. [3.45]

Question: General—come now, do you really believe that we invited attack through the appearance of timidity, and only strong countermeasures will end the threat?

Thucydides: Human nature is surely made arrogant by consideration, as it is awed by firmness. Let them now be punished as their crime requires. [3.39]

Question: No other way out of this mess, then?

Thucydides: If anyone sees a safe course, it is high time for him to change his mind. The side that is once attacked, whose own country is in danger, can scarcely discuss what is prudent with the same calmness of men who are in full enjoyment of what they have got, and are thinking of attacking an adversary in order to get more. [4.92]

Question: So do we go on to Iraq as well?

Thucydides: Those who are tempted by pride of strength to attack their neighbors usually march confidently against those who keep still and only defend themselves in their own country. But they think twice before they grapple with those who meet them outside the frontier and strike the first blow if opportunity offers. [4.92]

Question: That's pretty clear-cut. Let's turn again to matters here at home. I was struck especially by the bravery of the doomed passengers who rushed the hijackers, and also the firemen who went into the flaming buildings to rescue the trapped. Was their heroism all that remarkable? And if it was, why so?

Thucydides: None of these allowed either wealth with its prospect of future enjoyment to unnerve his spirit, or poverty with its hope of a day of freedom and riches to tempt him to shrink to danger. No, holding that vengeance upon their enemies was more to be desired than personal blessings, and reckoning this to be the most glorious of hazards, they joyfully determined to take the risk. [2.42]

Question: Go on, I'm enjoying your rather quaint idealism.

Thucydides: Well, choosing to die resisting rather than to live submitting, they fled only from dishonor, but met danger face to face and after one brief moment, while at the summit of their fortune, escaped not from their fear, but from their glory. [2.42]

Question: I guess you think their courage was somewhat different from the much ballyhooed determination of their suicidal killers, who piloted the jets into the towers?

Thucydides: It is not the miserable that would most justly be unsparing of their lives; these have nothing to hope for: it is rather they to whom continued life may bring reverses as yet unknown, and to whom a fall, if it came, would be most tremendous in its consequences. And surely, to a man of spirit, the degradation of cowardice must be immeasurably more grievous than the unfelt death that strikes him in the midst of his strength and patriotism! [2.43]

Question: Fiery words, General—I'd hope you would have tenure before saying that on a campus these days. Let's raise the issue of domestic terrorism for a minute. I've heard that some Americans are resolved to live for the day—given the uncertainty of the present, the sudden deaths of thousands, and promises of more deaths to come. And the anthrax scare certainly has panicked millions, especially in the first days of the news of the disease. Any remarks about what actually went on during that initial fright?

Thucydides: Men coolly ventured on what they had formerly done in a corner and not just as they pleased, seeing the rapid transitions produced by persons in prosperity suddenly dying. So they resolved to spend quickly and enjoy themselves, regarding their lives and riches as alike things of a day. [2.53]

Question: So that sort of panic is understandable?

Thucydides: Before what is sudden, unexpected, and least within calculation the spirit quails. And putting all else aside, the disease has certainly been an emergency of this kind. But born as you are, citizens of a great state, and brought up, as you have been, with habits equal to your birth, you should be ready to face the greatest disasters and still to keep unimpaired the luster of your name. [2.61]

Question: I hope so, at least. Let's go on to some brighter news. So far our leaders have been beacons of democratic resolve—particularly Mr. Rumsfeld. Looking back, can you shed any light on the secretary's formula for success with the press, or for that matter with the American people in general?

Thucydides: By his rank, ability, and known integrity, he was enabled to exercise an independent control over the multitude of them—in short, to lead them instead of being led by them. Since he never sought power by improper means, he was never compelled to flatter them, but, on the contrary, enjoyed so high a reputation that he could afford to anger them by contradiction. When he saw them unseasonably and insolently elated, he would with a word reduce them to alarm. On the other hand, if they fell victims to a panic, he could at once restore them to confidence. [2.65]

Question: High praise, indeed. Well, going beyond Mr. Rumsfeld, do you think in this age of cultural relativism, that gives us advantages over the enemy? Surely our institutions are different from those of our adversaries? What is it exactly that makes us strong?

Thucydides: We cultivate refinement without extravagance and knowledge without effeminacy. Wealth we employ more for use than show, and place the real disgrace of poverty not in owning to the fact but in declining to struggle against it. Our public men have, besides politics, their private affairs to attend to, and our ordinary citizens, though occupied with the pursuits of industry, are still fair judges of public matters. Unlike any other nation, we regard him who takes no part in these duties not as unambitious but as useless. And so we are able to judge if we cannot originate, and instead of looking on discussion as a stumbling block in the way of action, we think it an indispensable preliminary to any wise action at all. [2.40]

Question: I'm sure the U.S. Senate would agree. One last time, let's return again to the war. Afghanistan in general, the last three decades, seems an especially dangerous place, where almost anyone at any time will kill at will. And why have these tribes invited in so many terrorists?

Thucydides: In peace, there would have been neither the pretext nor the wish for such an invitation. But in war with an alliance always at the command of either faction for the hurt of their adversaries and their own corresponding advantage, opportunities for bringing in foreigners are never wanting. [3.82]

Question: You seem to be suggesting that we can expect further random killings over there? We've heard awful stories of torture, executions, and mutilations. Are there more to come?

Thucydides: In peace and prosperity states and individuals have better sentiments, because they do not find themselves suddenly confronted with imperious necessities; but war takes away the easy supply of daily wants, and so proves a rough master that brings most men's characters to a level with their fortunes. [3.82]

Questions: If you're right, won't it be hard to bring back law and order over there? I mean, it looks like continual cycle of tribal tit-for-tat.

Thucydides: Men too often take upon themselves in the prosecution of their revenge to set the example of doing away with those general laws to which all alike can look for salvation in adversity, instead of allowing them to subsist against the day of danger when their aid may be required. [3.84]

Question: Any chance of surrenders or private deals?

Thucydides: From a mob like that you need not look for either unanimity in counsel or concert in action. But they will probably one by one come in as they get a fair offer, especially if they are torn by civil strife. [6.17]

Question: And should we be pretty tough with those who hold out, even those who weren't directly connected to 9/11?

Thucydides: Make up your minds to give them like for like; and do not let the victims who escaped the plot feel less our injury than the conspirators who hatched it. But reflect what they would have done if victorious over you, especially as they were the aggressors. It is they who wrong their neighbor without out a cause, that pursue their victim to the death, on account of the danger which they foresee in letting their enemy survive. [3.40]

Question: Thank you for your candid, if occasionally brutal, assessments. I know it's getting late, but one last, rather personal question—do you really think any of your ideas will ever have relevance beyond that rather esoteric war between Athens and Sparta? I mean, aren't you worried that today's Americans will find all this far too dry? After all, you're competing in a relatively small market, with the likes of Danielle Steele.

Thucydides: The absence of romance in my history will, I fear, detract somewhat from its interest, but . . .

Question: Gotcha. Sorry, I interrupted you—please finish. . . .

Thucydides: But . . . if it is judged useful by those inquirers who desire an exact knowledge of the past as an aid to the interpretation of the future, which in the course of human things must resemble if it does not reflect it, I'll be content. In short, I have written my work, not as any essay which is to win the applause of the moment, but as a possession for all time. [1.22]

Thank you, General, and good night.

Written on November 23 and published in National Review Online on November 27.

28.

The More Things Change

THE WISDOM OF THE AGES

THERE ARE TWO types of military analysts—those who believe that the essence of war is unchanging, and others who insist that its very nature is constantly and forever altered by rapidly transforming technologies, mentalities, and physical realities. The former are mostly historians. They see the nature of man as fixed, and so identify real change only in the pump—the delivery system—not the water, or essence, of war. The latter are social scientists, technologists, and sometimes military men themselves, who believe new hydraulics pour forth an entirely novel liquid.

Social scientists have warned us that we are up against an entirely new enemy. His lethal brand of Islamic fundamentalism, parasitic use of Western technology, and propensity for mass murder borne on the wings of suicide are purportedly like nothing we have yet encountered. But traditionalists counter that terrorists—whether the *sicarii* in Roman Palestine, or nineteenth-century central European assassins—are hardly novel. Remedies for their defeat are time-tried and effective, since brutal force, coupled with hope for repentance and renewal, eventually extinguish the threat entirely.

Scenes of fanatics in the streets of Pakistan have startled and frightened some Americans. To my mind, far scarier are the half-educated here at home who analyze this "new" challenge on television, sternly lecturing us about Western ignorance and a decade of unstoppable massacre and killing ahead. But history teaches us that the most thunderous Islamic crowds—as is always the way of the mob—are nourished on false hopes, and scatter with real defeat. Such frenzied haters listen not to calls for more talk and understanding, but only to more B-52s and parachuted food. Mr. Musharraf scattered the Pakistani street not with the logic of reason or international cooperation, but with the warning that his government, his people, and his very nation might well have to face an America angry over their prior support of terrorists. In 1941, evil Nazis who slaughtered innocent Greeks in barbaric reprisals could only abate, but not stop, Communist commandos. Later, idealistic Americans who promised food for the innocent and guns against the guilty ended such insurgency.

Professors of Middle Eastern studies warn that radical reinterpretations of the Koran, aided by global technologies, will make these novel groups unstoppable, so powerful is their new brew of anti Americanism. In contrast, history sighs and advises to look at what they do rather than say. The past reminds us that most in Pakistan would prefer a nap and coffee after an afternoon's shouting on global television, to weeks of misery in Afghanistan's frontline bunkers amid the stink of shredded flesh—in a bankrupt cause, no less, to outlaw cameras, books, and videos.

It is an iron law of war that overwhelming military superiority, coupled with promises to the defeated of resurrection, defeats terrorists—in the past, now, always—whether they be zealots, dervishes, or Ghost dancers. We do not really care whether bin Laden and his thugs are real Islamic fundamentalists, old-time Mahdists, or Christian nuts in drag. Nor does it ultimately matter much whether they plan to poison water, hijack airplanes, spread germs, or throw spitballs at us—only whether we have the military power and will to kill them first, destroy their enclaves, strip away their money and refuges, and demonstrate to their followers that death and misery are the final and only wages of a terrorist's life.

If, like the Romans, we can inflict death on the violent and ensure peace and security to the repentant, then the Muslim world's lust for bin Laden will pass—as it has in the past with other such thugs and madmen. For all the much publicized talk of a new wave of fanatical suicide killers, most of the Taliban in Afghanistan—as in the case of most Christians—would duck out on a prayer service if a daisy-cutter was on its way down, and if hungry, skip the holy man's harangue for the chance of a square meal. That may explain why those who hate us in the streets of the Muslim world have been less, not more, bold since we began the bombing.

We were initially told that bombing would win this war, and then that it would not, and then that it almost has—punditry being proved wrong or right or again wrong, as it sorts out the latest hour's news from the front, never apologizing for the prior misappraisals, always ready to promulgate more. Historians, in contrast to social scientists and journalists, would instead seek constants across time and space, and so put our air campaign in the context of the ages.

Air attack—whether arrows, Greek fire, catapult bolts, or grape-shot—has always been a valuable ancillary to, but not a replacement for, ground troops. The Greeks defeated the Persians because eastern missiles could neither penetrate their armor nor distinguish friend from foe in the melee—even as enemy bowmen were helpless when hoplites charged ahead. Bombing in its original incarnation promised to win wars outright. It did not, but within three decades helped to smash the Germans and Japanese (despite the denials of the flawed postwar Strategic Bombing Survey). In Vietnam, our jets by themselves could not ensure victory; in Serbia they did—and in the Gulf and Afghanistan, almost. Why so?

There are precepts of the ages that determine whether aerial assault will be vital to victory, and these unchanging determinants hinge entirely on the attacker's degree of lethality, accuracy, and safety. Catapults were occasionally precise, but rarely deadly to the mass of infantry, always vulnerable to counterattack, and so seldom appeared on the battlefield outside of sieges—unlike rifled artillery, which was both exact and fatal, although equally vulnerable to counterassault. B-17s could be lethal, but they were not always accurate and often per-ilous to fly over Germany—and so were valuable, but not in them-selves deciding factors in our victory.

In Afghanistan, however, the American air force of the present age has for the moment quite miraculously met the age-old triad of suc-cess: our pilots, protected with an array of electric countermeasures and by the destruction of enemy planes, are relatively safe; their bombs, whether of one thousand or fifteen thousand pounds, are alike lethal; and their laser- and satellite-guided ordnance strike with real precision, ensuring that the evil are killed and the innocent mostly spared—again and again. And so they save us from the moral quandary of a Dresden, and the fiasco of a Schweinfurt alike. Will this edge always be the case?

Hardly. As we speak, tacticians seek to improve antiaircraft missiles, to craft new sorts of defensible bunkers, and to jam and confuse smart projectiles—hoping once more to ensure that the pilot is vulnerable, ineffective, and amoral. Our military knows all this, and so strives in turn to both make our planes ever more deadly and craft countermeasures to destroy aircraft more practicable.

Weapons change. Tactics are altered. But the prerequisites of war from the air—lethality, accuracy, and safety—remain the same. To the degree they are met, planes will either be superfluous, handy, or indispensable in our wars to come. The Taliban are ignorant of both war's laws and history—and so apparently thought this conflict was circa 1985, rather than a rare moment of aerial renaissance of the new century.

What are we to make of the thousands who are surrendering in Afghanistan? Kill them, capture them, or let them go? Call in the U.N.? The Northern Alliance's Islamic courts? American wardens? Johnnie Cochran? The wigged from England? Once more we are told that we are caught up in an entirely new dilemma—a new terrorist enemy who has no country to represent him, no home to return to, no oath to take, no apology to give, and no identity to proffer.

All defeated combatants—and the al-Qaeda terrorists are at least that—face the same age-old tripartite range of fates: death, incarceration, or conditional freedom. And such choices themselves always remain contingent on the circumstances of their surrender—the key ingredient for successful conclusions of wars being humiliation coupled with mercy; a true end to hostilities is impossible without both. World War I led to World War II because the German army was defeated, but not disgraced—and so it limped back across the Rhine, convinced that it had been defeated abroad, not at home, through a stab in the back rather than a bullet in the brow.

Yet nearly three decades later, Nazis and Japanese soldiers faced different fortunes: Neither could believe that they had fought to a near draw—when their armies were ruined, the homeland ransacked, and their spirits crushed. That surrender gave us peace, not round two. It was not necessary to kill surrendering soldiers of the Wehrmacht—many of whom would be working with the American army in the postbellum cleanup—just to ensure that they realized that they were bankrupt and utterly defeated, and their cause discredited. So too with the Afghanis of the Taliban.

Saddam Hussein thought he had survived the world's armada, and so defined the Gulf War as success, not defeat. The unbiased touchstone of success—Baghdad not stormed, Hussein's head not in a noose, and the Imperial Guard not liquidated—suggested that he, not we, knew better. And so, like Churchill in 1939, we now face the same enemy in the same place because of naïveté and the misplaced humanity of the past.

A defeated army—now and always—must not merely surrender. Rather it and its infrastructure must be dismantled and its ideology disgraced. Lee gave in not when he was merely beaten—Gettysburg had done that months earlier—but only when his army was decimated, his cause lost, and his adherents embarrassed. Grant and Sherman accepted no less—and so gave us peace, not decades of terror and counterinsurgency. The firebrand Nathan Bedford Forest once promised unending resistance, but after what he'd seen in Tennessee and Georgia, thought it better to quit and go on home.

The terrorists of al-Qaeda who give up and throw down their weapons must be embarrassed and dishonored as they are sorted to meet either hangmen, wardens, or rehabilitation. If caught alive, Mullah Omar and his Keystone Clerics, along with thuggish mercenaries from the Arab world, should ideally be shaved, paraded in stripes, and muzzled as they await destiny. Those found to be killers and accessories to murder must be dispatched; others who are veterans of the organization must be jailed for years, while the newly recruited ignorant, young, and misled so far without blood on their hands must be debriefed, photographed, fingerprinted, and cataloged before being sent home to their just desserts—their identities, the names of their families, their very homes recorded among the world's criminal archives, and available even for the novice on the Internet or at the local library. For the captured new recruits, it must become a shameful and foolish thing to have served with bin Laden. Anything less and we shall be back in Afghanistan and elsewhere in less than a decade.

We must not forget the wisdom of the ages in the noise and clutter of the present. In general, Plato, Sun-Tzu, and Shakespeare, who know the unchanging nature of man, are more valuable guides in our present war than the *New York Times* or the talking heads on MSNBC. So far we should be thankful that our military leadership is guided more by Thucydides than by Marx, Freud, or Foucault, and so believes that the more things change in war, the more the fundamentals remain the same.

Written on November 28 and published in National Review Online
on November 30.

IV.

December

(Mass surrender and capture of Taliban and al-Qaeda; last remnants flee to Tora Bora; Americans bomb bin Laden's hiding places in the mountain caves; creation of new government of national unity in Afghanistan; controversy over captured American al-Qaeda terrorist; more American troops pour into Tora Bora area; Europeans promise peacekeepers in Kabul; Americans discuss next theater of operations)

WITH THE PROGRESSION of American victories, a new picture of Afghanistan was now emerging quite contrary to the one presented by either the American media or our own cultural establishment. There was not mass starvation. Victory celebrations suggested a liberated rather than a captured populace. Collateral damage had not, as suggested in the Islamic press, killed thousands of innocents, but achieved a level of precision not seen in the history of aerial bombardment. The Middle East did not explode, but rather the specter of American resolve began to prompt governments to join in the effort to root out their own homegrown terrorists. Violence in the West Bank reached new highs as suicide bombers killed dozens in

Israel, who in return targeted both the elite of the terrorist organizations and also the infrastructure of Mr. Arafat's government.

Out of the conundrum of the war I argued three clear truths had emerged. The Middle East had suffered a serious blow to its global prestige, mostly through the universal recognition that its tacit complicity with the terrorists from the Gulf to Egypt now threatened all nations of the world. Moreover, supposedly moderate regimes were in fact more culpable for the creation of al-Qaeda than were more radical states like Syria, Libya, and Yemen.

Second, the American military had achieved a level of military lethality not seen in the last half century, and could now wage a new deadly type of war thousands of miles from home, at enormous injury to its enemies, and without major losses to its own combatants.

Finally, the waves of September 11 by December had further drowned out the constant criticism by the American far left and its supporters in Europe. For weeks America had been castigated as imperialist, warmongering, and murderous, but the facts of the war suggested that it had no real interest in Afghanistan other than finding mass murderers and preventing future terrorists enclaves. It provided humanitarian assistance even as it bombed killers, and the only large groups to die in the war so far were not Northern Alliance fighters, Afghani civilians, or American servicemen, but rather al-Qaeda terrorists and Taliban soldiers. The war was also reminding millions worldwide of a long-forgotten lesson about human nature—that zealotry and fanaticism, for all their shrillness and terror, fade before real military power when coupled with justice. Some Americans, at any rate, seemed stunned that vocal fundamentalists who had weeks earlier promised a century of mayhem were now nowhere to be found or in caves high in the mountains.

29

Questions Not Asked

ISSUES NOT RAISED

ONE OF THE more frustrating experiences of the ongoing war is the dearth of intelligent, in-depth questioning on the part of our media—especially television reporters, news anchors, and hired on-camera experts. Do our news people know anything of culture, history, or literature? Are they all trained in "Mass Communications"; did they without exception major in "Radio/TV"?

Or does their obtuseness reflect a desire to be politically correct, culturally relative, or overly polite? The failure to ask intelligent questions surely cannot be due to us, the American audience, because we appreciate bluntness, intellectual honesty, even eccentricity across the spectrum—from the refined Mr. Rumsfeld to the scrappy Bill O'Reilly. Why, then, do our television reporters accept what they are told and rarely think for themselves?

We are informed that millions in the Muslim world watch the programming of al-Jazeera, "the Arab world's CNN." Reports show clips of its ultramodern newsroom. Their telejournalists are interviewed and without cross-examination proclaim their affinity with the values of free exchange and real, Western-style reporting. Western professors brag of its "cutting-edge" talk shows, like *The Opposite Direction*. American networks gladly announce reciprocal news arrangements. And so when it comes to the real nature of al-Jazeera, the American people are told everything that is irrelevant—and nothing that is either important or true.

Is al-Jazeera really a news organization at all—or instead an ideological and largely government- (if not self-) censored infomercial of Muslim propaganda? Just because the sheiks of Qatar allow it to broadcast without a censor, with a Kalashnikov in the stationhouse, does not mean it is in any way free.

Terrorist attacks on Israelis are not covered by Arab reporters on-site in Haifa, in the manner of an NBC journalist sticking a microphone into the face of a Serbian or Afghani civilian hit by an American bomb. Does Mr. Mubarak face the equivalent of a celebrity like Mike Wallace, Tim Russert, or Bob Schieffer, all eager to catch him in a lie? Do secular novelists debate mullahs and castigate fundamentalism in front of millions?

High-tech, imported broadcasting technology does not make television—any more than a man with a tie who reads the news is the equivalent of Peter Jennings or Ted Koppel, whose stock-in-trade is to root out government, corporate, or religious laxity, hypocrisy, and perfidy, and thereby gain both themselves and their stations fame, respect—and market share. Talking heads on al-Jazeera who henpeck among themselves about their own degrees of anti-Americanism do not represent real diversity of opinion. Cannot our reporters simply ask al-Jazeera a few basic questions: Do Muslim clerics ever mix it up with rowdy secular intellectuals, resulting perhaps in the type of abuse rightfully heaped on Jerry Falwell and Pat Robertson? Do feminists engage imams over the air? Do reformists critique the sheiks of the Gulf, and make the case before millions that it is high time for real democracy from Kuwait to Qatar? Do Copts, Christians, Kurds, and Shiites, in the manner of American minorities, issue on-the-air critiques, grievances, and demands to the majority culture? Do al-Jazeera's reporters on the ground broadcast images of those cheering in Kabul, the annihilation of the Taliban, or clipped beards and piles of discarded *burqas*? Our public interrogators must press home the point further still—asking whether there is real habeas corpus on the West Bank; if "parliaments" in Iran, Kuwait, or Palestine really vote as they do in Europe or Israel to disband their governments; and if there are Christian preachers at work in the heart of the Muslim world as there are imams in Europe or America.

If not, why not?

We Americans give billions collectively to Egypt, Jordan, and Palestine as well as to Israel—but if we are to be in the subsidy business, it is one thing to banter with a free and constitutional allied dependent, and quite another to pay for ankle-biting from illegitimate autocracies who are at best neutral, and sometimes downright hostile. I do not mind an occasional lecture from a freely elected Mr. Sharon—but $100 million a year to help subsidize crowds in Nablus who cheer on the news that thousands of Americans were incinerated by murderers from the Middle East?

So cannot one honest American reporter ask, "We know of Mr. Sharon, Mr. Netanyahu, and Mr. Barouk—but who are the corresponding rivals in Palestine for Mr. Arafat's job?" Both states are, after all, at war; yet one elects, the other does not—and not one American reporter asks *why* this is so. We, the American people, need to be told why our critics should be listened to, when none of them are the products of a free society—not a novelist, not a journalist, not an ambassador.

Cannot reporters on the scene, such as Ms. Amanpour or Ms. Banfield, put the military campaign in Afghanistan—just one time, just for a second or two—in some sort of historical context? Our informants so often instead use the phrase "some believe." Then the inevitable follows (fill in the blanks): "*Some* believe that civil war will arise immediately following the Taliban surrender"; "*Some* believe that American bombing has continued to hit civilians"; or "*Some* believe that American casualties inevitably will begin now to mount." But we need to know exactly who are these mysterious and never identified "some"—for we suspect the "*some*" are none other than the glum reporters themselves.

In fact, the real truth of this war constitutes unbelievable news—inasmuch as the present campaign so far stands as one of the most amazing and lopsided victories in the annals of battle—in sheer operational terms reminiscent of the victorious Ten Thousand suffering a single casualty at Cunaxa, Alexander the Great a few thousand while destroying the Achaemenid Empire, or Cortés fewer than one thousand at the fall of Tenochtitlán. The facts of the Afghani War, both militarily and in its long-term historical significance, are quite stunning—comparable to anything found in either Creasy's or Fuller's classic compendia of great battles. As I understand the conflict, it could be summarized something like the following.

A surprised and unprepared United States, after a vicious and deadly attack on its shores, took on an enemy some six thousand miles away with only a brief three-week period of logistical and tactical preparations—in the face of powerful opposition from the Muslim world, real skepticism on the part of our European allies, and a strong vocal minority at home. America initially had *no* reliable allies in the region, *no* port of embarkation, and *no* free air space.

The enemy knew the countryside; controlled all the main cities; was ensconced among civilians; and mounted an effective propaganda campaign dubbing us invaders, Crusaders, Westerners, infidels, and worse. Veterans of warring with such people, from the Russians to the English, warned us of our peril to come in snowdrifts, caves, and street-to-street shooting. A cacophony of domestic voices daily chirped that we were fighting neither an identifiable enemy nor a hostile state per se—and so had no way of knowing when the war was, in fact, to be over.

Our indigenous allies on the ground in Afghanistan were fractious, poorly supplied, and—after years of fighting—in control of less than 10 percent of the country. The geography was rugged and mountainous, the weather uncertain, and the urban population initially hostile—and we were forced to fight during the holy month of Ramadan, with the promise that our attack would result in more Americans killed by terrorists on our own shores, a Muslim world in open war against us, and our enemies made into popular folk heroes for decades to come. Anyone who peruses an old stack of *Time* or *Newsweek* issues will come across little but pessimism from the purportedly grim months of September and October—the constant theme being how the odds all favored our enemies, with stalemate at best the likely outcome well into next spring.

The result? In less than two months the United States of America devastated its enemies, destroying them on the battlefield, in their homes, and in transit. Its allies have grown, not shrunk—and now control nearly the entire country. Civilians were joyous, not angry, at being freed from the Taliban. Worldwide hostile demonstrations evaporated on television, and did not flood the airwaves; neutral ambassadors queued up to visit the White House, rather than railing at the U.N. Millions did not starve, as warned, but are being fed and clothed right in the very midst of a deadly war.

Every bit as astounding as the dazzling success of the military campaign was the cost—so far very few civilians killed, fewer than a dozen Americans lost to accident and hostile action, and the military far stronger after, than before, the bloodletting. Critics who forecasted or even welcomed American defeat were left speechless, and their reputations as both pundits and seers completely ruined.

Surely all this is a story of the ages—How did the victory transpire? and Why? and By Whom? Is it not at least more important than tales broadcast to us about the lonely lion at the Afghan zoo, stray shrapnel in the posterior of an American journalist, and interviews with other reporters about properly stylish winter attire?

Written on December 2 and published in National Review Online *on December 4.*

30.

Dates in Infamy

DECEMBER 7 AND SEPTEMBER 11

IT IS ALREADY conventional wisdom to see the attacks on September 11, 2001, as something new in our nation's history. After all, our present enemy has no planes or tanks of its own. Indeed, no state claims al-Qaeda as its own military arm. Our adversaries wore no uniforms—at least as the terrorists went up the ramps of our planes and before they put on their macabre death headbands—and were seemingly innocuous as they sat among their victims.

In our response to the present surprise attack, we are told also that Americans may not know exactly whom we are fighting or how we are even to discover when our foes in Afghanistan and elsewhere are vanquished. All these concerns contain an element of truth, but they are hardly the Truth. In fact, the destruction of the World Trade Center and the attack on the Pentagon share much in common with the Japanese bombing of Pearl Harbor sixty years ago this week—and therefore explain why the nature of the American response in both cases is remarkably the same.

Both Pearl Harbor and September 11, for all our enemies' cowardly audacity in murdering unsuspecting Americans in a time of peace, were military blunders of the first order. The Japanese killed more than twenty-four hundred Americans, sank eight battleships, and destroyed 186 planes, but found no aircraft carriers, sent no real modern ships to the bottom, left most of the Pacific fleet's critical oil reserves intact, and made no further attempt to disrupt shipping between Hawaii and the West Coast—much less seriously shell and bomb a mostly unprotected and ill-prepared American mainland.

So too it is with the terrorists. After the initial shock, they have been unable to erode further American assets. Al-Qaeda has shown no ability to shut down a damaged Pentagon or ruin the cultural, political, or economic life of a scarred New York. While we have suffered a grave defeat—far more than the number of Pearl Harbor dead, $50 billion in property damage, trillions lost in financial capital, and millions out of work—the ability of the United States to maintain its role as a world power remains unquestioned.

In fact, bin Laden's terrorists, like the Japanese militarists, violated the chief tenet of military science of the ages—one should never attack a militarily superior enemy in a time of peace without inflicting such damage as to cause ruination and thus prevent retaliation. Admiral Nagumo himself later acknowledged that he had "awakened a sleeping giant and filled her with a terrible resolve"—a confession by the attacker of Pearl Harbor apparently unknown to the supposedly astute bin Laden.

Six months after Pearl Harbor, in June 1942, the United States off Midway sunk four Japanese fleet carriers, killed the enemy's most seasoned naval pilots, and prevented the occupation of the atolls. And within a year, Americans were fighting in Japanese waters, and there was no question that any warring—other than at a few frigid outposts in Alaska—would take place close to American shores. Afghanistan is thousands of miles from New York, but the theater of fighting in this war from now on is more likely to be over there than here.

Just as the Japanese, in their fanatical banzai yells, embrace of suicide, and promises of death to weak, corrupt, and soft Westerners, misjudged us, so too the terrorists bragged that we were either too wealthy, cowardly, or impotent to retaliate in kind. And just as in the months after Pearl Harbor—at Midway and Guadalcanal—we proved the fanatics wrong on all counts, so too our present-day fascist attackers in Afghanistan are mostly either dead, captured, or hiding in caves. Bin Laden has learned the same lesson as General Tojo: shouting, threats, and a brutal and maniacal creed are no substitute for West Point, GM, Cal Tech, Sears, the U.S. Senate, and the American soldier.

Again, in a mere three weeks the United States is on the verge of annihilating the purportedly elusive and near invincible al-Qaeda network, with plans on the boards for systematic attacks throughout the Middle East against terrorist havens, networks, and sympathetic regimes. In such audacity, our present planners resemble their predecessors of December 1941, who immediately began to draw up ambitious blueprints not merely to defend America, but to eliminate Japanese, Italian, and German fascism altogether and at once.

Apparently both our grandfathers and the present generation realized that there is no quarter to be given criminals, whether they be fascist states or murdering fundamentalists. Such is the self-righteous fury of democracies, past and present, when they fall victim to unprovoked attack. A culture that is characteristically slow to anger, shockingly ill-prepared in times of peace, full of domestic concern with the most trivial of issues suddenly awakes from its slumber, taps its arsenal of freethinking individuals, and then by consensus and law chooses not merely to defeat but to eradicate its enemies.

But there are a variety of other similarities between December 7 and September 11, and not all of them are merely military. The shock of World War I, followed by the boom of the 1920s and the depression of the 1930s, had created a self-absorbed and then apprehensive America, either unwilling or unable to marshal its resolve to destroy incipient fascism in Europe or Asia. So too with us: after setbacks in Vietnam and Somalia—and despite the clear victories of the Gulf and in the Balkans—Americans were still unsure of their real power, and once again had begun to listen more to what our enemies might do to us rather than to what we most surely could do to them. The earlier recession of 1991, followed by the recent dot-com boom and bust that created millionaires and then paupers, in the same manner as the Roaring Twenties and subsequent Great Crash, fostered insularity and absorption with domestic affairs.

"It's the economy, stupid" was hardly similar in magnitude to the scope of the New Deal, but both Clinton and the early Roosevelt tended to ignore events abroad in the belief that their political future hinged on solving problems at home—hoping all the while that the fumes of past American prowess would deter foreign aggression. While the explosive growth in the American population and sophisticated technology of the last half century suggest that our contemporary recessions and military cuts were not comparable to those more drastic of the 1930s, both eras nevertheless shared a psychological affinity with isolationism—and both illusions were shattered by Pearl Harbor and the September 11 bombings.

Politically, September 11 offers the same lessons as did December 7.

It really is folly to cut radically one's defenses in times of peace—if for any other reason than that enemies appear out of nowhere and view even moderate and apparently responsible disarmament as impotence and an invitation to aggression. Just as we ignored Manchuria until Zeros reached Oahu, so too the bombers in Lebanon, Saudi Arabia, Somalia, Sudan, and Yemen were the godfathers of the September terrorists. Appeasement, now and then, is a prescription for disaster. While we may still have plenty of muscle to deal with both Afghanistan and Iraq, let us hope that our taxed and weary carriers in the next six months are not also needed off Palestine, North Korea, China, or Cuba. Since September 11 we have relearned the depressing lesson of human nature that six decades ago we had also rediscovered after Pearl Harbor—in the interval "suffering" what the Roman satirist Juvenal once dubbed "the evils of a long peace."

Landmark events like Pearl Harbor and the recent attack do not invent new mentalities so much as return us to the wisdom of the ages—predictably forgotten during the luxury of tranquility and prosperity. Americans woke from their slumber on December 8 and soon fathomed that prior international agreements on arms reduction had not stopped the building of the behemoth battleships *Yamato* and *Musashi*, that the League of Nations did not save Ethiopia or Manchuria, and that summit talks on the eve of Pearl Harbor led to disaster, not reprieve. So too we will learn once more that most of the Cold War accords on bio-weaponry were violated most egregiously by the former Soviet Union and others, that Saddam Hussein honored few of the 1991 armistice agreements, and that the United Nations can do nothing to prevent terrorism. Utopian internationalism has its uses among squabbling equals during peacetime, but only military preparedness and a willingness to use force stop aggressors from killing the innocent.

Of course, in a rapidly changing and global culture, there are also many superficial differences between these attacks on America six decades apart. We are interviewing aliens, not interring citizens; our ancestors were asked to sacrifice for the war effort, we to spend our way out of a recession; few then had any qualms about hitting the Japanese back; our cultural elite talk of the moral equivalence between terrorists deliberately killing the innocent in a time of peace and soldiers consciously avoiding civilians in a time of war.

Yet human nature and democracy are constants over time and space, and so the real lesson of Pearl Harbor teaches us that fanatics, autocrats, and fascists, out of perceived rather than real grievances, will always envy, fear—and eventually hate a culture of freedom and prosperity. The surprise attacks from such bankrupt cultures will always be encouraged by complacence aided by dereliction of vigilance—the terrible price of amnesia that affluent and self-absorbed democracies so often pay.

The ultimate verdict—still unfathomable to many of America's cultural elite—likewise is not in doubt. Mr. bin Laden should remember that the wrecks of Battleship Row led to the cinders of Berlin and Tokyo; the fall of the Twin Towers and the firing of the Pentagon will in the same manner bring al-Qaeda and its abettors a similar oblivion. Pearl Harbor set off a chain reaction of mobilization, war production, and national resolve in America, as an energized response at Coral Sea led to Midway to Guadalcanal to Iwo Jima to Okinawa and finally Tokyo Bay. Each week after December 7 we learned that our initial vulnerability was ephemeral, our rejoinder deadly and enduring. Because we are still our grandfathers' children, the Taliban, Saddam Hussein, and perhaps Mr. Arafat, Mr. Assad, and others of their ilk should understand that September 11 was not the end, but the very beginning. We did not want this war and as a people abhor killing, but history teaches us that by God we shall surely end it—and on our terms, not theirs.

Written on December 6 and published in National Review Online
on December 8.

31.

The Pied Piper of Tora Bora

STANDING ALONE

RUSSIA, EASTERN EUROPE, and most of South and Central America and Asia have accepted the demise of Communism and caudillos alike. Most states of the world have conceded that dumas, politburos, and the Praetorian Guard do not give people hope or freedom, and so are beginning to entertain free elections and unbridled speech. Similarly, people in the real world recognize that widespread poverty more often is state-induced than a result of racism, colonialism, or global exploitation. Mature nations have learned that Communism proved no paradise, but instead left millions of corpses in its wake and dearth as its legacy. Even China seems determined to adopt free markets—while fighting a desperate, and probably hopeless, rear-guard action against liberty and democracy. The world has always had its share of religious zealots and crackpot fundamentalists, but most states now acknowledge the truth that God did not intend to directly govern man.

So, outside of university economics, English, and anthropology departments—and similar fundamentalist churches—we know that there is no solution for starvation, continual violence, and chronic chaos other than the adoption of consensual government, open economies, personal freedom, and secular rationalism. Everywhere at the millennium, the human community agrees that fascism, theocracy, Communism, tribalism, statism, and fundamentalism lead nowhere but to misery—everywhere, that is, except the Islamic world of the Middle East.

Iraq is a hooligan state, Algeria chaos incarnate. Iran is run by a fraudulent theocracy; Afghanistan preferred a more lunatic brand. Syria and Libya have fancy murderous dictatorships, while the tribes and monarchies of the Gulf embrace fundamentalism at home, blondes and booze abroad. Sudan, Somalia, and Lebanon remain as chaotic as Yemen and Egypt are bankrupt. Morocco is sort of trying. All this tragedy is proof enough that it did not take Israel to ensure that Jordan, Palestine, and Gaza would be as unfree as they are broke.

Rather than looking to itself—by emancipating women, holding free elections, opening markets, drafting constitutions, outlawing polygamy, curbing fundamentalism, insisting on secular education, and ending tribalism—the Islamic world has more often cursed others. And, consequently, a musician has been welcomed into town—one not conversant with the true tune of salvation, but arriving as a sinister player, whose narcotic chords of resentment have captivated the Muslim world and so tragically led it, singing as it went, right over the precipice of disaster.

Bin Laden's mesmerizing jingle of a sinister Israel and conspiratorial America has stampeded an entire culture. At the vanguard of the enthralled were the terrorists and the piper's own al-Qaeda gangsters. Thanks to bin Laden's insane and cowardly attack on the world's sole superpower, his cells have been rounded up in nearly every European country; their Middle East nests are burning; and hundreds of his supporters have been torched or blown to bits. Bullets or bars await them and any other self-loathing killers in the Muslim world who believes the West—not their own conduct and culture—brought them their misery. The siren song of bin Laden has done more to destroy terrorism than has any cruise missile or Interpol operative in the last decade.

Close behind the terrorists in the shuffling, spellbound multitude was the purportedly formidable Taliban, who bragged and postured all the way to the abyss—not so much a religious order as a crass guild of bloody incompetents that hijacked an entire country through bribes, random assassination, and old-fashioned terror. These vicious bureaucrats believed their irrelevancy, remoteness, and sheer lunacy might make their cruelty relatively unimportant and therefore safe from retribution, until bin Laden, the mad minstrel, seduced them— with dollars and half-baked schemes of grandeur—to countenance one hit job too many. And so the Taliban also followed at his heels, screeching and threatening right over the cliff and into the nothingness below.

Next in line in the entranced swarm was the puffed-up Muslim street—the millions of illiterate and unemployed in Islamabad, Cairo, Damascus, Gaza, and the West Bank who sadly cannot vote, cannot read, and cannot talk freely without the nod of a mullah or a government thug. When news broke that thousands of Americans were butchered, skyscrapers toppled, the Pentagon afire, and jets blown apart, they too joined the ranks of the piper's pack. For three months the world has recoiled in both horror and embarrassment as thousands of the ignorant have cheered on their mass murderer, hawked his posters, and rushed into the bazaar to shake their fists and wave their pathetic, misspelled banners and kindergarten scribblings. Europe, the Americas, Russia, India, and even China have all stared in disbelief at their trance—and rightly or wrongly decided that these are rather crazy, dangerous folk, better left alone in their lockstep march to paradise than allowed to visit or immigrate to the more sober nations of the world. No Israeli, no rogue CIA agent, no Christian or Hindu fundamentalist could have done so much damage to the global image of the Islamic populace as Mr. bin Laden, whom the Muslim masses so mindlessly follow—indeed elbowing each other to be first over the edge.

We should not forget the center and rear of the performer's frenzied host, who were just as hypnotized—and are meeting the same fate as those who rushed out in the front rank. The so-called moderate governments of the Middle East listened, though rather coyly, to the sweet lyrics of "Islam ascendant" married with the chorus of an "America in flames." A Saudi sheik gave lectures to us at Ground Zero. Those who were once rescued in Kuwait snickered a decade later on *60 Minutes* about the American inferno. Moderates from Egypt to the Gulf cried crocodile tears for our dead—before immediately publicly resisting requests for financial records, travel logs, or antiterrorism intelligence. All their hostility was packaged with polite "but" speeches: "We do feel for the victims of September 11, but—" (fill in with comments on either "Israel" or "your government's foreign policy").

Yet news has leaked out to the American people (to the embarrassment and chagrin of our own government) that many of the Saudis were rather amused at what happened to our innocent, and that the Palestinian elite was not all that unhappy with the idea that thousands of Americans had been murdered—victims whose taxes helped to pay

$100 million a year in subsidies to the West Bank kleptocracy. Consequently, it will take millions of dollars in slick ads in *Time* and the *Financial Times* to bring back confidence in Kuwait; thousands of glossy infomercials of gleaming airports and highways in Saudi Arabia to reassure us that it is civilized; and hundreds of bought-and-paid-for retired American generals, ex-diplomats, defense contractors, and oil men to lobby and mislead us that the *real* Middle East didn't mean it at all. And still the damage wrought by bin Laden to the "moderate governments" will not be undone.

You see, hidden among the thronging mob—slightly embarrassed, shuffling rather than skipping, with canes rather than jogging shoes—were the geriatric sheiks and the unelected autocrats in ties and suits. Bobbing in and out of the crowd, at last they really did join the hypnotized columns, and so have hobbled right to the brink of the chasm of no return—never realizing that the music of jihad was dooming them, not us.

Finally, of course, was the opportunistic rear guard, who caught only a stanza now and then of bin Laden's mad piping. Liking much of what they heard, they tagged along nonetheless, thinking they could fall out before reaching the cleft. And they too are now going over with the rest. These were the so-called intellectuals in Egypt, Jordan, Palestine, and the Gulf who knew better. These novelists, newspaper editors, lobbyists, and the other assorted glib and sophisticated were no fundamentalists; indeed, they claimed that they knew the West, and sometimes resided in America and Europe. Afraid to confess openly that they also found the music of bin Laden's entertaining too clever by half, they called the mad piper a "symptom," "a wake up call," or a "barometer"—anything other than a megalomaniac looking to murder the helpless.

So those who brought up the rear of the hypnotized mob were not the ignorant but the educated. When not drugged by bin Laden's melodies, they understood the freedom, prosperity, security, and power of the West—knew it and, of course, wanted something like it for themselves. Worse still, they not only desired us, they knew exactly whence our superiority arose—not from the legacy of colonialism, not from racism, not from the Jewish state of Israel, and not from the foreign policy of America—but from the institutions of democracy, capitalism, and individual liberty: the very ideals of the West that they were so attracted to, and that thus left them so angry at their own unquenchable desire.

The educated of the Middle East hid in the dust and melee of bin Laden's entranced throng, but joined in at the back nonetheless. Did their ears prick up to his wafting notes out of envy—and with it, a sense of inferiority? Or was their behavior explicable—because they merely lacked the courage to demand of their own culture an end to fundamentalism, polygamy, sexual apartheid, the clan, statism, and all the other pathologies that prevent Islam from moving ahead in the modern world?

In their equivocation, contortions, and passive-aggressive circumlocutions, the educated too are close to going over the edge with all the rest of the piper's zombies. Every time a novelist or journalist—whether the respected Nobel laureate Mr. Mafhouz or Abdul Rahman al Rashed of the state-owned *Al Sharq al Awsat*—announces that the American bombing of Afghanistan was as much an act of terror as September 11, the piper smiles and plays on. No Western chauvinist, no crazed nativist or half-educated xenophobe has done so much to discredit the Middle Eastern intellectual as has the snickering minstrel bin Laden.

Now bin Laden is perhaps safely—for a time—holed up in his cave, while most of his hypnotized herd has already plummeted into the gorge. The rest of the world—Europe, the Americas, Russia, China, India, Japan, and the Pacific—grimaces at their fate, sad at the plunge of the deceived flock, but ever more determined not to listen to the cacophonous songs of hate, lies, and envy that have led them only to catastrophe.

Written on December 9 and published in National Review Online *on December 11.*

32.

Our Jurassic Park

THE FOSSILS OF WARTIME
CONVENTIONAL WISDOM

WE HAVE BEEN lectured sternly for the last three months by hordes of "experts." From a variety of sometimes wacky angles, they have predicted stalemate and even well-earned American humiliation in our war against terrorism. Magnifying our enemy's scant power, while deprecating our own real strength, some gloomy pundits—especially abroad, and particularly in Europe—have offered neither retractions nor apologies for their flawed analyses, even as events in Afghanistan have proved their glum prognoses completely wrong.

Week after week, we have been subjected to one scolding after another: Afghanistan is unconquerable. The Russians and British perished where we will too. The snows are coming to freeze us. The Taliban are too firmly entrenched and must be included in any postwar government. Only a pan-Islamic peace force will restore order. Al-Qaeda is impossible to root out. We need better proof of bin Laden's complicity in September 11. The bombing is not working. We are in another Vietnam quagmire. Oil will go sky-high. We dare not fight during Ramadan. The Northern Alliance is a paper tiger. The Arab street will explode. Mr. Arafat and the *intifada* will ignite the Middle East. The moderates in the Islamic world will turn on us. And so on.

Like the fossils of *Jurassic Park* dinosaurs, skeletons of the now unclaimed conventional wisdom of the last few months are strewn everywhere. From the shards of these old bones it is hard to believe such animals just a few weeks ago stalked our country and were cloaked in real flesh. Perhaps we can go back to the pile, sort out the bleached teeth, rib cages, and skulls, and so remember the brief lives of these absurdly silly beasts.

Afghanisaur

ALL RECALL THIS flesh-tearer! Purportedly an especially fearsome hunter, with curved teeth and snapping jaws, this beast's "Texas-sized" hulk and endlessly bloody appetite—we were told—gobbled up entire herds of unwary and lumbering trespassers. *Afghanisaur* was a tribal, unpredictable carnivore, an all-terrain quadruped who bellowed loudly among the skeletons of his past victims, lurked in snow, ignored wind, preferred high altitudes, and was reportedly as cannibalistic as he was indomitable.

Ramadanoceros

AH, RAMADANOCEROS, WE knew ye well. His large, seasonal horn supposedly sprouted each fall to root out and spear any who dared disturb this mystical and sullen recluse during his fall hibernation. Although some scientists believed that the *Ramadanoceri* were more likely to go on devouring each other throughout their annual autumn cycle of quiet, many swore that their unquenchable fury was reserved solely for other unwary species who dared to prowl in their restricted domain.

Vietnamapous

MYTH SURROUNDED THIS ubiquitous, smelly, and lethal marine predator, conjectured to be able to produce ten to fifteen litters per year. Prone to enticing large, bumbling dinosaurs into shallow reefs, the creature's innumerable and nearly invisible tentacles would then hamstring clumsy opponents and leave them wriggling for mercy, as other opportunistic scavengers fed off their paralyzed carcasses. *Vietnamapous* was said to be the most fearsome predator of the bumbling and once-stung *Americanaderm*. How the remains of *Vietnamapous* ended up in the arid dry land of Afghanistan no one knows.

Bombadactyl

REMEMBER SILLY BOMBADACTYL? His hollow bones were proof of a rather pathetic airborne flapper, a lightweight and often frail bird who—no doubt ineffectively—dropped small pebbles from his clumsy, horned beak. But his forays were more likely to result in hitting other innocent vegetarians than in ever hurting his targeted prey—the far more clever *Alqaedatron*. Quite unlike the *Arafator* in evolutionary terms, he had a preference for air assault that was an utter failure, apparently never defeating his enemies or even protecting the friendly Northern *Allianopus*.

Talibanus rex

WHO COULD FORGET the king of the dinosaurs? *T. rex* was a foul, two-legged, bellowing omnivore who purportedly would swallow anything in his immediate vicinity, and was nearly impossible to kill. His wild fits and teeth-gnashing were no doubt horrendous spectacles, and spelled death for any who approached him without careful consideration and specialized knowledge of his unique habitat and unpredictable moods. Apparently, these unstoppable *Talibani reges* were autogenous—inasmuch as no females of the species have yet been found.

Northern Allianopus

ALL DURING SEPTEMBER, experts lamented the poor *Allianopus*. These rather unimpressive, gaunt, rodentlike crawlers of the north, we were told, were natural fodder for flesh-eaters of all sorts. Often malnourished and nocturnal, the tiny and shy *Allianopus* on occasion was forced to make feeble night forays against both *Talibanus rex* and *Alqaedatron*—usually ending in an easy feast for his more advanced and specialized carnivorous enemies. No doubt related to the equally unimpressive and perhaps even more frail Southern and Eastern *Allianopus*.

Alqaedatron

WE ALL TREMBLED in fear of this monster! From his carcass it is hard to remember that this snapping, cave-dwelling iguana—who was seldom seen and almost never successfully cornered—was akin to something like the modern ferocious Gila monster. *Alqaedatron*—the very name was to send shivers down our spines—was prone to appearing from almost anywhere, spewing forth instantaneously lethal venom, and then scurrying unscathed back into crevices. Parasitic on unsuspecting hosts, often protected by *T. rex,* this devilish lizard brilliantly camouflaged himself among the unsuspecting vegetarians on whom he fed without fear of retaliation.

Fundamenippus

THE WORLD JUST lately shuddered before the collective neighing of thousands of these hoofed ungulates. The now extinct beasts were allegedly formidable herders—a social species believed to muster mindlessly on rumors of perceived insults in order to swarm, bite, and kick to death their prey. Their curious donkeylike ears allowed them to hear sounds from above not otherwise detectable to other species. Once an unsuspecting quarry provoked the frenzied throngs of *Fundamenippi,* he would be pulverized in a sea of crunching molars and wild kicks. The only salvation was to accommodate these unpredictable herds through careful backpedaling, clear expressions of homage, and periodic offerings of food and rangeland.

Arafator

WE SHOULD NOT be misled by the scant remains of that hornetlike stinger. On the slightest sign of conflict, the *Arafator* would dive out of nowhere to buzz and poke the combatants until he was given ample honey and air space. At the sound of his droning, both the deadly *Alqaedatron* and *T. rex* were likely to join in to snap at the *Arafator's* prey—and so most adversaries preferred to pay or run before this unstoppable and deadly hell-diver.

Oilodile

LONG-SNOUTED OILODILUS was the most temperamental, sensitive, and savvy of all our extinct creatures. His myriad eyes missing nothing, this ever ready siphon was quick to slither out at the first sight of commotion, suck up all the primeval goo of the forest, and then retreat back to his lair to horde it, as the distracted—and soon-to-be-hungry—dinosaurs devoured each other. As recompense for the fouling of his nest, the Oilodile would mete out his ever scarce, stockpiled nourishment only to those famished beasts that queued and paid proper obeisance—in some sense, he was the real *rex* of the age, and had to be coddled at every opportunity.

Americanaderm

OH, POOR *AMERICANADERM!* It is hard to conceive that this somnolent and lazy mammoth plodded about just a few months ago. This thick-skinned behemoth was by all accounts plagued with a pea-sized brain; no visible horns, teeth, or trunk; and an innocuous disposition prone to eating and idle amusement—teased mercilessly by the vicious *Oilodilus*. Only one specimen has been found, suggesting a rather isolated and parochial existence, and reflecting the *Americanaderm*'s perhaps legitimate fears of his more aggressive and lethal competition. This powerless but attractive target was conjectured to be clearly a Darwinian mistake; experts said it probably served as an opulent feast for the *Alqaedatron* and *Talibanus rex* alike.

Bushanthropos minor

HARVARD RESEARCHERS SHOOK their heads, dumbfounded, at poor *B. minor.* Once thought to be related to the purportedly Neanderthal *Bushanthropos major,* this apparently mute and indecisive hominid was felt to be even more underdeveloped. Recall that he was believed to have no discernible survival mechanisms—at least according to conjectures about his unimpressive mental capacity, arrested analytical skills, and only vestigial vocal facility. Yale experts surmised that *Bushanthropos minor* was an idle, happy creature who survived only due to long periods of sleep and careful avoidance of the surrounding treacherous landscape. Some Oxford anthropologists believed that he may have found solace in the company of the equally unthinking *Americanaderm*—a likely symbiosis given their similarly infantile and unobtrusive natures.

Iraqisaurus

NO, NO! MY God, not him! From his shattered skeleton, it is now hard to imagine that, just days ago, this wily and unpredictable serpent coiled, rattled, and slithered unmolested thanks to the plethora of his unstoppable weapons and numerous allies. With his infectious, venom-laden fangs, *Iraqisaurus* perhaps also emitted toxic gases, lethal spittle, and poisonous dung. Or—heaven forbid—even worse! Even more frightening still, the once deadly snake's lair was occasionally a safe haven for both the deadly *Alqaedatron* and the unspeakable *Fundamenippus,* with deadly *Arafator* humming in the distance—raising the specter of an unstoppable, multifaceted assault on any dinosaur imprudent enough to approach his hole.

As difficult as it is to believe, from the fossils of these extinct creatures, that any of them were really alive, we should take note of their brief existence all the same—so that we can recognize the offspring no doubt to arise among us in the days to come.

Written on December 12 and published in National Review Online
on December 14.

33.

Odd Couple Out

LEFTOVERS IN A NEW CIVILIZATION

LATELY BOTH MR. Arafat and Saddam Hussein—who shocked the world in the late 1970s and 1980s with their threats, terrorism, and anti-Americanism—look like stunned deer in the headlights. Their creased visages are not merely explicable because they are aged and worn by their own self-induced catastrophes. Nor do their paunches and lines reflect recognition of their checkered pasts that finally have burdened their souls; both have far too much blood on their hands for any such remorse. No, all the epaulettes, sidearms, and occasional ceremonial headdresses cannot disguise that they at last have figured out that we are in an entirely new world that has little use for any of their ilk.

We forget that both originally rose to power through either the tacit or explicit help of the communist bloc—the Soviet Union and its Warsaw Pact supplying clandestine money, refuge, and intelligence to the radical Palestinians and overt military hardware to Iraq. No matter how incendiary either tyrant was, both Arafat and Hussein—who kissed and hugged each other during the Gulf War—could at least count on Russia to confront the United States, and thereby clean up the detritus from misadventures in Palestine and the Gulf. Provoke a war with Israel? The Soviets will step in before Palestinians and their allies are annihilated by an Israeli counterattack. Rattle sabers among the oil sheikdoms or Iran? The Russians will make good any losses and sell or give away almost any nightmarish weapon that could be used against America or its allies.

But with the breakup of the Soviet Union, and the increasing anger of a new Russia and its allies at the Islamic fundamentalists, there is no succor left. Even the opportunistic Chinese are more worried about their own fanatics than about propping up these two rather bothersome and aging provocateurs. No state has the willingness to make good their gaffes; those few firebrands in the Middle East that might secretly wish to lend military support have neither the audacity nor the wherewithal. The younger Assad and the aging Khadafi these days sound either shrill or irrelevant—and often both at the same time. It says something when Arafat and Hussein find support from the nut in North Korea or the windbag in Havana.

With the demise of the outlaw states of the communist world, there simply are no longer friendly East German intelligence agents, Soviet arms-peddlers, safe houses in Budapest, Czech mouthpieces at the U.N., phony KGB passports, or any of the other assorted harbors that the PLO and the Bathists used to sail into once their self-created storms broke. We have not had a real war in the Middle East since 1973. Should it break out again—God forbid—the only obstacle between Israeli tanks and Damascus is the United States—not Russia, not the Arab world, not the Chinese. If Saddam Hussein thought the tottering Russian communists ignored him in 1991, he can only imagine what Moscow in 2001 would be like.

The bleak situation for these waking anachronisms is worse than the mere fall of communism and the end to state-organized anti-Americanism. The United States not only defeated Marxists, but successfully spread its own culture abroad. The result is that South America, Asia, and Eastern Europe rather like free elections, capitalism, and secular tolerance. For all the brutishness of the new globalism, even its most recalcitrant critics welcome international banking, communications, air travel, and intellectual exchange. In other words, outside of Mr. Arafat's own close circle and a few sycophants in Baghdad, hardly any worker in any state wishes to see continual suicide bombers and poison gas plants on the evening news when there is a chance to catch a Schwarzenegger movie, read spirited newspapers over coffee, and put a little away for a VCR. Indeed, even individual Arabs at Ground Zero in Jerusalem and Baghdad—if they could speak freely without repercussions—would perhaps prefer an end to their own state's sanctioned terror and a chance to join the rest of the world in the effort at living comfortably and securely.

In the past Mr. Arafat and Mr. Hussein as a last resort could always triangulate with Europe, where opportunism and fashionable anti-Americanism used to bring either kudos, arms sales, cash subsidies, or at least threats to pull out of assorted coalitions should the United States act forcefully. But September 11 has changed all that. Europeans are rather proximate to North Africa and the Middle East, and no longer seem to like what they see across the Mediterranean.

Europeans once seemed proud of the New Age multiculturalism of their union, and welcomed thousands of Muslims to their shores without requirements or even promises of eventual assimilation; yet now they are not all that eager to sleep so soundly in the lumpy beds they have made. In the months ahead, Interpol will be more likely to wiretap than wink at Hamas operatives, Hezbollah fund-raisers, and Iraqi consular officials in Bonn, Paris, and Rome. After the murder of thousands of Americans, threats of dirty bombs, and anthrax scares, no European company will be eager to ship anything to Iraq. A few may even reexamine funds sent to the PLO that they know are shared among suicidal terrorists who are blowing apart children.

Nor can Arafat or Hussein put much currency in the rantings of the European cultural elite. In the last ninety days it has been proved absolutely intellectually and morally bankrupt—and now occupies the same insolvent position as British rightists circa 1939. Euro-leftists' ominous promises of American incompetence were proved wrong by the liberation of Afghanistan; of American evildoing, by the shaved beards, *burqa* piles, and female newscasters in Kabul; and of American isolation, by the sudden warmth of India, Russia, and dozens of states in the former Soviet Union. If an endorsement of Mr. Arafat in the *New Statesman* or a *Le Monde* op-ed urging restraint—if not friendship—toward Saddam once momentarily bothered Americans, such antics now barely warrant a chuckle.

The last bastion of tacit aid was always the American university, a tiny clique of Arabists in the State Department, and some of our elite media, who all could be counted on to chastise us for U.N. sanctions or Israeli reprisals, or simply be against whatever America was for in the Middle East. But I think September 11 has also crippled such knee-jerk support for homegrown anti-Americanism as well. When an anchorman catches the scent from the ruin of the Twin Towers, he is less, not more, likely to listen carefully to Mr. Arafat's contorted explanation of why the blasting apart of Israeli teenagers is morally equivalent to Israeli retaliatory missile attacks on PLO police officers. When tenured professors hear of stories about dirty bombs planned for Boston or New York, have their mail disrupted by anthrax scares, and wait three hours in line at the ticket counter on the way to the next conference, silently they wish that Arafat and Hussein would just disappear, no questions asked.

For all their posturing about independence and principled opposition, the American intelligentsia has always wished foremost to be liked, envied, and courted—Orwell once said of their similar opportunistic counterparts in England that if it paid better they would be fascists. Yet now 90 percent of Americans support the current military response; Americans by a margin of four to one think the PLO, not Israel, is the problem in the Middle East; and 70 percent wish to remove Saddam Hussein. Our airwaves are full of thoughtful and serious ex-officers, idealistic young enlistees, and sober senior planners in the Defense Department—quite a contrast from the occasional appearance of some whiny, often hysterical professor, activist, or high-priced lawyer lecturing us about voluntary interviews of Middle Eastern aliens, the confusion of John Walker Lindh, or the certain advent of a police state. Bill O'Reilly usually makes short work of them on national television—if not first enticing them to reveal their rather harebrained ideas to millions of shocked listeners. Academics were always somewhat irrelevant—but never more so than during the last ninety days, when the country at large, their own students, and many on the campus itself have simply stopped listening to them. With fickle friends like them, who needs enemies?

What does this brave new world mean for the odd couple? They have one—and only one—final chance of survival. With careful wrangling the PLO could about-face, deplore the bombers they once tacitly sanctioned, and accept something like the generous terms once offered by the Clinton State Department—forcing on Israel either a humiliating acceptance or an even more embarrassing rejection. An apologetic Hussein still could open up his country to U.N. inspectors and appear on global television as solicitous of international cooperation in the new post–September 11 world. Both actions would be insincere; they would be abjectly disingenuous—and very dangerous. Yet, given the opportunistic and often cowardly nature of world opinion, they would most likely work and perhaps even allow Mr. Arafat and Mr. Hussein to fade away peacefully into their dotage as heads of illegitimate states. But far more likely both autocrats, as is always the nature of such tyrants, will do neither—and so in the coming weeks they will find themselves without friends and at the mercy of an increasingly angry and powerful United States.

In turn, we should be especially careful. In their eleventh hour the two are beginning at last to grasp the new realities of this altered universe in which their terror invites not reprisal but the specter of their utter destruction. In their final desperate throes, they will for a brief moment be more, rather than less, dangerous as they sadly try to take others down with them and openly revert to their original natures. "Who cares about the Americans?" Mr. Arafat now scoffs; "America will face disaster," Saddam rants.

Yet, despite their rhetoric and perhaps the chance of some unforeseen last gambit to come, the final verdict is clear—a suddenly confident civilization has rejected both leftovers, bored with, rather than afraid of, them. So the odd couple shall soon vanish, with a few penultimate shrieks as the fresh wind of a brave new world blows their shades away forever.

Written on December 15 and published in National Review Online
on December 18.

34.

Pillars of Ignorance

SINCE SEPTEMBER 11, we have heard mostly slander and lies about the West from radical Islamic fundamentalists in their defense of the terrorists. But the Middle Eastern mainstream—diplomats, intellectuals, and journalists—has also bombarded the American public with an array of unflattering images and texts, suggesting that the extremists' anti-Americanism may not be an eccentricity of the ignorant but rather a representative slice of the views of millions. For example, Egyptian Nobel Prize–winning novelist Naguib Mahfouz reportedly announced from his Cairo home that America's bombing of the Taliban was "just as despicable a crime" as the September 11 attacks—as if the terrorists' unprovoked mass murder of civilians were the moral equivalent of selected air strikes against enemy soldiers in wartime. Americans, reluctant to answer back their Middle Eastern critics for fear of charges of "Islamophobia" or "Arab smearing," have let such accusations go largely unchecked.

Two striking themes—one overt, one implied—characterize most Arab invective: first, there is some sort of equivalence—political, cultural, and military—between the West and the Muslim world; and second, America has been exceptionally unkind toward the Middle East. Both premises are false and reveal that the temple of anti-Americanism is supported by pillars of utter ignorance.

Few in the Middle East have a clue about the nature, origins, or history of democracy, a word that, along with its family ("constitution," "freedom," and "citizen"), has *no* history in the Arab vocabulary, or indeed any philological pedigree in *any* language other than Greek and Latin and their modern European offspring. Consensual government is not the norm of human politics but a rare and precious idea, not imposed or bequeathed but usually purchased with the blood of heroes and patriots, whether in classical Athens, revolutionary America, or more recently in Eastern Europe. Democracy's lifeblood is secularism and religious tolerance, coupled with free speech and economic liberty.

Afghan tribal councils, without written constitutions, are better than tyranny, surely, but they do not make consensual government. Nor do the Palestinian parliament and advisory bodies in Kuwait. None of these faux-assemblies is elected by an unbound citizenry, free to criticize (much less recall, impeach, or depose) their heads of state by legal means, or even to speak openly to journalists about the failings of their own government. Plato remarked of such superficial government-by-deliberation that even thieves divvy up the loot by give-and-take, suggesting that the human tendency to parley is natural but is not the same as the formal machinery of democratic government.

Our own cultural elites, either out of timidity or sometimes ignorance of the uniqueness of our own political institutions, seldom make such distinctions. But the differences are critical, because they lie unnoticed at the heart of the crisis in the Muslim world, and they explain our own tenuous relations with the regimes in the Gulf and the Middle East. Israel does not really know to what degree the Palestinian authorities have a real constituency, *because the people of the West Bank themselves do not know either*—inasmuch as they cannot debate one another on domestic television or campaign on the streets for alternate policies. Mr. Arafat assumed power by Western fiat; when he finally was allowed to hold real and periodic elections in his homeland, he simply perpetuated autocracy—as corrupt as it is brutal.

By the same token, we are surprised at the duplicity of the Gulf states in defusing internal dissent by redirecting it against Americans, forgetting that such is the way of all dictators, who, should they lose office, do not face the golden years of Jimmy Carter's busy housebuilding or Bill Clinton's self-absorbed angst. Either they dodge the mob's bullets or scurry to a fortified compound on the French coast a day ahead of the posse. The royal family of Saudi Arabia cannot act out of principle because *no* principle other than force put and keeps them in power. All the official jets, snazzy embassies, and expensive spin masters cannot hide that these illegitimate rulers are not in the political sense Western at all.

How sad that intellectuals of the Arab world—themselves given freedom only when they immigrate to the United States or Europe—profess support for democratic reform from Berkeley or Cambridge but secretly fear that, back home, truly free elections would usher in folk like the Iranian imams, who, in the manner of the Nazis in 1933, would thereupon destroy the very machinery that elected them. The fact is that democracy does not spring fully formed from the head of Zeus but rather is an epiphenomenon—the formal icing on a preexisting cake of egalitarianism, economic opportunity, religious tolerance, and constant self-criticism. The former cannot appear in the Muslim world until gallant men and women insist upon the latter—and thereby demolish the antidemocratic and medieval forces of tribalism, authoritarian traditionalism, and Islamic fundamentalism.

How much easier for nonvoters of the Arab world to vent frustration at the West, as if, in some Machiavellian plot, a democratic America, Israel, and Europe have conspired to prevent Muslims from adopting the Western invention of democracy! Democracy is hardly a Western secret like Greek Fire of the Byzantines to be closely guarded and kept from the *mujaheddin*. Islam is welcome to it, with the blessing and subsidy of the West. Yes, we must promote democracy abroad in the Muslim world, but only they, not we, can ensure its success.

The catastrophe of the Muslim world is also explicable in its failure to grasp the nature of Western success, which springs neither from luck nor resources, genes nor geography. Like third-world Marxists of the 1960s, who put blame for their own self-inflicted misery upon corporations, colonialism, and racism—anything other than the absence of real markets and a free society—the Islamic intelligentsia recognizes the Muslim world's inferiority vis-à-vis the West: but it then seeks to fault others for its own self-created fiasco. Government spokesmen in the Middle East should ignore the nonsense of the cultural relativists and discredited Marxists and have the courage to say that they are poor because their populations are nearly half illiterate, that the governments are not free, that their economies are not open, and that their fundamentalists impede scientific inquiry, unpopular expression, and cultural exchange.

Tragically, the immediate prospects for improvement are dismal, inasmuch as the war against terrorism has further isolated the Middle East. Travel, foreign education, and academic exchange—the only sources of future hope for the Arab world—have screeched to a halt. All the conferences in Cairo about Western bias and media distortion cannot hide this self-inflicted catastrophe—and the growing ostracism and suspicion of Middle Easterners in the West.

But blaming the West, and Israel, for the unendurable reality is easier for millions of Muslims than admitting the truth. Billions of barrels of oil; large populations; the fertility of the Nile, Tigris, and Euphrates valleys; invaluable geopolitical locations; and a host of other natural advantages that helped to create wealthy civilizations in the past now yield an excess of misery, rather than the riches of resource-poor Hong Kong or Switzerland. How could it be otherwise, when it takes bribes and decades to obtain a building permit in Cairo, when habeas corpus is a cruel joke in Baghdad, and when Saudi Arabia turns out more graduates in Islamic studies than in medicine or engineering?

To tackle illiteracy, gratuitous state-sanctioned killing, and the economic sclerosis that comes from corruption and state control would require the courage and self-examination of Eastern Europe, Russia, South America, even of China. Instead, wedded to the old bromides that the West causes their misery, that fundamentalist Islam and crackpot mullahs have had no role in their disasters, that the subjugation of women is a "different" rather than a foul (and economically foolish) custom, Muslim intellectuals have railed these past few months about the creation of Israel half a century ago, and they have sat either silent or amused while the mob in their streets chants in praise of a mass murderer. Meanwhile millions of Muslims tragically stay sick and hungry in silence.

Has the Muslim world gone mad in its threats and ultimatums? Throughout this war, Muslims have saturated us with overt and with insidious warnings. If America retaliated against the mass murder of its citizens, the Arab world would turn on us; if we bombed during Ramadan, we would incur lasting hatred; if we continued in our mission to avenge our dead, not an American would be safe in the Middle East. More disturbing even than the screaming street demonstrations have been the polite admonitions of corrupt grandees like Crown Prince Abdallah of Saudi Arabia or editor Abdul Rahman al Rashed of Saudia Arabia's state-owned *Al Sharq al Awsat.* Don't they see the impotence and absurdity of their veiled threats, backed neither by military force nor cultural dynamism? Don't they realize that nothing is more fatal to the security of a state than the divide between what it threatens and what it can deliver?

There is an abyss between such rhetoric and the world we actually live in, an abyss called power. Out of politeness, we needn't crow over the relative military capability of one billion Muslims and three hundred million Americans, but we should remember that the lethal, twenty-five-hundred-year Western way of war is the reflection of very different ideas about personal freedom, civic militarism, individuality on the battlefield, military technology, logistics, decisive battle, group discipline, civilian audit, and the dissemination and proliferation of knowledge.

Values and traditions—not guns, germs, and steel—explain why a tiny Greece of fifty thousand square miles crushed a Persia twenty times larger; why Rome, not Carthage, created world government; why Cortés was in Tenochtitlán and Montezuma, not in Madrid; why gunpowder in its home in China was a pastime for the elite, while when stolen and brought to Europe, it became a deadly and ever evolving weapon of the masses. Even at the nadir of Western power in the Middle Ages, a Europe divided by religion and fragmented into feudal states could still send thousands of thugs into the Holy Land, while a supposedly ascendant Islam had neither the ships nor the skill nor the logistics to wage jihad in Scotland or Brittany. Much is made of five hundred years of Ottoman dominance over a feuding Ortho-dox, Christian, and Protestant West, but the sultans were powerful largely to the degree that they crafted alliances with a distrustful France and the warring Italian city-states, copied the Arsenal at Venice, turned out replicas of Italian and German canons, and moved their capital to European Constantinople. Moreover, their "domi-nance" amounted only to a rough naval parity with the West on the old Roman Mediterranean; they never came close to the conquest of the heart of Western Europe.

Europeans, not Ottomans, colonized central and southern Africa, Asia and the Pacific, and the Americas—and not merely because of their Atlantic ports or oceangoing ships but rather because of their long-standing attitudes and traditions about scientific inquiry, secular thought, free markets, and individual ingenuity and spontaneity. To be sure, military power is not a referendum on morality—Pizarro's record in Peru makes as grim reading as the Germans' in central

Africa; it is, rather, a reflection of the amoral dynamism that fuels ships and soldiers.

We are militarily strong, and the Arab world abjectly weak, not because of greater courage, superior numbers, higher IQs, more ores, or better weather, but because of our culture. Between Xerxes on his throne overlooking Salamis and Saddam on his balcony reviewing his troops, between the Greeks arguing and debating before they rowed out with Themistocles and the Americans haranguing each other on the eve of the Gulf War, lies a twenty-five-hundred-year cultural tradition that explains why the rest of the world copies its weapons, uniforms, and military organization from us, not vice-versa.

Many Middle Easterners have performed a great media charade throughout this war. They publish newspapers and televise the news, and thereby give the appearance of being modern and Western. The chief dailies in Algiers, Teheran, and Kuwait City look like the *Pravda* of old. The entire Islamic media is a simulacrum of the West, lacking the life-giving spirit of debate and self-criticism.

As a result, when Americans see a cavalcade of talking Middle Eastern heads nod and blurt out the party line—that Israel is evil, that the United States is naive and misled, that Muslims are victims, that the West may soon have to reckon with Islamic anger—they assume the talk is orchestrated and therefore worth listening to only for what it teaches about how authoritarian governments can coerce and corrupt journalists and intellectuals.

A novelist who writes whatever he pleases anywhere in the Muslim world is more likely to receive a fatwa and a mob at his courtyard than a prize for literary courage, as Naguib Mahfouz and Salman Rushdie have learned. No wonder a code of silence pervades the Islamic world. No wonder, too, that Islam is far more ignorant of us than we of it. And no wonder that the Muslims haven't a clue that, while their current furor is scripted, whipped up, and mercurial, ours is far deeper and more lasting.

Every Western intellectual knows Edward Said's much hyped theory of "Orientalism," a purely mythical construct of how Western bias has misunderstood and distorted the Eastern "Other." In truth, the real problem is "Westernism"—the fatally erroneous idea in the Middle East that its propaganda-spewing Potemkin television stations give it a genuine understanding of the nature of America, an understanding apparently deepened by the presence in the Middle East of a few McDonald's franchises and hired U.S. public relations firms. That error—which mistakes ignorance for insight—helps explain why Osama bin Laden so grossly miscalculated the devastating magnitude of our response to September 11.

Millions in the Middle East are obsessed with Israel, whether they live in sight of Tel Aviv or thousands of miles away. Their fury doesn't spring solely from genuine dismay over the hundreds of Muslims Israel has killed on the West Bank; after all, Saddam Hussein butchered hundreds of thousands of Shiites, Kurds, and Iranians, while few in Cairo or Damascus said a word. Syria's Assad liquidated perhaps twenty thousand in sight of Israel, without a single demonstration in any Arab capital. The murder of some one hundred thousand Muslims in Algeria and forty thousand in Chechnya in the last decade provoked few intellectuals in the Middle East to call for a pan-Islamic protest. Clearly, the anger derives not from the tragic tally of the fallen but from Islamic rage that Israelis have defeated Muslims on the battlefield repeatedly, decisively, at will, and without modesty.

If Israel were not so successful, free, and haughty—if it were beleaguered and tottering on the verge of ruin—perhaps it would be tolerable. But in a sea of totalitarianism and government-induced poverty, a relatively successful economy and a stable culture arising out of scrub and desert clearly irks its less successful neighbors. Envy, as the historian Thucydides reminds us, is a powerful emotion and has caused not a few wars.

If Israel did not exist, the Arab world, in its current fit of denial, would have to invent something like it to vent its frustrations. That is not to say there may not be legitimate concerns in the struggle over Palestine, but merely that for millions of Muslims the fight over such small real estate stems from a deep psychological wound. It isn't about Lebensraum or some actual physical threat. Israel is a constant reminder that it is a nation's culture—not its geography or size or magnitude of its oil reserves—that determines its wealth or freedom. For the Middle East to make peace with Israel would be to declare war on itself, to admit that its own fundamental way of doing business—not the Jews—makes it poor, sick, and weak.

Throughout the Muslim world, myth and ignorance surround U.S. foreign policy toward the Middle East. Yes, we give Israel aid, but not that much more than the combined billions that go to the Palestinians and to Egypt, Jordan, and other Muslim countries. And it is one thing to subsidize a democratic and constitutional (if cantankerous) ally but quite another to pay for slander from theocratic or autocratic enemies. Though Israel has its fair share of fundamentalists and fanatics, the country is not the creation of clerics or strongmen but of European émigrés, who committed Israel from the start to democracy, free speech, and abundant self-critique.

Far from egging on Israel, the United States actually restrains the Israeli military, whose organization and discipline, along with the sophisticated Israeli arms industry, make it quite capable of annihilating nearly all its bellicose neighbors without American aid. Should the United States withdraw from active participation in the Middle East and let the contestants settle their differences on the battlefield, Israel, not the Arab world, would win. The military record of four previous conflicts does not lie. Arafat should remember who saved him in Lebanon; it was no power in the Middle East that brokered his exodus and parted the waves of Israeli planes and tanks for his safe passage to the desert.

The Muslim world suffers from political amnesia, we now have learned, and so has forgotten not only Arafat's resurrection but also American help to beleaguered Afghanis, terrified Kuwaitis, helpless Kurds and Shiites, starving Somalis, and defenseless Bosnians—direct intervention that has cost the United States much more treasure and lives than mere economic aid for Israel ever did. They forget, but we remember the Palestinians cheering in Nablus hours after thousands of our innocents were incinerated in New York, the hagiographic posters of a mass murderer in the streets of Muslim capitals, and the remonstrations of Saudi prince Alwaleed to Mayor Giuliani at Ground Zero.

Saudi Arabian and Kuwaiti westernized elites find psychological comfort in their people's anti-American rhetoric, not out of real grievance but perhaps as reassurance that their own appetite for all things Western doesn't constitute rejection of their medieval religion or their thirteenth-century caliphate. Their apologists in the United States dissemble when they argue that these Gulf sheiks are forced to master a doublespeak for foreign consumption, or that they are better than the frightening alternative, or that they are victims of unfair American anger that is ignorant of Wahhabi custom. In their present relationship with the terrorists, these old-fashioned autocrats are neutrals only in the sense that they now play the cagier role of Franco's Spain to Hitler's Germany. They aid and abet our enemies, but never overtly. If the United States prevails, the Saudis can proclaim that they were always with us; should we lose a shooting war with the terrorists, the princes can swear that their prior neutrality really constituted allegiance to radical Islam all along.

In matters of East-West relations, immigration has always been a one-way phenomenon. Thousands flocked to Athens and Rome; few left for Parthia or Numidia unless to colonize or exploit. People sneak into South, not North, Korea—in the same manner that few from Hong Kong once braved gunfire to reach Peking (unless to invest and profit). Few Israeli laborers are going to the West Bank to seek construction jobs. In this vein is the Muslim world's longing for the very soil of America. Even in the crucible of war we have discovered that our worst critics love us in the concrete as much as they hate us in the abstract.

For all the frothing, it seems that millions of our purported enemies wish to visit, study, or (better yet) live, in the United States—and this is true not just of Westernized professors or globe-trotting tycoons but of hijackers, terrorists, the children of the Taliban, the offspring of Iranian mullahs, and the spoiled teenage brats of our Gulf critics. The terrorists visited lap-dancers, took out frequent flier miles, spent hours on the Internet, had cell phones strapped to their hips, and hobnobbed in Las Vegas—parasitic on a culture not their own, fascinated with toys they could not make, and always ashamed that their lusts grew more than they could be satisfied. Until September 11, their ilk had been like fleas on a lazy, plump dog, gnashing their tiny proboscises to gain bloody nourishment or inflict small welts on a distracted host who found them not worth the scratch.

This dual loathing and attraction for things Western is characteristic of the highest echelon of the terrorists themselves, often Western-educated, English-speaking, and hardly poor. Emblematic is the evil genius of al-Qaeda, the sinister Dr. al-Zawahiri: he grew up in Cairo affluence, his family enmeshed in all the Westernized institutions of Egypt.

Americans find this Middle Eastern cultural schizophrenia maddening, especially in its inability to fathom that all the things that

Muslim visitors profess to hate—equality of the sexes, cultural free-dom, religious tolerance, egalitarianism, free speech, and secular rationalism—are precisely what give us the material things that they want in the first place! CDs and sexy bare midriffs are the fruits of a society that values freedom, unchecked inquiry, and individual expression more than the dictates of state or church; wild freedom and wild materialism are part of the American character. So bewil-dered Americans now ask themselves: Why do so many of these anti-Americans, who profess hatred of the West and reverence of the purity of an energized Islam or a fiery Palestine, enroll in Chico State or UCLA instead of *madrassas* in Pakistan or military academies in Iraq?

The embarrassing answer would explain nearly everything, from bin Laden to the *intifada*. Dads and moms who watch al-Jazeera and scream in the street at the Great Satan really would prefer that their chil-dren have dollars, an annual CAT scan, a good lawyer, air-conditioning, and Levis in American Hell than be without toilet paper, suffer from intestinal parasites, deal with the secret police, and squint with uncor-rected vision in the Islamic paradise of Cairo, Teheran, and Gaza. Such a fundamental and intolerable paradox in the very core of a man's heart—multiplied millions of times over—is not a healthy thing either for them or for us, as we have learned after September 11.

Most Americans recognize and honor the past achievements of Islamic civilization and the contribution of Middle Eastern immi-grants to the United States and Europe, as well as the traditional hos-pitality shown visitors to the Muslim world. And so we have long shown patience with those who hate us, and more curiosity than real anger.

But that was then, and this is now. A two-kiloton explosion that incinerates thousands of our citizens, planned by Middle Easterners with the indirect financial support of purportedly allied governments, the applause of millions, and the snickering and smiles of millions more has had an effect that grows, not wanes.

So a neighborly bit of advice for our Islamic friends and their spokesmen abroad: topple your pillars of ignorance and the edifice of your anti-Americanism. Try to seek difficult answers from within to even more difficult questions without. Do not blame others for prob-lems that are largely self-created or seek solutions over here when your answers are mostly at home. Please, think hard about what you are saying and writing about the deaths of thousands of Americans and your relationship with the United States. America has been a friend more often than not to you. But now you are on the verge of turning its people—who create, not follow, government—into an enemy: a very angry and powerful enemy that may be yours for a long, long time to come.

Written on December 1 and published in the winter issue of City Journal.

35.

The Iron Veil

FACING THE NEW GLOBAL REALITY

THE MUSLIM MIDDLE East is baffling. Americans are exhausted by the use of the word "but." Remember the nightly choruses: "We deplore September 11, BUT . . ." "We do not approve of the suicide bombings against Israel, BUT . . ." "Osama bin Laden does not represent Islam, BUT . . ." Adversative clauses then follow that damn us and almost every manifestation of American foreign policy.

Overt threats and frenzied hostility—whether in the Arab street or in the chic enclaves of Gulf sheiks—rise and fall as little more than a barometer of current American military strength. Clinton's few Tomahawk missiles invite big talk against our national character; B-52s and daisy-cutters prompt quiet respect and pampered grandees scurrying to Washington to assure us that they really like us after all.

How is America to deal in a methodical and intelligible fashion with such a contradictory and incendiary—and maddening!—region of nearly half a billion people? Complete disengagement from such unpleasant regimes and hostile peoples is a very attractive idea—until we remember that the Middle East and its surrounding area is home to the world's three great religions. It occupies a strategic nexus of three continents, holds a sizable percentage of the world's oil reserves, contains the Suez Canal, and lies in close proximity to Europe. Yet, we must accept the sad truth that our present ad hoc policy has been an unmitigated disaster. Giving billions to Egypt and providing military hardware to Saudi Arabia did not prevent their citizens from spearheading the murder of thousands of our innocents—to cheers and quiet approbations of their own millions back home.

So we need a new direction that is logical, time-tried, and designed to be enduring and systematic in its treatment of *all* the countries of the Middle East. In other words, America must remember its past successful approach toward Eastern Europe—accepting that Islam in its increasingly radical manifestation, along with its twin of military dictatorship, represents the same dire threat to freedom and civilization, both at home and abroad, as did the iron curtain of Soviet totalitarianism.

No Soviet nuke, after all, incinerated three thousand Americans. Even Khrushchev's metaphorical "We will bury you" was not as bad as "Kill every American." The Polish never blew up four airliners in flight, nor did the Hungarian communists bomb the Pentagon. Rather than continue to give billions to illegitimate regimes in Jordan and Egypt, cozy up to fundamentalists in the Gulf, and label vast areas like Syria, Iraq, Libya, and Lebanon as supporters of terrorism—while doing nothing to prevent them from killing more Americans—we should treat *the entire region* uniformly, as we once did Poland, Hungary, Romania, East Germany, and the other members of the old Warsaw Pact.

Just as an American-led NATO was ready for anything that came west, so too must we be ever vigilant against the Middle East Bloc. Militarily, America should increase its forces in the region. The United States must accept the grim reality that at any given moment we can be on the verge of war with almost *any* country of the Islamic world. Remember that in the last two decades alone, we tried to use armed force to free our hostages in Iran, fought the Iraqis, had shootouts in the streets of Somalia, bombed terrorists in Libya, and tried to retaliate against killers in Lebanon and the Sudan—all this quite apart from supplying weapons to Israel in the not too distant past to fight the Syrians, Jordanians, and Egyptians. If we throw in Bosnia, Afghanistan, the Sudan, Yemen, and the barracks in Saudi Arabia, are there very many countries in the Islamic world where Americans have not been in the line of fire?

Politically, we must accept that there is not a real democracy in the entire subcontinent. And what elections are proclaimed, as occurred in Iran and on the West Bank, are quickly subverted into little more than referenda for autocracy. The only mystery hinges on whether unelected mullahs or authoritarian councils shall allow either "radical" or "moderate" candidates to take over the reins of government.

Are purportedly friendly governments in truth either moderate or neutral? Just as the supposedly maverick states of Romania and Yugoslavia proclaimed their independence from the Soviet Union and falsely postured as nonaligned countries who were not practitioners of totalitarianism, so we are told that the nonelected governments of the Gulf, Egypt, Jordan, and Saudi Arabia are not as bad as Libya and Syria—even as they thwart us, and their young men crash airliners into our skyscrapers. "Friendly" Saudi citizens have killed far more Americans than have "enemy" Cubans.

So, we must return to a comprehensive and systematic approach that recognizes America cannot be allies with *any* existing government in the Middle East—that an Iron Veil has fallen across the region preventing all free intercourse—until the entire region has been liberated from mullahs like those in Iran, killers such as Saddam Hussein, Assad, and Khadafi, plutocrats like the sheiks, and even the benevolent dictators in suits and ties in Jordan and Egypt.

In the past, Radio Free America and our official policy made it clear to the Eastern Europeans that we saw them as captive peoples of commissars, who someday could rejoice under democracy. America should treat the unfree millions of the Arab world the same way. The more we hate their governments now, the less they will hate us later. We did not seek military alliances with communist Hungary, sell weapons to Czechoslovakia, welcome in students from Bulgaria, or encourage cultural ties with East Germany.

So also after September 11, we should not expect such reciprocal exchanges with countries that are either theocratic or autocratic, in which hate-mongering mullahs and servile media are either subsidized or at least government-sponsored. Neither students nor intellectuals from undemocratic countries of the presently constituted Middle East should come to the United States. Nor should regular air flights continue in either direction. Nor should Americans be allowed to travel freely to visit Bethlehem, the Pyramids, or the bazaars of the Gulf.

In other words, we should begin to see *all* the governments of the Middle East as we do Iran and Libya, keeping only minimum, thoroughly frosty ties on an official level—even as we wage a desperate political and cultural war to appeal directly to the people themselves so that they might rise up and fight for legitimate government. On the theory that Eastern Europe prior to Soviet-installed communism had a distinguished pedigree, so too we must at least profess that before the recent batch of dictators and theocrats, the Middle East at least had no prolonged history of exporting terrorists to kill Americans.

Critics on the right will no doubt dub such efforts to promote democracy in areas without literacy, secularism, the rule of law, or viable economies as naive, while leftists will dismiss a new cold war as retrograde or worse. But we must remember that the Cold War was a victory. Our faith in the people on the other side of the Iron Curtain proved to be warranted, and half a continent is now legal rather than renegade—a bulwark, not a nemesis, to Western Europe.

Nor must we sigh that our vigilance will bear no fruit until a half century has passed. Ad hoc strongmen and even bloodthirsty mullahs do not possess the power or resilience of Soviet-inspired terror. The world is also a different place from 1946. Nearly all the promised utopias of the past—fascism, communism, third-world liberationist kleptocracy, and Islamic theocracy—have now had their day and failed miserably before the eyes of billions. A Westernized and secular minority in the Middle East knows that the future lies only with freedom and democracy. While hostile in a variety of ways to America, it is perhaps still the only hope of millions. America must stand ready to go to war with any country of the region that kills our citizens, and stand aloof from all the illegitimate governments of the Middle East Bloc—even as it wages a desperate fight over the airwaves, through thousands of agents and dissidents, and with subsidies and encouragement to thousands more democrats in exile to free an oppressed population.

If we adopt principled and tough resistance to Middle Eastern governments while at the same time offering the carrot of honest friendship and material support for any of their silenced citizens who aspire to democracy, then what once happened among the enslaved peoples of the Warsaw Pact could occur again in the Middle East—and in a decade or less rather than in fifty years. The same old dominoes of repression are now tottering. With a concerted push they could set off a chain reaction as quickly and unexpectedly as they once did in Eastern Europe.

Written on December 17 and published in National Review Online
on December 21.

36.

Glad We Are Not Fighting Ourselves

WHAT WERE THEY DRINKING?

AMERICA NOW ENJOYS a level of global military and political influence not seen since the Roman Empire in the age of Trajan. Besides the obvious preponderance of carrier battle groups, strategic bomber wings, and tactical fighters unrivaled by any other military, much of the current power of our armed forces is attributable to the Western military tradition itself.

But in the last two decades America, for better or worse, has evolved beyond the traditional Western paradigm, in reaching the theoretical limits of freedom and unbridled capitalism to create a technologically sophisticated, restlessly energetic, and ever changing society—whose like has never been seen in the history of civilization. Unlike the more staid consensual nations of both Europe and Japan, America has no real class system. It has transmogrified from a nation of European immigrants into a truly multiracial society. Despite the energy of the contemporary race industry and the efforts at disunity by multiculturalists and separatists, America is emerging more united than ever—if not by a vision of shared values, at least more pragmatically through intermarriage; the vibrant popular culture of music, television, fashion, and sports; and the shared breakneck quest for material security and affluence.

The result of such an open, pulsating society is sometimes a weirdly insidious civilization that drives our enemies crazy. Write polemical diatribes about the West from your unfree university on the West Bank? As a reward for your anti-Americanism, Harvard or Stanford is likely to offer you a cushy year of subsidized invective firsthand—making the freedom and affluence of the modern American university campus hard to give up when your annual tenure expires. Do Middle Easterners allege that we are European crusaders? It won't fly when the troops who are blasting apart the al-Qaeda terrorists are Americans who look like Asians, Mexicans, Africans, and Europeans and about every combination in between. Need analysis about Iraqi bombs, Russian germs, or Afghani politics? Most likely just those native experts who were knee-deep in such deadly business are living right now in northern Virginia or New York, well paid in government, universities, and foundations, and eager to share the insights of their checkered past for the benefit of their newly adopted leaders.

Have problems locating an Afghani cave in one of bin Laden's videos? Somewhere there is an American geologist who wrote his thesis on Afghani caves. And his knowledge will be corroborated, supplemented, challenged, refuted, or modified by an array of botanists, engineers, and anthropologists who will add that the background flora, the type of the terrorist's clothes, and the nature of his video transmission suggest he is not in place A, but rather at B or even C.

We have seen just such flexibility in the deadly evolution of our military response—a strike force unlike even what we saw in the Gulf or Kosovo. Quite literally the entire nature of our present war-making has been reinvented through a novel four-step formula. In its first stage, indigenous resistance is encouraged by gifts of arms and supplies, immediately followed by precision bombing, leading to a third phase of Special Forces using new laser and GPS technology to "shoot" bombs even more accurately right into the laps of their enemies a few thousands yards away—followed by a fourth step in which larger groups of highly trained Marines and Mountaineers set up base camps to facilitate hunter-killer patrols, launch helicopter attacks, and interrogate and process prisoners.

But unlike Soviet infantry and armor doctrine of the 1960s and 1970s, which had changed little from World War II, our new tactics are not static. We are just as likely to see armored divisions on the ground in Iraq, storms of cruise missiles in Lebanon, or covert assassination teams in Somalia—or the return once again of the Afghani mode—depending on the changing nature of our adversaries.

Why are we so deadly? Like European armies, American weaponry and Special Forces reflect the fruits of secular research, the bounty of capitalism, the discipline of civic militarism, and the spirit of egalitarianism sanctified by America's real concern, both spiritual and legal, for its soldiers in the field. But there is also something rather new in our military that makes it even more lethal than the forces of our European cousins, and it is a dividend of America's much more radical efforts to destroy the barriers of class, race, pedigree, accent, and any other obstacle to the completely free interplay of economic, political, cultural, and military forces.

Our Secretary of State and National Security Advisor are African-American; our president is a proud Texan but also the son of an Ivy League blue blood. Geraldo, formerly the ultra-liberal defender of Bill Clinton during the dark days of impeachment, is now reinvented as Fox News' new patriotic Ernie Pyle come alive—more, not less, controversial than his prior incarnation—to supplement the stories of the once indicted Ollie North, himself hardly a pariah, but now a national hero, beloved by Marines in the field. One's past in America fades before the present, as ideology, degrees, parentage, and breeding mean little in the here and now—the present pulse of the market of ideas and consumption being the sole arbiter of success. No wonder most of the world fears, envies, and is dumbfounded by us.

I was recently reminded of the unique nature of this topsy-turvy country in a brief car trip to Los Angeles, witnessing firsthand the terrifying energy, resilience, and power of the United States. Driving south down Freeway 99, I passed myriads of self-employed truckers, linoleum installers, plumbers, salesmen, and electricians, their various vans and trucks weaving in and out at high speeds, fleeting reflections of thousands of private agendas scurrying for the next dollar, flags waving, and their drivers of nearly every race on the globe. Arriving at 5 P.M. in downtown Los Angeles, which purportedly has neither an efficient transportation system nor an impressive skyline—I drove into concrete canyons at rush hour from the orchards of the Central Valley to the Jonathan Club in less than three hours—I was struck by the beauty of its massive skyscrapers and the ingenuity of the freeways.

There I spoke to an alumni group of Navy and Army graduates. Few countries in the world could collect more educated, disciplined, diverse, and spirited men and women in a single room. Their questions were far more astute than those asked by university professors, their ideas about the present war hardly one-dimensionally bellicose, but deeply embedded in culture, history, and philosophy. The next morning on the way home I stopped at UCLA—once again reminded that Los Angeles's premier university is, in fact, a stunningly beautiful place, to the unaccustomed eye more a horticultural park than the nexus of thirty thousand students.

Across the freeway, I visited the Getty Museum, a strange cross between Hearst Castle and the Gardens of Babylon, and a receptacle of civilization's great work—spotlessly clean, meticulously manicured, staffed by hundreds of professionals from every class, and all privately subsidized for the public good. As I left, a Mexican-American docent was lecturing in Spanish to a small group of immigrants on the Old Masters, while two staffers not over twenty were politely escorting aged German tourists through the museum bookstore, everybody speaking heavily accented English. Twenty-five hours later I drove into the farm, amazed at the military, cultural, educational, economic, and aesthetic restlessness of this civilization in a period so often labeled by its critics as one of material and moral decline.

I came away with the impression that September 11 has super-charged rather than short-circuited this frightening, multifaceted engine of America. What were bin Laden, the mobs in Pakistan and the West Bank, the nuts in al-Qaeda, and their opportunistic support-ers in the Middle East drinking? We shall never know, but their attack on a country such as this was pure lunacy. Thank God we do not have to fight anyone like ourselves.

Written on December 19 and published in National Review Online
on December 21.

37.

It Really Is Your Father's Europe

SOME OF US in the heartland must confess that we were raised with our fathers' old and rather predictable prejudices against Europe. Whether out of a sense of cultural inferiority, ignorance of the wider world, or the twentieth-century tendency of wild men in Europe to disrupt our peace, the older generations once embraced a certain suspicion of things French, German, and English. Each unappreciated generation of twentieth-century Americans, in their view, went over to Europe either to be killed, gassed, or shot at—or to the Pacific to fight various wars spawned by a tumult that had begun in Europe.

So our supposedly blinkered fathers once had a lurking suspicion that, while we had inherited our democratic ideals from the European Enlightenment, our forebears across the water were a much different people from us. In this line of thinking, they imagined that Europeans had privately concluded that we pushy Americans had simply gone too far in our experiments with unchecked capitalism, class mobility, and freedom. In our efforts to welcome radical egalitarianism, material well-being, and massive immigration, Americans had more or less obliterated ideas of landed gentry; the importance of breeding, class, ancestry, and accent—and perhaps high culture altogether.

The postwar peace of the last half-century was to have ended all the needless suspicion and downright ignorance about a supposedly aristocratic and jealous Europe. Millions of Americans served in wars overseas. Millions more traveled to London, Paris, and Rome in the boom and affluence of the last fifty years. Not only was our generation of Americans impressed by the European propensity to eat better and slower, preserve their inner cities and hallowed buildings, promote their small farms and towns, and build an efficient and humane infrastructure of mass transit and medical care, but Europeans in turn admired our idealism—if not naïveté—and energy, and so came to appreciate that in a single century we had saved the continent from Prussian militarism, German and Italian fascism, and Soviet communism. And so we two more or less got along well—as should the twin offspring of a shared Western heritage.

The recent war, however, is revealing how far America and Europe have drifted apart just in the past decade. In the last few days, we have been lectured by the Spanish—whose record of freedom and the protection of individual rights the last few centuries is not stellar—that we cannot expect extradition of those enemy warriors implicated in the conspiracy to kill our thousands. Instead, we must assure Franco's children that these alien soldiers of war who tried—and will try—to kill us will be processed solely through our civil courts.

Even some British leaders—whose troops comprise a small percentage of those fighting on land and in the air to free Afghanistan—have announced that should their men catch bin Laden first (hardly likely), they will *not* ship such an odious mass murderer to America to answer for his killing of our innocents. You see, we still have the death penalty. To British sensibilities we thus cannot be trusted to mete out fair justice to the CEO of Terror, Inc. True, a few years ago we were reluctantly welcomed to fly into central Europe, destroy fascism in Serbia, and stop an ethnic holocaust a few hours away from Berlin and Rome—but surely all that should not suggest that we can be let loose on our own turf to try killers of thousands of our innocent.

The French recently made a convicted cop-killer, Mumia Abu-Jamal, an honorary citizen of Paris—although he was condemned by a jury of his peers and has produced no evidence that either his fingerprints or witnesses contradict the court's verdict that he blew out the brains of a prostrate policeman. Neither Jane Fonda nor Noam Chomsky ever warranted that honor.

European papers in the first few weeks after September 11 sounded themes of the "chickens coming home to roost" in their efforts to suggest either that American "imperialism" had prompted such attacks, or that our distrust of international accords fashioned at Kyoto and Durban had made our appeals to create coalitions against terror hypocritical and vain. Antiwar demonstrations in London and Paris were large and overtly anti-American. What, then, is going on, if our NATO allies, in a time of war no less, do not trust our courts, our culture—or us!

Anyone who has followed the growth of the European Union over the last decade—eighteen thousand bureaucrats with the equivalent of an $80 billion budget—could offer answers. Increasingly, Europe is no longer democratic in the American sense, but ever so insidiously creating a sprawling regime of appointed rather than truly elected officials to override nationhood in order to create a utopian culture—with all the arrogance, smugness, and authoritarianism that such pipe dreams always entail.

The result is that although sizeable majorities of Europeans support the death penalty, it cannot be enacted in any EU country. All states prove their seriousness by their ability to protect themselves, and so Europeans publicly boast of new pancontinental armies and air forces on the drawing boards that will supplement NATO. Privately, of course, most Europeans concede that it's far better to rent us bases in Spain, Germany, Naples, and Crete so that their own security is assured and paid for by someone else—and with the added bonus of voicing anti-Americanism on the cheap when our planes take off on a necessary but unpopular mission to bomb in Kosovo or Afghanistan. This is a continent, after all, now squabbling not about sending troops into battle, but over the relative dangers of stationing them in a conquered capital.

Perhaps it is the rather small confines of Europe, the pressures on its resources, its history of internecine war—who really knows?—that prompts it to welcome a paternalistic government of highly educated elites to distill utopian bromides without real grass-roots audit or public scrutiny. The reality, however, is that in exchange for giving up its sovereignty and autonomy, European states have opted for the assurance of a comfortable lifestyle, subsidized by American defense, cheap immigrant labor across the continent, and generous social welfare spending—and all of it fine-tuned by highly educated and aristocratic bureaucrats who more and more will answer to no one except their immediate supervisors.

What should we Americans do when such novel political developments over there result in such poorly disguised disdain for us—and at a time when we are fighting for our very way of life? Nothing and everything. We must maintain our de jure NATO membership, but de facto accept that it is no longer an alliance. Rather, it is a mere informal understanding that the United States can base troops in Europe in exchange for unilaterally defending the West and protecting the type of world that Europe so desperately depends on but so rarely will admit to.

Mutual heritage and tradition insist also that we seek common ground when the enemies of Western civilization promise to destroy us all. And we should listen fairly to European concern about environmental problems and third-world hunger. But we must nevertheless realize how different America is from Europe, rediscovering in the process why our strange country appeared in the first place. The United States was not merely a refuge for the oppressed and destitute from Europe. It was also created as its antithesis in its insistence on the right of popular government and a willingness to defend a new way of life at all costs. In that regard, the Europeans' kudos to an unctuous Clinton, not their disparagement of a principled Bush, should cause worry.

Our muscular commitment to liberty and economic freedom explains why we probably will be even more at odds with Europe in the future. Accused of being imperialist, America in fact has little colonial heritage—but rather a strange habit of intervening in very dangerous places where there is on occasion no clear national interest other than the protection of isolated states like Israel, the starving in Somalia—or Europeans themselves who are being butchered, whether in 1941 or 1997. We Americans must not be shy in accepting the truth that we execute terrorists like Timothy McVeigh, while Europeans released them after the Munich Olympics. Communists were welcomed into European coalitions even as Americans spent billions to ensure that Russian tanks did not make it to the Atlantic.

While we should do nothing overt to end our special relationship with the Europeans, in the meantime we should be attuned to the radically different world that September 11 has ushered in. There are emerging powers in the world that are nuclear, democratic, capitalist, and continental. India and Russia, for example, share some of our own multiracial and multicultural challenges, remain suspicious of militant Islam, pay for their own defense, and are trying to flee, not welcome in, an all-intrusive state power. We should seek stronger ties of friendship with both, if not their overt alliances in the future. Japan and Germany, again whether we like it or not, inevitably will seek military status and a world role commensurate with their natural power. Both must be dealt with on occasions as near equals in ways that are mostly unconcerned with the European Union per se.

This perplexing relationship with the Europeans also sheds light on many of our own paradoxes here at home. Throughout this entire war, our cultural elite has taken a stance toward the war incomprehensible to the vast majority of Americans—in an uncannily similar manner that Europe has appeared so haughty to America at large. Are professors, the hierarchy at CNN, and Hollywood so similar to the Spanish, Dutch, Belgians, French, and Scandinavians, because they both pose as sophisticates shuddering at what bumbling blue-collar, flag-waving Americans have gotten themselves into?

Maybe. But the real truth is that a small, privileged group in America no longer has any idea from whence their very sustenance, freedom, and leisure arise. Upscale liberals are safe because hundreds of thousands of less polished, but quite smart people join their armed forces, put out their fires, and arrest criminals in their neighborhoods. They are affluent because millions of less educated but very industrious laborers cut their grass, lay their cement, pick their fruit, pave their streets, and unclog their drains. And they are smug because they have found a way to get good money, plenty of free time, and personal security without having anything to do with those who give them so much of what they expect as their birthright. And so either out of guilt, old-fashioned aristocratic arrogance, or simple naïveté and stupidity, a very large class of utopians promotes pie-in-the-sky solutions to distant problems that only undermine others less fortunate under their noses.

We are not supposed to say this—class is now the third rail of affluent conservatives and liberals—but we see these antitheses in America almost every day of this war: a heroic, middle class, and now dead Johnny Spann versus a spoiled, traitorous, and "mixed-up" Marin County Johnny Walker; Sarah Jane Olson, an upscale suburbanite with almost no concern about the past bombing of blue-collar policemen; a smart-alecky ex-terrorist and now tenured Bill Ayers with little remorse about past dynamiting aimed at soldiers and public employees of the working class. Repeatedly, we witness mostly upscale Americans flirting with the forces of destruction—but only for a while, always with mitigating circumstances, and ultimately with the ready sanctuary of a nearby progressive legal or academic enclave, supported in its comfort and security by the working classes.

In the same manner, an affluent and spoiled Europe hectors a brutish United States, which, like some Neanderthal of the past, still executes murderers, bombs terrorists, and sets up military tribunals to try killers. And like our own elite, Europeans preach such easy morality always and only with the assurance that this other America with its dirty fingernails—as it once blocked Soviet divisions from storming into Germany—will continue to keep Greeks and Turks apart, provide neighborhood security off the North African coast, take out their garbage in Serbia, keep the noise down across the street in the Middle East, prune back the annual growth of Saddam, and scrub away al-Qaeda.

Written on December 21 and published in National Review Online
on December 26.

38.

Winners and Losers

TO PARAPHRASE CHURCHILL, with the conclusion of hostilities in Afghanistan we are *not* at the beginning of the end, but rather at the end of the beginning in our fight against the terrorists. Although judgments in medias res are always hazardous, we can perhaps look back over the last four months and size up winners and losers that appear on the national scene in clear-cut antitheses. War takes away the luxury of peace, and so shows things for what they are rather than what they seem.

Before September George W. Bush was dismissed as inarticulate and worse. Pundits constantly and often cruelly reminded Americans that their leader had not mastered the intricacies and nomenclature of world politics. But September 11 revealed the president as quite a different person from his critics' caricature. Mr. Bush is, in fact, the Greek iambic poet Archilochus's proverbial hedgehog, the allegorically wise beast, who, unlike the supposedly clever foxes of the world, knows one—but one big (*hen mega*)—thing: how to galvanize his nation to fight back relentlessly and powerfully against evil in the hour of its greatest peril.

In contrast, his predecessor's impressive and near encyclopedic knowledge of names, dates, and places now appears little more than thin veneer, a glossy lamina that scarcely hid his real ignorance about the nature of the human condition. Mr. Clinton, not the current president, wished to be liked at all costs and therein possessed a flaw fatal for a leader of the world's greatest power. Mr. Clinton's inability to pursue the terrorists and keep his country on guard against its noxious enemies is now judged as the last amoral straw that broke his camel's back of security lapses, unwise military cuts, impeachment, personal scandal and perfidy, and tawdry sales of White House visits and eleventh-hour pardons alike. The more Mr. Bush is terse and to the point, the more Mr. Clinton frantically flits from one public forum to another—whining about his legacy, lecturing the citizenry about its purported sins from the Crusades to the Civil War, and thereby ensuring that he is no longer a tragic, but rather a comically absurd, figure.

Before September 11 popular wisdom suggested that bin Laden and his terrorists represented a new, vibrant, and deadly threat to a tired, soft, and decadent West. But the past four months have shown just the opposite. The true weaklings and cowards were the al-Qaeda leadership. They, not us, cynically sent the deluded and young to suicidal murdering while they hid in caves, planned their escape, and churned out pitiful and self-serving videos.

The worst indulgence for a fanatical and "committed" terrorist is to appear worldly, gossipy—and petty. Bin Laden's tapes revealed all three sins. He brags of his rising ratings among the mosques of the world, but then, like a toddler in his terrible twos, bellyaches that our bombs were bigger than his and therefore not fair in his infantile game of tit-for-tat. He slurs blacks—as revealing as his chuckles over the fate of his naive henchmen who boarded the planes of death on September 11—which must send a chilling message to Africans anywhere who might think that an anti-Western radical Islam offers the proper home for their own unhappiness with America and Europe.

In contrast, the United States military and its war-makers loom as not merely deadly, but overwhelmingly so in a manner that reduces bin Laden and his ilk as unworthy of combat between equals—and therefore deserving not an honorable duel between real soldiers, but a quick incineration befitting criminals and cutthroats. Far from appearing overly worried about losing soldiers in a ground war with terrorists, America's ability to kill without danger from high in the skies comes off as Olympian: the omnipotent do not think it worth their time to wrestle below with weak and shrill miscreants when they can dispatch them at will with thunderbolts.

The Left, both on and off campus, has been reduced to a state of ethical insolvency—followed by silence—in the aftermath of September 11. The roll call of published remarks by the likes of Mary Beard, Eric Foner, Frederic Jameson, Barbara Kingsolver, Arundhati Roy,

Edward Said, Susan Sontag, Alice Walker, and a host of others has revealed that the luminaries of today's Western cultural and intellectual establishment are not merely ignorant of politics, history, and culture, but often downright immature, hysterical, and inarticulate. And now we see that the only skeleton of an ideology remaining that feeds the elite far Left is a reactive anti-Americanism. But those old bones have little taste left given our power and humanity in waging this present awful war that we did not ask for.

How different are their antitheses. Over the past decades others have perhaps garnered less glitter—scholars like Bernard Lewis, Fouad Ajami, Daniel Pipes, Donald Kagan, and others—but in the present crisis they have in contrast offered blunt, unsparing, and sober appraisals grounded in history, an understanding of human nature, and clear and precise prose. The former intellectuals are of the moment and of no relevance, even as needed critics of their culture. The latter scholars prove to be engaged, principled, and prescient. Ironically, the traditionalists, not the universities' darlings, have done far more to salvage the entire notion of liberal education and the reputations of the great schools themselves.

The binaries of this war, then, also involve institutions as well as people. For two decades we have been worried about the ultimate harvests of the diseased groves of academe. The present war has exposed for public view young people in the military as knowledgeable as college students, their officers as well-spoken as professors, and the high command perhaps more well-rounded and engaged than university administrators. Again, we are not talking merely of common sense and practicality, which we expect from a military culture, but rather those visible and manifest signs of learning—logic, lucidity, and information—that is the supposed monopoly of our schools.

If this apparent paradox is true, the dichotomy presents a host of further disturbing consequences. Is our defense budget, then, complementary, rather than antithetical, to social expenditure on education? Here I do not invoke just the negative notion that more money for guns means less funding for foolhardy programs in our schools that do real harm to our youth. Rather, in a positive sense, can it be that a few critical years in the military produce youth as well-spoken, disciplined, and worldly as those on our college campuses? Do campuses need to learn from the military as much as the latter has from the schools? Seriousness, literacy, and written and oral communication must be shared by dozens of young people in order to safely catapult a jet plane off a rolling carrier—let us for a moment ignore questions of maturity and teamwork—skills hardly inculcated by counseling, journal writing, and gender studies so often found on the contemporary campus.

The war, however, has not embarrassed the Left alone. Many on the Right come in for needed reexamination. The officers of the Enron conglomerate appear not merely felonious, but biblically amoral in draining off money for themselves while destroying the life savings of thousands of loyal employees. In a time of war, such an energy corporation, which provides the lifeblood for a technologically advanced society, proves itself much more than duplicitous and incompetent. It is near treasonous as well, and has done its nation far more damage than the teen traitor from Marin County. Enron's leadership should be named often, and then roundly condemned by both the president and the Congress—as preliminaries to well-publicized indictments by the Department of Justice.

And under the false guise of "national security"—a slight against the very struggle we are in—our Congress is about to pass the largest farm bailout in history. Yet we know that family farms are rarely the beneficiaries of such ill-conceived largesse; that the present legislation simply makes liars out of the architects of the "absolutely final" multi-billion-dollar 1996 Freedom to Farm bill; and that the more the Department of Agriculture has grown, the more rapidly real agrarians have been obliterated. The latest gift to a few thousand corporate farms is little more than an insult to the memory of the rural vanquished. Faced with congressional passage of this monstrosity, any true conservative would either abolish the Department of Agriculture altogether; eliminate once and for all its welfare policy for select, campaign-donating agribusiness concerns—or, barring that, in the interest of fairness, bring back the equally inequitable and dishonest giveaway programs for the urban poor of the past.

War is merciless in the manner it cuts through cant and traditional wisdom. When men and women risk their lives to save their brethren, and the power of arms, not brag, decides who lives and dies, then truth emerges to expose pretense in ways we could scarcely imagine when the fighting broke out. And if the last four months are any guide to the next year, then we are likely to see far more unexpected winners and losers in the days ahead.

Written on December 22, 2001, and published in National Review Online
on January 2, 2002.